"Princess is emerging as one of the justly inspiring leaders of our time. Her faith and courage will challenge us to be the change we want in this world. This is a truly moving account of one woman's unique ability to find purpose in adversity."

Hugh Evans, director and cofounder, The Global Poverty Project

"I prayed with Princess in the lobby of a hotel in Lusaka, Zambia. I walked beside her and watched the sun set over the village where she grew up. I listened to her 'preach' to community leaders in the beautiful Bemba language, and sang while she led worship. Princess Kasune Zulu is a woman of passion, strength and wisdom. She has challenged me to engage more deeply with my global sisters and to speak more clearly on their behalf. I am grateful for the example she has been to me and glad that this book will allow her story to inspire many others."

Lynne Hybels, advocate for Global Engagement, Willow Creek Community Church

"*Warrior Princess* is a beautifully written, powerfully moving story. As we follow Princess on her extraordinary journey from a poor Zambian village to the corridors of global power, we find ourselves learning a great deal about the critical issues of our time how and why extreme poverty affects Africa, and what life is like for the world's 15 million children orphaned by AIDS. The humbling lesson from *Warrior Princess* is that AIDS affects people just like you and me, who through an 'accident of latitude' were born into the world's poorest countries. AIDS affects mothers and fathers, brothers and sisters, teachers, doctors and nurses with hopes and dreams and families of their own. The great moral question of our time is, just how will we choose to respond?"

Tim Costello, CEO, World Vision Australia

"Princess Zulu's story is one of significant suffering, profound courage and great hope. Princess is not willing to be conquered by death or disease, but instead holds on to the hope of a greater purpose. She is a warrior, one who has embraced her life completely. I am utterly amazed at the joy found in her story. *Warrior Princess* is deeply moving and inspiring, reminding us of the life-giving truth of the gospel and provoking each of us to live out our God-given purposes. Read expecting to be challenged and encouraged by Princess's story of hope and great joy."

Mae Elise Cannon, author of *Social Justice Handbook: Small Steps for a Better World*

"This is the story of the life of Princess Kasune Zulu—from very humble and simple beginnings in a little village in Chibombo central Zambia, through early marriage, infection with HIV, fiery AIDS activism to meeting with the world's most powerful men and women—is a compelling story of a warrior woman's determination not to be defeated by a deadly virus. Princess says of her infection that the HIV running in her bloodstream is a mere guest in her body and her life; she has refused to let the guest take over her life! This is the story of a Zambian woman who is positive about being positive. It is a story everyone must read."

Dr. Mannasseh Phiri, HIV and AIDS activist, Zambia

"This book is a compelling and inspiring story of suffering and hope that will motivate, empower and challenge you to believe that the impossible is possible in our lifetime—even in the face of poverty, HIV and AIDS. *Warrior Princess* is a must-read for every person who wants to make a real difference in the world."

Rev. Dr. Brenda Salter McNeil, president and founder, Salter McNeil & Associates, LLC

"The first time I met Princess Zulu I was impressed by her physical beauty and her effervescent personality. But I was equally taken with her deeply spiritual, intensely personal relationship with God born out of suffering and difficult situations. She is an amazing woman! If we speak at the same event, I do my best to make sure I speak before her so that I don't have to live up to her ability to capture a crowd! I'm proud to call her my friend and sister."

Kay Warren, founder, HIV/AIDS Initiative, Saddleback Church

"In person, and now in this book, Princess puts a beautiful, honest and strong face on HIV/AIDS. Her story stirs us all to personal action, taking us past awareness or even heartfelt sympathy that still accomplishes little. Zulu has challenged me to a restless search for my role in this battle for life and death. She is a bridge between those of us born into privilege and health and those in deepest pain and despair. Bring on the movie!"

Steve Madsen, pastor, Cornerstone Fellowship, Livermore, California

WARRIOR PRINCESS

Fighting for Life with Courage and Hope

PRINCESS KASUNE ZULU

WITH BELINDA COLLINS

IVP Books

An imprint of InterVarsity Press
Downers Grove, Illinois

InterVarsity Press
P.O. Box 1400, Downers Grove, IL 60515-1426
World Wide Web: www.ivpress.com
E-mail: email@ivpress.com

InterVarsity Press® is the book-publishing division of InterVarsity Christian Fellowship/USA®, a movement of students and faculty active on campus at hundreds of universities, colleges and schools of nursing in the United States of America, and a member movement of the International Fellowship of Evangelical Students. For information about local and regional activities, write Public Relations Dept., InterVarsity Christian Fellowship/USA, 6400 Schroeder Rd., P.O. Box 7895, Madison, WI 53707-7895, or visit the IVCF website at <www.intervarsity.org>.

All Scripture quotations, unless otherwise indicated, are taken from the Holy Bible, New International Version®. niv®. Copyright ©1973, 1978, 1984 by International Bible Society. Used by permission of Zondervan Publishing House. All rights reserved.

Picture of Princess with George W. Bush on p. 256 courtesy of Thomson Reuters. Used by permission.

Design: Cindy Kiple
Cover Images: Girl walking to school in rural Natal, South Africa: Per-Anders Pettersson/Getty Images
Princess Kasune Zulu: Andrew Jacob/World Vision Australia

ISBN 978-0-8308-3725-0

Printed in the United States of America ∞

Library of Congress Cataloging-in-Publication Data

Zulu, Princess Kasune, 1975-
  Warrior princess: fighting for life with courage and hope /
Princess Kasune Zulu; with Belinda Collins.
    p. cm.
Includes bibliographical references.
ISBN 978-0-8308-3725-0 (hardcover: alk. paper)
1. Zulu, Princess Kasune, 1975- 2. Christian biography—Zambia. 3. AIDS (Disease)—Patients—Religious life. 4. AIDS (Disease)—Africa. 5. HIV infections—Africa. 6. AIDS (Disease)—Religious aspects—Christianity. I. Collins, Belinda A., 1974- II. Title.

BR1725.Z85A3 2009
276.894'083092—dc22
[B]

2009032097

P 21 20 19 18 17 16 15 14 13 12 11 10 9 8 7 6 5 4 3 2 1

Y 27 26 25 24 23 22 21 20 19 18 17 16 15 14 13 12 11 10 09

This book is written to honor the memory of . . .

Every life lost as a result of AIDS and all left in its wake—your courage and hope gives me strength.

My mother, Joyce Mwanamusulwe Kasune, my father, Goodson Moffat Kasune, my baby sister, Linda, and my brother, Kelvin.

Moffat David Tombosangu Zulu, the father of Joy and Faith, whose life will forever be part of mine, who gave me not only my beloved daughters but a story to tell. Without Moffat, there would be no story.

My cousin Beatrice, my dear friends Betty, Brian and many other close friends and family members whose names cannot be mentioned—this book is for you.

I wish that this story was mine and mine alone, but unfortunately, it echoes that of millions. I hope that by sharing my story I am sharing the story of Africa; for the story of each and every girl, boy, woman and man is equally important.

Our children need to know there is someone waiting to listen, they need to know we care, that we are ready to respond to their cries.

Princess Kasune Zulu

Contents

PART FOUR: THE AMERICAN FLAG STANDS STILL

About My Story

When a generation of parents dies they take with them the precious childhood stories of the next generations.

Having lost my parents so many years ago, I have done my best to capture and retell the stories of my childhood in an accurate way, though there is no one left to verify the details. Wherever possible I have filled in the gaps with knowledge from other family members and older folk who knew my parents, grandparents, Moffat and our family. Learning these stories of my childhood has been moving and deeply rewarding.

When you recall your own place in history there is a danger of romanticizing your role, the way you carried yourself, the statements you made. I have tried not to do this. I hope I have portrayed my strengths and weaknesses, the courageous woman and the frightened young girl, the strong and the naive, for these qualities live within us all.

To bring light and life to this story I have reconstructed conversations as I recall them. At times it has been necessary to put words into people's mouths, but I have thought long and hard to ensure the words reflect the spirit and intent of the people who originally spoke them.

While many of the people in my life have been happy to have their names and stories reflected, other names have been changed to protect identities.

Much has been written by the media over the years about the origin of my name, timing of events and the death of my parents. Some of it is accurate, some of it is not.

Now that my story has been written in the way I wish it to be told, please accept that this book, to the very best of my abilities, is the true and accurate record of my life so far.

From the Coauthor

The journey that became *Warrior Princess* began for me in 2002 when I met Princess Kasune Zulu, a woman who would go on to change my life in the richest, most beautiful way.

I had packed up the communications business I ran for four years and accepted a media role with an international humanitarian agency in my home country, Australia. With World AIDS Day approaching, my first task was to make the AIDS pandemic "real" to a country of around 20 million people, with a comparatively low figure of around 15,000 HIV-positive.

Make it real? It wasn't real to me. Forty million people were HIV-positive, twice Australia's entire population. This number didn't make sense, and I didn't want it to.

To become real, AIDS needed a name and a face. I did some research and came across Princess. Similar in age to myself, she was one of the few in southern Africa proudly admitting to being HIV-positive. Down a crackly phone line, plans were made for her to come to Australia. I had no idea what to expect.

At first I was struck by Princess's physical beauty, only magnified by the striking African outfit she wore. Her royal lineage is very plain to see. As we drove along the Beach Road, the endless blue sea to our right, Princess asked with a childlike smile, "Belinda, does the roof come off your car?" It did, and soon Princess was standing tall in my car, the long red fabric of her head wrap flapping freely in her hand. Full of the joy of life, she laughed a free, childlike laugh.

While it was clear I had met someone special, I could never have imagined the journey we had begun that summer day.

I watched in awe as Princess captivated every person she met. While her natural manner is warm and gentle, she quickly switches gears when the fiercely intelligent, innate leader needs to shine. She speaks articulately, with the most touching humility and courage, about things that are difficult to discuss.

By the week's end, Princess had indeed given the AIDS pandemic a face and a name. It was the face and the name of my friend. Now it was personal.

The following years saw me travel to Africa on a number of occasions. I wanted to see for myself, and what I saw tore me apart. Sometimes I traveled alone, but much of the time I was with Princess, who held my hand as I awkwardly came to terms with the complex realities of southern Africa. We met children, some as young as eight years old, orphaned by AIDS, heading their ramshackle households; frail grandparents caring for grandchildren whose parents had perished. We visited the putrid water sources where children walk to fetch drinking water. On subsequent trips escorting journalists, I even met poor little children who had escaped fighting in grown-up wars. One carried an AK-47 to protect himself on his three-day walk to safety.

There but for the grace of God go I, I thought. The saying repeated itself over and over throughout my travels. *This could have been me.*

These travels took me to sites of some of the greatest human suffering. Yet it was in these places that I experienced some of the greatest joy and beauty imaginable. I felt I had taken so much from the families I met but left so little in return. My heart was broken. I would never be the same again. The AIDS pandemic was real.

Bono aptly describes the place we are born as "an accident of latitude." Born into my loving family in a land of opportunity, my birthright was a joyful childhood, healthy parents, hot and cold water flowing to my big, safe, warm home, an abundance of fresh food, an education I took for granted, and a great job on graduation. Where I happened to be born puts me in the luckiest 1 percent of the world's people. *It could have been very different.*

My relative privilege became more apparent as my husband, Darren, and I welcomed our baby boy, Samuel, into the world. If he were born in Zambia, there's a one in five chance Sam wouldn't see his fifth birthday and one in three chance he would be orphaned by AIDS. Watching over him as he sleeps, I weep in this knowledge. Is this the same world we live in? While I thank God for his health every day and I pray with all my might to keep him safe from harm, I don't understand why the forecast for my son, for my family, should be so much brighter, just because we happened to be born in Australia.

What truly begs belief is that it doesn't have to be this way. As you read *Warrior Princess* you will learn about the globally agreed plans to end extreme poverty and eliminate preventable diseases. The plans were made in the year 2000, but so few even know of their existence. Once you know about these plans it will become clear that the way we choose to respond becomes one of the great moral questions of our time.

It has been my great privilege to coauthor *Warrior Princess*. It's a daunting responsibility to write the story of someone infinitely more wise and articulate than yourself. Princess only agreed for her story to be shared as the suffering in her story is echoed in millions of homes across southern Africa with every new sunrise that dawns. She hopes that sharing her story will awaken people to the plight of the children AIDS has left in its wake.

This book is meant to move you and inspire you. It should make you cry, laugh and question. We want you to get angry and be moved. We want you to join the fight.

Thank you.

Belinda Collins

PART ONE

A CHILD OF
COURAGE AND HOPE

1

Positive

M<small>RS. Z</small>ULU<small>, YOU ARE</small> HIV-<small>POSITIVE.</small>"

As the words touch my ears, the roof smashes open and the brightest ray of light bounces straight into my heart, or so it seems. The most wondrous sense of peace and calm fills my body. I am floating on a cloud and my heart wants to shout, "Praise God!"

When I recall that day, it's like I'm watching a collection of scenes from a movie. As the next scene unfolds, I see the kind, sorrowful face of my doctor. Short in stature, Dr. Tembo is dressed in a crisp white coat that lets you know you are in safe hands. He is heartbroken. In his eyes I am a condemned woman: he has handed me a death sentence, the diagnosis of a disease he is powerless to cure. Here he is, a gentle, humble man whose passion is saving lives, who has dedicated his own life to curing the sick. With a health system as brittle as Zambia's this was always a challenge, and now this HIV has begun a systematic, deadly march through his country where it claims young lives at every turn. The doctor is at a loss for words. So how can I tell him my heart is filled with the greatest sense of hope? While the words aren't audible, I can hear them clearly: say "Praise God."

Now words and images from my past are flooding into my mind: the skeletal frame of my baby sister as she wastes away, the faces of the sick I nursed in the hospital, my mum coughing and struggling to carry a sack of maize, a series of photographs from a pink book, my dad lying alone in a hut and above all a string of words that has remained a mystery to me for some time: "I will go before you and I will level the mountains; so you will know it is me who has called you by name." *Aha! So, this is it? After all this time, here it is—my mountain.* At once I know this virus is my reason for being. *This* is why God put me on earth. HIV is my cause, my mountain to climb.

In January 1998 most Zambians know very little about the Human Immunodeficiency Virus. But having read a pink-covered book lent to me by a nurse, I now know. I know what Dr. Tembo's diagnosis means. I had read the book several times over, had studied its pictures and reeled at the list of symptoms this virus causes as it takes over a body. I had tried for months to be tested myself; first the hospital turned me away and then my husband denied me permission. But finally we made it, and I am HIV-positive. I know what this means—yet here it is, my heart beating strong and an inaudible voice beckoning me to shout "Praise God!"

I try to refocus, as Dr. Tembo is about to give my husband the results of his own test.

With his eyes respectfully cast down at the floor, Dr. Tembo delivers the news: "Moffat Zulu, I am sorry, you are also HIV-positive." Moffat remains silent.

Feet firmly back on the floor I ask, "What next, Doctor?"

"Well . . . I am so sorry to inform you there is nothing that can be done, not here in Zambia. The treatment is just too expensive. You may only have six months to live."

Just one year earlier a Taiwanese-born researcher named David Ho, the son of refugees, had created a cocktail of drugs that successfully suppressed HIV. *Time* magazine had named Dr. Ho "Person of the Year." But Ho's drugs had yet to make their way to the poor, remote township of

Luanshya where few, if any, could have afforded the ten-thousand-dollar annual price tag. Even five years after Dr. Ho's discovery, only eight thousand people in Africa were taking these life-saving drugs.[1] By the time the cocktail of drugs became more widely available, millions would have already died.

When Moffat and I emerge from the drab atmosphere of the hospital into the clear light of day, Moffat looks shattered. His shoulders slump, his feet plod. At first his eyes seem to search for answers, for hope, for a miracle, but within seconds a dull look of hopeless resignation takes hold. He says farewell as he sets off for work. To me, though, Luanshya looks brighter, different somehow. I see the world with new eyes as I make my way toward the road to hitchhike home.

As always, it doesn't take long to get a ride, and I am soon riding in an old blue car. The padding has been pulled from the inside of the doors, revealing rusty blue metal and the workings of the worn-out door latch and window handle. Not long after we set off, my driver hints I might like to pay for my ride with sex. "Sir, please. I am a married woman," I protest. But I learn it's going to take something more to deter this relentless driver as he tells me, "I am married too. That's okay."

"Well, sir, I am a child of God. I am faithful to my husband."

"We are all God's children, my dear."

He's not giving up. I know it's time to drop my bombshell. "Sir, I am also HIV-positive."

While this man's attitude is extreme, for me, a beautiful, voluptuous twenty-one-year-old woman, the proposition is not uncommon. It has never troubled me before as it seems like just another part of life. But not today. Today things have changed. *How many of these drivers carry the virus around our country and back home to their family?* I find myself pondering.

I look at the run-down old cars and trucks driving all around us and shudder in disbelief. *My beloved Africa.* I now see this vast land taking the form of a woman. If Zambia is her landlocked heart, I picture her long legs stretching out across Zimbabwe and Mozambique and down into

South Africa, Botswana and Namibia while her arms embrace Malawi, Tanzania and Angola. Her elegant neck and head rest comfortably in the Democratic Republic of Congo. I am struck by the image of her roads and highways serving as arteries, pumping an endless flow of virus-carrying vehicles from her hands, feet, arms and legs through her heart and back again. If fighting this virus is my calling, it is clear I have my work cut out for me.

So how did I get here? What journey did a hopeful young girl take to arrive in Dr. Tembo's office on January 2, 1998, to be given the news I am HIV-positive? My story begins like this.

2

"Princess Is Her Name"

Hᴇʀ ɴᴀᴍᴇ ɪѕ Pʀɪɴᴄᴇѕѕ. She will be a princess among princesses. She will meet with the leaders of this world." These are the words my bataa (that's what I call my dad, in the language of my tribe, the Lenjes) said underneath the shady leaves of a mango tree at our home in Kabwe, about a week after the sixth of January 1976—the day that I was born.

I know this story because it was repeated again and again as I grew up. When I think back now, I can almost picture the scene: Bataa's voice, proud, strong and sure, and his dark head held high as he made this grand announcement.

The subject of my name had been greatly discussed, for I was the first-born child of my parents. We had a privileged, modern lifestyle by Zambian standards. I was born in Kabwe General Hospital and delivered by a nurse, rather than in the village, where I would have been delivered by family or a traditional birthing attendant. But still, my parents followed many of Zambia's traditional customs. In the lead-up to my birth, my mother was surrounded by the women of her family. Bataa was not allowed to be present.

As Bamaa and the nurse worked to deliver me, the women who had traveled from near and far concentrated on finding a suitable name for the new arrival. Once I had made my way out and was all cleaned up, it was time to meet my extended family. "Freda. She is so like Freda, this must be her name," Bataa's aunt remarked. While the story was repeated many times over, it was never explained to me who Freda was or what the aunt saw in me that so reminded her of Freda; maybe it was the way my face smiled, for they also told me that when I was born I laughed rather than cried. I guess now I'll never know.

Bataa had heard this suggested name and was torn. As the father of the baby and the head of the household, he was within his rights to choose my name. However, our culture demands great respect for our elders, and as his aunt was some years older, he was tempted to go with the name of her choice. Throughout this discussion, I am told, Bamaa stayed silent, finding it too problematic to take sides.

Why did it take a whole week to name me? Well, another important Lenje tradition states that a baby can only be named once her umbilical cord falls off and is buried safely under a tree. On the day this happened, as soil was being shoveled over the tiny cord that was my lifeline for nine months, my bataa made up his mind. "I will hear no more. Her name is Princess. I tell you now this child is destined for great things."

Now Freda is a beautiful name, but to this day I am glad my bataa was so insistent. I have come to agree there is something magical about one's own name. Later in my life, the name Princess has opened many doors that may not have opened were I called Freda.

My bataa felt free to name me Princess because, through him, my lineage traces back to the chief of our tribe. In my country, this name and relationship gives me a royal connection. Our chiefs are like our royal family. Being called Princess does not, however, mean I shall become queen; Zambia does not have a queen, and in any case, my connection is not so close.

I belong to the Lenje tribe, as this is Bataa's tribe. In my country it is customary for children to take their father's tribe. The Lenjes' ancestry and connection to Zambian land can be traced back further than any other tribe without migrating from another country, so we believe we have the greatest claim to indigenous status. With a gentle, mocked arrogance we say, "So bene chishi": "We are the owners of the land." Other tribes call back to us, smiling, "Kulibonesha," which means, "You are too proud," or "You like showing off." There are more than seventy tribes in Zambia today, blending together seventy dialects, though the most common languages are Nyanja and Bemba. The main tribes are the Bemba, the Ngoni, the Tonga, the Lozi, the Lunda, the Luvale and the Kaonde Ila.[1]

In some small ways the Lenje tribe has grown even further in prestige since the advent of modern society, as the railway passes through our land in the central part of the country. When the capital city was moved from Livingstone to Lusaka this new capital city fell in our land, so as a tribe we also became known as city people.

I remember a time when I was growing up and one of the Lenje chiefs passed away. My uncle came visiting from the village and, while he was sad for the loss, he was also all excited at the idea that my brother Muyani, my parents' next-born after me, should be put forward for consideration as the new junior chief. This great honor was seen as appropriate for our family because of our father's relationship to the chiefdom.

Bamaa, however, had other ideas. On hearing my uncle's suggestion, she took Muyani and went into hiding for what seemed like weeks. She hoped that if she could keep her son hidden long enough, my uncle would leave and take his wild ideas with him.

Of strong Christian faith, Bamaa could not bring herself to accept the traditional life of a chief for her son. First among the list of things Bamaa found uncomfortable was the chief's initiation ceremony. While none of us had attended such a ceremony, we understood it involved calling on the spirits of the chief's ancestors to protect his rule. We had also heard that chiefs had spiritual guides who would use witchcraft and voodoo to protect him and to deal with his enemies. Whether this was true or not, it was enough to scare Bamaa.

Witch doctors were and still are commonplace in Zambia today. They were believed to change a person's fortune using a combination of potions, roots, powders, animal blood, curses and rituals. Witch doctors are called on for everything from spiritual guidance to curing disease, crop failure and exacting revenge on wrongdoers. They even have small boats and planes made from grasses and brooms that are said to transport people to another place and time. This was all too much for Bamaa, who only returned home with Mugani once she was sure another chief had been selected and her son could stay safe in her arms.

In addition to the traditional lifestyle of a chief, I am sure Bamaa worried about her son taking on so much responsibility at such a young age. People from far and wide call on their chief for guidance and wisdom, and Muyani was just a young boy. While Bataa may have had held lofty dreams for his children, Bamaa's role was to protect her young family.

Suppose for a minute that Muyani had become chief. He would have lived in a chief's palace, though this is not like the palaces typically portrayed in the movies. It is common for a tribal chief's palace to be made from mud bricks and roofed with grass, although some chiefs have palaces made from brick, iron sheets and asbestos, still a commonly used building product in Zambia today. Sometimes a chief's palace will even have electricity. People would have to pay homage to my brother when they visited, bringing him gifts such as oil, sugar, cornmeal or other worthy items of their choosing. The life involves many rituals. As chief, my brother would have a kapaso, a kind of village bodyguard or messenger, and people would have to speak to the kapaso before they spoke to him.

The village chiefs still retain authority to this day. If our president visits a chief, it's the president who bows. To an extent, they have been incorporated into our British model of government, and today there is a House of Chiefs in Parliament where chiefs can share their views. While

Zambia's towns and cities are run by members of Parliament, the villages are still largely run by chiefs, who feed the views of people through to Parliament. Among all chiefs there is one leader. He is the only chief the British colonists chose to recognize during their rule; he is the chief of the Lozi tribe who we call the Litunga. Fortunately, when we regained our independence, the chiefs once more took their rightful place.

Yes, Goodson Moffat Kasune, my bataa, felt strongly about his royal lineage. It could be seen in the way he walked, his head held high with pride, and in the careful, dignified way he spoke. Bataa would often tell us in Lenje, "Muli bana babami": "You are children of the royal family." Bataa instilled in me the greatest respect for our traditional chiefs. He showed me that, while they may lack material wealth compared to their Western counterparts, they are our leaders and the preservers of our culture. Their role cannot be minimized, he used to tell me often. Zambia's chiefs are our guardians and our gatekeepers. Without them we are lost people.

Bataa's teachings also shaped my view of myself, as Bataa continually told me I had an important connection to this critical part of our culture. Even from a tender age, while I had no idea what twists my life would take, Bataa's teachings made me proud of my Lenje heritage and instilled in me a responsibility to care for others—a trait that would shape my life in ways I couldn't have imagined.

My Big Family

I REMEMBER ASKING MY BAMAA about the time she met Bataa. Her eyes glowed, reflecting the light of the campfire, as she told me the story of how she fell in love with my father. "When I met him, your father was such a man; I knew I wanted to be with him always. There are not many men like your father. Taller than six-foot-seven, he was the most handsome, slender, intelligent and well-dressed man I ever met."

Bataa boasted about Bamaa too. One night when I was fifteen or sixteen Bataa took me to our first dance together. I am so glad we had this chance as it was the only time we danced together. Here, a single lady came and asked him to dance. "You had better sit down or choose someone else. You are not as beautiful as my wife. She is the most beautiful woman in the world. She is the one for me," he told her. I was so embarrassed for the woman, but I cherish the memory of that night and the way he loved Bamaa.

My father had had several wives before he married Bamaa. However, when they met, my bataa was divorced and had no wife. So, beautiful, young Joyce Mwanamusulwe, a devoted Jehovah's Witness, felt free to follow her heart and marry Goodson Moffat Kasune, a man roughly twenty years her senior.

I say roughly twenty years because at that time it was not common for Zambian men to tell their age. Regardless of the ups and downs they faced, it was obvious to everyone how Bataa had captured Bamaa's heart and he hers.

Goodson Kasune was a great man, I agree with Bamaa: he was the most handsome man I ever met. He had light skin and a solid African body. Growing up, I measured all men against my handsome father. It still amazes me, the power of a father over a child, especially a daughter. In my world, he was the best man in the whole universe.

Bataa's nickname was Ronald Reagan because he was stylish and self-assured. I'm not sure if we knew anything at all about the real Ronald Reagan; we just knew this was the name of an important man in a far-off place called America. While he had little formal education, our own Ronald Reagan was hard-working, charming and tenacious.

Unlike fathers in the village, Bataa was not too traditional in the role he took raising his children. As long as we behaved, Bataa liked to play the good guy of the household. He would spoil us and buy us expensive things. If Bamaa went visiting the village, Bataa would cook special meals for us. While Bamaa knew the importance of rationing food, our father would cook meats and many dishes with no thought of the expense. Little did we know, Bataa was blowing the household budget buying so much meat. In time I would learn it was indicative of his personality, not to think of the future.

Bataa also took us children on outings. His role as senior superintendent of the railway police required us to move from time to time between Ndola, Kabwe and Livingstone. My favorite home was in Livingstone, since there Bataa took us on the best outings. Livingstone is the home of one of the seven natural wonders of the world—Victoria Falls. Bataa would take us to view the falls or take us cruising up the Zambesi River, where we would spot crocs and hippos. Or we'd head to the

Maramba Culture Village where traditional villagers danced and performed ancient rituals for tourists. On one occasion we had to flee a stampede of wild elephants as the hypnotic boomba, boomba, boomba of the Maramba drums had attracted a passing herd.

It was generally seen as taboo for a growing girl to hug her father, but I always hugged Bataa and he hugged me back. Still, as the head of the house, Goodson Moffat Kasune played a firm role in enforcing good behavior in his children. He was the disciplinarian and never hesitated to administer a spanking if we were naughty.

Bamaa rarely spanked us. She was happy for us to play as children. She was a gentle, tender woman, though strong in her own way. Whenever I did something wrong, her soft voice sparkled, "Princess. Stop what you are doing."

If we really misbehaved, Bamaa—like, I have come to realize, so many mothers around the world—could simply say, "I'll tell your father," and we would instantly behave. I never heard her cuss anyone. If you really upset her, it would not take long to see tears form in her eyes. Her heart was so tender and her tears came so easily.

※

My favorite time each day was when Bamaa would tell the children a story, which she sang in her Bamaa's tongue. Stories would either be told around a fire or in our bedroom. In most of our homes, I shared a bedroom with anywhere from four to six of my sisters, half-sisters and female cousins; the other girls all shared one or two double beds while I slept on the floor with my mat made from empty mealie meal sacks. I had to sleep on the floor because I had an embarrassing night problem: I wet the bed up until the age of thirteen. Still, I forgot my nighttime problems as all the children gathered around for Bamaa's stories.

Most African stories told by Bamaa were designed to teach us morals and values. She did not tell stories of Cinderella or Snow White, the tooth fairy or Santa Claus; there were no expensive cars and gifts, no gallant knights or ninjas fighting. Bamaa's stories taught us that our actions would have consequences. She taught us to respect our elders, to always tell the truth and not to steal. One of my favorite stories was "Munge Munge," which she told interchangeably between her various languages.

"Kwakalinga," or "Once upon a time," it began, there was a young girl whose beauty was the talk of the village. When her time came to be married, her father sourced the very best suitors to parade in front of his daughter. He searched for men with great wisdom, humility and love for their family from villages near and far. But the daughter refused every man chosen by her father.

Men continued trying to win her heart, but she was not moved until a young man came, dressed in finery with tricks and looks like no other. He talked of his great wealth and the lavish life they would lead together. That was it; the girl was taken. She told her father this was the man she had been waiting for, but the father was not convinced. Something troubled him about this young man.

The strong-willed daughter persisted, and her father finally agreed to allow the relationship with the provision that the girl's young sister live with the couple as a chaperone, as was custom in our culture. The bride-to-be agreed but was always resentful of her sister's presence and therefore mistreated her.

Once they were married, the husband would set out from his village each and every night, hunting to provide meat for his wife and her sister. He would return deep in the night calling out, "Munge, munge." His wife would answer, "Tushinkwele Bamuyama bamazangazanga bene batwele mwane, mbwane bahile nakwisamba chuni." The husband would enter with the finest meats, and occasionally the wife would share rations with her sister.

Knowing she had not treated her sister well, the wife thought the sister was simply being spiteful when she came to her and said, "Your husband is a monster. He turns into a hyena every night when he goes hunting. How else do you think he could kill so many large animals?"

At this point in Bamaa's story, all the children would be filled with fear. Bamaa would ask if we had heard enough, but we would squeal for her to continue.

Of course the wife did not believe her sister. Her husband could not possibly be a hyena. The sister knew it was up to her to protect them both against this monster. And so she secretly set about making a drum that, when beaten, could carry the girls away, up into the air. They would use it to escape when the time came.

Of course the sister was right. The new bride's husband did indeed turn into a hyena every night. It turned out that his true intent was to fatten up his bride and her sister in order to eat them. All his hyena friends kept asking him when the day of the big feast would come, for they were growing tired of waiting.

"They do not yet have enough meat on them. We need to be patient," was the reply from the husband. The other hyenas could wait no longer. The girls looked so tasty. They decided to disobey the husband and prepared to attack and eat the young ladies, who were fattening up nicely, especially the bride. When they could wait no longer, the other hyenas made their move.

The sister, who had taken it upon herself to sit on watch twenty-four hours a day, saw them coming in the distance and began to beat her drum: "mbitibiti kalikoma kamabingoma kalikono, beat, beat, beat." The young bride, unaware of what was happening, turned to see an angry group of hyenas coming faster and faster after her. She screamed and froze.

No matter how many times I heard the story, at this point it was like watching a thriller movie. I sat upright, my chin in my hands, just waiting to hear what happened next. I'd stare enthralled at my mother's face as she shared her story. She was a true African woman—not too skinny and not too fat, with velvet chocolate skin and a soft pink tongue that danced in her mouth as she lovingly sang to her children.

If we became too scared, she would simply calm us by saying, "Shhhh, my children. It is only a story." On other nights, if we were too noisy, she would make us really frightened so we could not wait to go to bed.

On she continued: "Mbitibiti kalikoma kamabingoma kalikon," sounded the drum, as the youngest girl grabbed her older sister and flew off into the air.

The husband was furious when he came home to find his plump bride and her sister missing. The next day he headed for the village of their family to retrieve them. Once again, he wore the disguise of the handsome, dashing young man.

But, by the time he arrived at the village, the girls had already told their family the awful truth. Their family quickly understood the situation and formulated a plan. When the husband arrived he was greeted lovingly, lulling him into a false sense of security. The family did not let on that they knew his awful secret. Instead they put on a show, outwardly treating the groom with great respect. They offered him a seat, a drink and some food, which the groom accepted. He didn't realize that he had been tricked. The villagers had placed his seat over a deep, deep ditch, which the chair tumbled into, ending the hyena's life.

The story ends with the older sister thanking her younger sister and apologizing for treating her so poorly. With that, Bamaa would encourage all her children to sleep, leaving us to ponder the message that would one day become so relevant.

�֍

As I grew, Bamaa searched for opportunities to spend time with me. She'd let me help her make a lemon cake or Victoria Sandwich cake. Or she'd show me how to sew clothes that she'd make for our family and to sell. I loved sitting on the floor with her as her scissors sliced through colorful sheets of fabric. The voom, voom, voom, chicka, chicka, chicka of the sewing machine that stitched the shapes together hypnotized me as it formed beautiful new clothes.

My mother's Christian faith was strong. If she wasn't telling me African tales, she would read to me from my book of Bible stories; my favorite was the story of baby Moses. I loved to hear of the baby found in the reeds who grew to perform such spectacular feats. At Bataa's recommendation I attended Roman Catholic church but Bamaa also took me to her church. While as a little girl I did not understand the teachings, I saw the godliness in my bamaa and I wanted to be like her.

I rarely saw Bamaa relax. It would be late at night before she finished preparing our meals, assisting with our homework and putting us to bed. Her last task each night was to carefully lay out her clothes in preparation for the day ahead.

Bamaa was among the few women of her time who had a paid job outside the home. She worked as a secretary to a senior government official. Even our frequent relocating did not stop Bamaa from working. Since she was such a good worker, the government was usually able to find her a role where we lived. I never heard her complain; she loved her work.

I don't know what Bamaa did for fun, or if she ever even had time for fun. She never spoke on the phone to her friends; she rarely went on outings, other than to see her family in the village. When she wasn't working, her time was filled with reading the Bible, gardening and caring for her family. Looking back, I know my bamaa was amazing to do all she did in a house so full of people. At any one time, there were between fifteen and twenty of us living under our roof. We were a mixture of my parents' children, cousins, visiting family members and anyone who needed a place to stay.

My father and mother had four children together, of which I was the eldest. Next was my brother, Muyani, then my sisters, Caroline and Linda. Bamaa had two older sons, Kelvin and Felix, who grew up knowing my bataa as their own father. And then there were Bataa's other children; he had twenty-four total, to different mothers.

One of these women was Jennifer, my bama banini, my small mother, who lived in our home with us. You see, my bataa was a polygamist. I am unsure how long into his marriage to my bamaa it was before Bataa took a second wife. Together Bataa and Jennifer had a daughter, Sheila, who also lived with us and who Bamaa treated as her own. In theory, when a man wishes to take a second wife he can only do so with the first wife's permission. I am uncertain how often this permission is granted. (As I understand it, in many cases when permission is denied the second marriage still proceeds.)

Those of his children who did not live with us would sometimes visit, and whenever they did Bataa would insist, "These are your brothers and sisters. Love them and respect them." Some of them I only ever knew by name. From time to time Bataa would take a piece of paper and proudly draw a family tree, showing each of us in our birth order. I wish I had kept the drawings as I now find it hard to remember where we all fit. Like any little girl, though, I had thought my bataa would always be around to explain things to me. How could any of us have imagined what lay ahead?

❧

For several years we were fortunate to have a television in our home. Most families did not have a television at that time. I understand that in 2003 there were still only around five hundred thousand televisions between twelve million people in Zambia.[1] Any home with a television would always have a collection of neighborhood children in it at the times of *Tom and Jerry*, *Zorro*, *Bozo* or *The Muppet Show*. Owning a television was a great way to make friends. Before we had our own television, our friends would leave their blinds open so we could peek through their windows to watch our favorite shows. Once or twice when the blinds were closed, I still stood outside with my brothers and sisters, trying to make out what was happening on the little screen.

Once we got a television of our own, we were allowed to watch until 8 p.m., when it was time for bed or time to review our homework. Every night I was so excited as the news began and Maureen Nkandu appeared. *Do-do, do-do, do-do* came the start of the national anthem and then the coat of arms and slogan: One Zambia, One Nation. I can't remember much of what Maureen Nkandu said during the news; I was more taken with the way she carried herself, her demeanor. I wanted to be like her.

When the bathroom was empty, in my mind it became the studios of Zambia's national broadcaster. I would hide away and earnestly commence the song "One Zambia, One Nation"—and then it was time for "Here's the latest news from Maureen Nkandu." Standing in front of the mirror with a hairbrush for a microphone, I would begin, "Thank you and good evening. Here is the news of the day." I so wanted to be Maureen. On I would go, mimicking her and making up news stories.

My childhood nickname given to me by my family was "The Reporter." It came about because I had a loud voice as a child (and still do), and I was fond of informing my parents whenever my brothers and sisters did anything wrong.

I was also very outspoken as a child. If my bataa was in the wrong or if he didn't treat my bamaa properly, I would always find myself speaking for Bamaa. Even though Bataa felt he was the boss and no one should speak back to him, I was different somehow; as I grew, I was always brave enough to confront him. When I did he would ask, dumbfounded, "What are you made of, my daughter? There is something about you." I would answer impudently, "I don't know. You gave birth to me." It is said the traits of children only grow stronger in adulthood. For some reason, even at a young age I had an instinct to protect the weak; that was why I wanted to protect Bamaa.

Sometimes great love is hard to understand as a child. As I became more aware, I watched my parents and learned that you have to work hard to continue loving each other. From them I learned that relationships can be complex; I came to learn that marriage must be based on more than just a feeling, as feelings fade away. It takes real commitment to love someone when it is not easy to love them. From them I also learned the importance of family and community; I learned to welcome all people into my heart and into my home. It is around family you can be naked and vulnerable; you can make mistakes and not be judged. If not around family, then where shall we learn?

4

The Short Life of
a Baby Named Linda

As a young girl I loved school and took it upon myself to teach the younger children everything I was learning in class. I, however, learned easily and quickly, and I expected the other children to do the same, forgetting their tender age. If they didn't know an answer, I would spank them until they ran away from class.

Bamaa encouraged me to be gentle, but I was frustrated that they wouldn't learn quicker, and I didn't see the need to slow down. She was right, though; my pupils stopped attending class, and for some time after, I was forced to teach the small canon flower bushes instead of real students. Teaching the bushes soon became boring and I begged for my students to recommence school, promising better treatment in future.

In 1984 it seemed my luck had changed when my mother gave birth to a baby girl named Linda. This noisy baby with fine curly hair was my parents' fourth born together. My sister Caroline and I have light, chocolate-colored skin but Linda was a dark, dark baby, slender, with beautiful features like a child from Ethiopia or Somalia. Bamaa loved her so much.

"Black is definitely beautiful," she would say as she made little circles with her finger on Linda's stomach and admired the small baby in her arms.

As for me, I loved Linda too; she was the most precious treasure in my life. There had always been children and babies around our home, but when brand-new baby Linda was born, I was bursting with pride that I was now old enough and responsible enough to actually care for her. I would carefully wrap baby Linda and carry her in a *chitenge* on my back, the way African women carry babies as they do their chores.

Even more importantly Linda became another student for my school. While I didn't hold formal classes for her, I taught her from time to time. *One day when Linda grows up she will get all the answers, far better than the other students,* I thought to myself. I loved Linda so much I wanted to carry her with me wherever I went, but Bamaa had to draw the line at baby Linda climbing mango trees.

There were two other reasons I wanted to carry baby Linda with me. First, she always seemed to be the same size as a baby doll. She never seemed to grow in size or weight so she was easy for me to carry. I had watched other babies grow so fast but baby Linda's size remained the same. She kept sucking from my mother's breast, but she just didn't get any bigger.

I also wanted to carry Linda because if she was left alone for even a few minutes she would cry and cry as if she was in great pain. While she was in someone's arms she would mostly sleep or whimper, but occasionally she cried so hard, and no one could stop her from her crying, no matter what tricks we tried. I could tell from the look on Bamaa's face that she was beginning to worry.

While my bamaa was a quiet woman, she had always had a sparkle in her eye; she would laugh, joke and smile tenderly. But a deep sadness took over her eyes when Linda failed to grow. I would sometimes find her sitting, rocking back and forth on a mat on the floor holding tiny Linda in her arms and staring into the distance. Looking back, I see that look of

Bamaa's as the desperate sadness of a mother who knows her child may not survive.

Bamaa had Linda in and out of the hospital in search of a treatment or a cure, but no doctor could explain her condition. While Linda was in the hospital my bamaa would sleep there, just so she could remain close to her baby. She tried everything she could to care for Linda. She prayed deep into the night, she asked the church to pray, she tried all sorts of foods—vegetables, fruits, eggs, meats, anything she could lay her hands on that might restore her baby's health. But no matter what she did, Linda was never well.

By age one, Linda could barely walk; she would move a little and fall back down. Then we started noticing that her hair was falling out. None of us understood Linda's sickness but each of us felt it every day. Soon after her first birthday she became too fragile to come outside with me.

Bataa, too, loved baby Linda and would have done anything to cure her, to ease her pain. To give Bamaa a break, he would wrap Linda in Bamaa's *chitenge* and carry her on his own back. He would even give the baby his own breast—though he knew it could not provide milk—in an attempt to calm her.

One day, I recall, without telling Bamaa or any of the children, Bataa took Linda to a traditional healer. Traditional healers are still common in Zambia today, for reasons related partly to culture and tradition and partly out of necessity due to a crippled health system that has only one Western doctor for every ten thousand Zambians, or a total of 1,264 doctors in the entire country.[1] Whatever the reason, Bamaa disliked and mistrusted these healers. Her religion (and later mine) forebade them in the same way it forbade witch doctors. In this instance, Bataa felt Western medicine had failed to give us answers, so he turned to tradition in case someone was witching his baby.

Returning home with Linda, Bataa asked all the children to go outside and play. We didn't know why, but he looked serious, so we all ran outside. As I so often did, I pretended to run off and play but instead hid close by, but out of sight, so I could eavesdrop on the conversation. What I heard was Bataa reporting the traditional healer's diagnosis.

"This is serious," he began. He was whispering nervously, huddled close to Bamaa. "There is a neighbor who has put a curse on this baby. A large, poisonous snake with a flickering tongue is swallowing this baby every day." I'd never heard Bataa's voice sound like this before. From my vantage point, just outside the room, I could see his eyes darting around as if he expected someone to be following him. He had seen something very dark and disturbing, and he was struggling to break the terrible news to his young wife.

"Joyce, you will recall we found a frog in her baby cot. Since she was born there have been owls flying around the place. Those things are sucking the blood and the life from our baby. Someone has placed a curse on this baby that has been with her since the day she was born."

The healer had spoken. Baby Linda had been cursed. Bataa was right; there had been a frog and lizards in her room and owls around the house. The healer had tried to reverse the curse but was not sure he had been successful; it was a powerful curse cast long ago, so perhaps it was too late. For me, that was it. I had heard the truth of what was taking my baby sister and I had to get my revenge.

One day soon after, I was going to my friend Mainza's pink house opposite our home at One Mushili Way in Livingstone when I spotted the culprits: two large owls and one small owl perched in the big tree by the side of the road. I was so angry and upset that I found myself throwing rocks to stone the owls as they slept. In the naive mind of a child, someone or something has to be to blame. The healer had said it had something to do with the owls, and I was with Bataa on this one—I believed him. These birds were sent to kill my baby sister and now I wanted to kill them.

Despite the best combination of traditional and Western medicines and our family's deep love and prayers, baby Linda died in 1986. She was just like a visitor: one day here and the next day gone, without the chance to stay too long.

I was ten years old when death first visited my family to take my baby sister. My relative level of privilege meant my protection from the death of a loved one had lasted longer than it does for most others in a country where one in five children dies before their fifth birthday[2] and the average adult life expectancy is just forty years.[3]

I found that the sadness consumed me, and it seemed to make my bamaa weak. My bamaa tried to ease my pain: "Even though you are sad, my Princess, Linda is at peace and no longer has to suffer. Please let this comfort you and be happy for her."

I tried to find comfort in my bamaa's words. My heart had broken watching baby Linda die for no explicable reason. At the end of her short life she was little more than a skeleton, her teeth rotten from toxic medicines that could not save her. She never grew to walk or talk; she barely had the strength to smile. I remember thinking how unfair it was that a tiny child should have to live and die in such pain, how unfair it was for my parents who loved her so dearly and how unfair it was for me to lose my precious baby sister. The heartbreak I endured as a ten-year-old watching a child in pain has not eased. It grows ever stronger, burning inside me.

When you look back on your life, there are a few key moments that change your life's direction. Sometimes it hits like a bolt of lightning, and you know life has changed forever. At other times you may not even be aware you have walked your first steps down a new path. You just keep living each day as the day before without realizing that you have passed through a different doorway and life will never be the same again. The too-soon death of my baby sister from a mysterious illness was such an event for me.

With distance and perspective, these are the times you know your life's path was set before you were born. Some call it fate; some call it destiny. Me, I marvel at the power of a God who knows our whole life's journey long before we walk it.

5

Bataa's Gun Goes Missing

Shortly after baby Linda was buried in the Livingstone Graveyard, something happened to Bataa. He went from being our Ronald Reagan to someone not like Bataa at all. It's hard to remember clearly just when it began, but I recall him becoming a bit wobbly, and doing strange things. He also had some episodes of sickness—colds and bugs—which stand out in my childhood memories because Bataa never got sick.

It didn't make much sense at the time, but as an adult, a scrapbook of memories comes together: feelings, snippets of conversations overheard, a nervous look and muffled arguments all take their place on its pages.

The trouble, as I recall it, started when Bataa's gun went missing. For as long as I could remember, Bataa had a railways-issued firearm that he carried while at work. He was always very careful of his gun, polishing it meticulously and locking it out of sight when he wasn't working. Then, mysteriously, one day it could not be found.

We heard Bataa searching the house saying, "Joyce, where could that gun have gone?" It troubled him for several days and nights. He retraced his steps time and time again, walking out to the car, then inside again as though he was returning from work. Bataa knew that if the gun wasn't found, serious trouble lay ahead.

Of course it didn't take long before rumors spread among the railway workers that Goodson Kasune had lost his firearm. Naturally, he suspected everyone he worked with. But whatever the cause, my father was held responsible, which meant he lost his job. I'm guessing he told Bamaa Bamini when it happened, but it was some time before he could bring himself to tell his children. We were left to try to work things out for ourselves. And with Bataa around the house more, we noticed more and more things happening that didn't quite make sense.

One day soon after the episode with the gun there was a knock on the front door. Once again, the other children and I were ordered to play out in the garden while some serious-looking men went inside to speak to Bataa and Bamaa. After some time, the men came back out, walked up to Bataa's beloved Land Rover, opened the door with a key and drove it away in front of our eyes. Bataa had recently given up his personal car and now the car provided by the railways was taken as well. *Did this mean we were to have no car? Just what could be happening?* No one spoke about the incident at the dinner table that night. The look on Bataa's face warned us off asking. But even at my tender age it was very clear to me something was wrong.

More signs of trouble emerged. Partly because the railways had always provided us with homes, partly because my father was a self-educated man, but mainly because he was a man who lived for the moment—a man who had twenty-four children and two wives, and who liked to spend his money—Moffat Kasune was never inclined to plan for the future. He never invested in property or saved money in a bank. So you guessed it . . . losing his job meant losing our home.

Since this time, I have often found myself wondering if my father's employers fired him because they were afraid of his illness. After all, his health was clearly deteriorating. If, as a child, I could tell he was not quite right, surely his employer was aware that something was wrong with the commanding officer of the southern region of the railways police? After all, it wasn't just obvious in Bataa; he was not the only one becoming sick.

At this time, Zambians were becoming nervous about a mystery illness that was taking the lives of people who seemed perfectly healthy not so long before. Most of us could recognize the symptoms of malaria in the summer months, TB and cholera when it rained in the townships, dysentery and the distended bellies of bilharzia patients, but this disease was something else.

Not even smart adults or doctors seemed able to diagnose the symptoms, which sometimes seemed to be a mixture of so many diseases. As we experienced firsthand in the case of baby Linda, the witch doctors and traditional healers fueled fears with their talk of curses and witching, igniting rumors and discrimination.

Fortunately, because my bamaa was still working as a secretary for the government, we were able to stay in one of the government-owned homes for a short time, but soon this too was taken away. These unexpected hardships placed a great strain on Bataa and Bamaa's relationship, and they were arguing often by this time.

My father's confidence that he could provide a good city life for his family was jolted out from underneath him with his prestigious job gone. It was painful to see my proud Bataa, who once had so much, who traveled around Africa for work, now broken. His only option was to bundle his family and possessions together and return to a life in the village.

6

Be Strong and of Good Courage

THE DAY WE LEFT FOR THE VILLAGE Bamaa took little Muyani, Caroline and me on the train. Bataa and the others would follow some time later. Our furniture would travel by truck once we reached our destinations. By now Bamaa and Bataa were fighting so badly that it was agreed Bataa would go to the village of his own bamaa, taking Bamaa Banini and some of the children with him. Bamaa's other children, Kelvin and Felix, would spend some time with us and some time with our grandparents. For the time being at least, my parents would live separate lives and we children would be split up.

Life in the village was very different from our comfortable city life. I still remember being woken in the dark that first morning in my cold, breezy hut to go and fetch water. I remember the sight of my reflection in that dirty, shallow hole that was our water source; the cow lapping our water with its long tongue; the laughter of the other children as I learned to carry the yellow water container on my head.

But by far the most difficult part of village life for us children was missing Bataa. Every other Friday as school ended, and on school holi-

days, a group of us that would include some combination of my brothers
Muyani and Kelvin, my sister Carol, my cousin Beatrice and me, would
set off on the long walk across the sandy soil to Chipopo Village, where
Bataa and old Grandmother Shantantu lived. We were always ecstatic to
see him when we arrived.

Bataa kept himself busy in the village. He had been able to reclaim
some land on which he grew crops. He called his farm *Tula Twabane,*
meaning "make a stop so that we can share," but while proud of this farm,
it was clear he missed his life and important job in the city. He continually tried to create opportunities to regain his former glory. Wherever
there was a village meeting, he was there. The village folk must have
thought him odd, as he wanted to meet with the chief, the governor, the
councilor, then with this group or that. The staff at the Chibombo Boma
rural government office had certainly not met any village person like
Goodson Moffat Kasune, who they now encountered on at least a weekly
basis. For him the busy life of meetings was the only life he knew, and he
would not let go. Preparing for and attending meetings was Bataa's opportunity to shine. His eyes would come alive once more and he would
begin to hum as he carefully pulled a suit out of the wardrobe.

"No-bana Sandabota—Children, do I look smart today?" This was
Bataa's British-influenced way of asking whether he looked handsome
and distinguished, though he believed he already knew the answer. "Ehe
mwabota," we would reassure him.

Occasionally his tie needed adjusting, and I loved helping Bataa with
this. His eyes beamed with pride that his young daughter was helping
him to look even more handsome and distinguished. Then he would set
off, bobbing his head to pass through the low door of the hut into the
dusty village.

Walking proudly, with a spring in his step, I knew Bataa would be
singing to himself as he so often did, "No-bana sandabota. Ehe, mwaabota.
So ba Lenje sobapale. So balomfu nshingo. Nakatwenda bantu balebela,
ba bombwe baleemikana, Insoka kuchicha mukuyuba muchilindi. Atu

sweko besa ba sankwa balamfu nshingo, basankwa bapaale, ba Lenje bataanshi," meaning, "Here I come, handsome Lenje man with a long neck. When I come people watch, the frogs stand to attention to marvel and the snakes run for their lives saying 'here comes the handsome man with the long neck, the Lenje man, Goodson Moffat Kasune.'"

But the truth was that, while still handsome, my father seemed to be losing a lot of weight. His aging suits seemed baggier each time he put them on. I didn't think much about his weight loss then; it seemed to make sense. In the city, Bataa had driven his Land Rover everywhere, but now he walked long distances visiting us and the government offices, and he was actively tending his land most days.

His physical health wasn't the only thing that seemed to take a beating from village life, however. Though Bataa kept busy, and though life for my family was still not as tough as it was for many poor rural Zambians, the stark contrast between village life and that which we were used to stung my proud parents every day. Bataa could not forget his city life; he held on tight to his memories. He wanted to be sure his children didn't forget either. One day he took me for a long walk to the top of a big hill in his village where he pointed out across the plains and said, "Look at this. You have the right to this land. You are royalty and this is your land. Please do not forget this, my child." The whole way home he kept repeating, "Always remember you lived in a big house in the city. Don't become comfortable in the village and don't forget I was once a commanding officer, one who rose from a gardener to high heights."

Bataa was right to continually remind us of our city lives, to remind us that there was another way to live. The longer we spent in the village, the more this other life faded to a distant memory. My behavior began to change; I started sitting at the back of the class at school, disrupting other students. I would still score high marks in English, but my math marks grew steadily worse. I think I excused myself with the misguided belief that girls are not good at math, which of course is not true. Despite my bad behavior, when my seventh-grade exam results came out I had scored some of the highest marks in our school, which got me accepted to one of the finest boarding schools in Zambia.

When I came home for my first holidays and saw Bamaa and Bataa in their separate villages, I couldn't believe how much each of them had changed. Seeing them with fresh eyes, I noticed they had both lost a lot of weight and looked unwell. We didn't discuss it; health is just not something most African parents talk to their children about. Besides, it was the holidays; once I got used to seeing them, they began to look normal enough, and I was off playing with my friends.

But the pattern persisted. After each three-month-long school term I returned home to the village to notice Bamaa and Bataa growing thinner. For a while I convinced myself they were simply lean and fit from village life. But their appearance soon became more haggard than fit. Something about their faces, their appearance and their demeanor made them look unhealthy too. I became worried. *What was wrong with my parents?*

On one of my trips home, Bamaa and I went to buy some cornmeal. With her now twig-thin arms, she hauled the forty-four-pound sack up to her head. She began to walk, but I noticed her neck struggling to support the weight. She was coughing and clearly unwell.

"Bamaa, please let me carry this for you," I asked her gently.

"No."

"Please, I would like to carry the bag."

"No, Love."

I stopped walking until she gave me her bundle to add to my own twenty-two-pound bundle, which meant I was now carrying over sixty-six pounds on my head. The weight hurt but I didn't let it show. More than my head and my neck, my heart ached with the confirmation of how sick my dear Bamaa must be. I was stronger than she was now, and I was happy to help. In Zambia we have a proverb that says *Iyakota—yonka mu bana:* "parents take care of their children when they are young, but as they grow it is the children's turn to take care of their parents." At fourteen, it was time for me to begin caring for my bamaa.

We took Bamaa to Liteta Rural Hospital where she was diagnosed with tuberculosis and admitted. Bamaa's sister Violet and her bamaa helped nurse her because she was so weak. She was treated for tuberculosis and she returned home, though her health was still not good. This pattern was repeated several times.

Several more terms passed at boarding school, and each time I returned home I was pained to see my bamaa losing even more weight. She must have been weak and so very tired, but she still maintained the garden, growing tomatoes, pumpkins, cassava and ground nuts.

Sadly, I continued to be playful at school, and when I returned home at the end of ninth grade I had failed all my grades. This Bamaa could not tolerate. She removed me from boarding school and sent me to live with another aunt, this time in Chililabombwe on the Copperbelt, the mining town that borders the Democratic Republic of Congo, formerly known as Zaire.

I failed because I was worried about my parents. I chose to rebel and misbehave to distract myself, and my grades suffered. I couldn't say this to Bamaa so I accepted her decision and went to live with my aunt some hours away. This was a particularly bitter pill for me to swallow. Not only did I have to leave boarding school, but there was no place for me in ninth grade at Chililabombwe Secondary School. The only place available was in the eighth grade. So, an intelligent but playful girl who should have been progressing to the tenth grade found herself in a small, regional school repeating eighth grade. I was so disappointed in myself. Of course, I found the work simple, but every time I answered a question the other students would say, "It's easy when you've gone two years backwards." This was a valuable, painful lesson for me.

❋

While I was staying with Aunt Erika, I was pleased that Bamaa negotiated to move back to a humble government house in the Chibombo district. The house was still in the rural area and it was surrounded by huts,

so she always had family close by. Her health was just too fragile to remain in a hut, and she seemed to recognize this.

One night during an April holiday visit to Bamaa she called me to her
side in the small home. "My girl, I need to leave this message with you. I
want you to be strong and be of good courage even though what I am going to tell you will be hard for you to know."

Next she told me a story. "There was a man who was rich. He had
butcheries, a bakery and a red car and when his time came to die he left
everything to his son, asking him to take care of his mother, brothers and
sisters. As his father lay dying, his son promised, 'Father, I will do this,
you have my word.'

"But when the father died, the son spent all the money on girls and
drink and the family went bankrupt. All the work the old man had done
was in vain, the whole family struggled, and the children never went to
school."

Holding my hands, she looked into my eyes and confirmed my worst
fears: "Princess. The reason I told you that story is because I am going to
die." Her coughing took over for a minute or two. When she was able to
catch her breath, she continued.

"I am going to leave you in charge of the family. You need to care for
your brothers, sisters and my other dependents, try to make sure they all
continue school. It is the only way they will have a future. And also never
forget your grandparents, for without them you would not be here. I
don't have the money of the man in the story. But as you can see, money
comes and goes. It will be hard for you. I don't know how much money
will be left, or if there will be any at all. Almost all the money I had has
been spent on medication. I leave you to care for your brothers and sisters
with almost nothing. Princess, I am sorry. Life will be hard but I know
your heart, and I know you will be strong. You are a child of courage and
hope and I know you will make it."

I was in shock. I don't know why Bamaa chose me. I guess she knew I
had motherly instincts, as I had helped care for baby Linda, and she knew

I had protective instincts, as I defended her when my father argued with her. Perhaps as the oldest girl she felt she had little other choice.

I loved my bamaa, but like most teenage girls I often answered back when she asked me to do things. But that night I remember sitting quietly, nodding a few times as if to say, *I am listening and will do as you have asked.* I wondered why we couldn't stay with Bataa but didn't ask the question. While I was with her I controlled my tears without saying a word, but as soon as she finished talking I ran to my own room and cried. With my head in the pillow to muffle the sound, I sobbed that night. I couldn't catch my breath—the air wouldn't reach my lungs but I couldn't let my bamaa or anyone else hear me.

I wanted to pray but I didn't know how to pray properly, because Bamaa always prayed for me. I managed to speak just six words: "Lord, give me strength and courage." I kept sobbing until eventually I cried myself to sleep. I didn't tell anyone what happened. I wanted to be strong and of good courage. I was seventeen.

※

While we will never know for certain, today I can make an educated guess at what was taking place inside Bamaa's failing body. HIV and AIDS was first officially "discovered" in Africa in the early 1980s, although retrospective studies of blood samples indicate the virus was already thriving in at least Congo, Rwanda and Burundi in the 1970s.[1] History shows that by the late 1980s the virus already had a firm grip over much of sub-Saharan Africa, and indeed, in 1986 Rwanda became the first country in the world to do a national survey of HIV prevalence. The results indicated that a staggering 17.8 percent of people in cities were already infected.[2] Anything above 1 percent is considered a generalized epidemic, indicating that a disease is spreading in the population as a whole and is already difficult to control.[3]

We now also understand the very firm relationship between tuberculosis and HIV. The World Health Organization estimates that two billion people around the world carry the TB bacillus; in most cases it lies dormant and harmless. But having HIV more than doubles the chance a person will develop the disease. In Zambia today, three-quarters of new tuberculosis cases are in people with HIV.[4] The Human Immunodeficiency Virus is clever—and insidious—this way; if left untreated it destroys your immunity and lays down a red carpet to welcome other infections that eventually claim your life.

Somehow Bamaa got up and went to work the next day. I still don't know if she was aware just what was killing her. Looking back, the fact that she always focused so hard on the vegetable garden and eating nutritious meals makes me wonder if she did in fact know. I think it is more likely the doctors said, "You need to eat a healthy diet to fight against this mysterious disease we cannot yet identify."

Sometime in October of 1993 while staying with my aunt I received the dreaded phone call from the village: "Your bamaa is very sick. You need to come now." I was on the first available bus.

When I reached Bamaa hours later, she was once more in Liteta Rural Hospital. She asked my family not to locate Muyani as he was writing his ninth-grade exams, and she was determined her children would be educated. Caroline had to stay with Aunt Violet in the village because she was too young to be at the hospital, but my Bakaapa Banakashi, my Grandmother Selina, was already at Bamaa's bedside. Even when my aunts and other family members were there, my Bakaapa Banakashi insisted on being there herself to care for her baby girl, her firstborn out of eight children.

My bamaa was an amazing woman, full of kindness, always joyful, full of integrity and strength. She had such a beautiful smile, and she was beautiful both inside and out. Wherever she was it was a peaceful place to be. She showed me how to love people, not by saying but by being.

Now she lay like a skeleton in the hospital, just as baby Linda had done seven years before. As I looked at her lying there, weak, in this unfamiliar, narrow hospital bed, she caught my gaze for a moment but then turned away. Each time our eyes met, she turned her head from me. Sensing she wanted to watch me, I deliberately looked away—at the ceiling, out the window, across to the other beds—respecting her silent wish to avoid painful eye contact. With my gaze diverted, I could sense Bamaa's loving eyes taking in their last glimpses of her daughter.

I can't describe the foul smell in that ward. Many patients, including Bamaa, suffered from chronic diarrhea, and they didn't have the strength to get to the bathroom; most looked to be suffering the same disease. The hospital didn't even have running water in the wards. Bakaba Banakashi, my aunts and I had to fetch water to wash my bamaa's dirty linen.

Also, like many Zambian hospitals, particularly those in rural areas, Liteta couldn't afford to serve meals. I'm not sure whether this has changed, but at the time, it was up to the families of patients to provide meals for their sick. My aunts sent food from the village in with me each morning, though by now Bamaa ate little.

My grandmother was so strong through it all. While others came and cried I never saw her cry in front of her daughter, for she kept on hoping for life for her child. On a practical level she also had a lot to fear. After all, Bamaa had been the only breadwinner in her family. In addition to losing her precious daughter, she was losing her only source of income.

Bakaba Banakashi was not alone. Women are affected disproportionately by HIV and AIDS. Our biology makes us more susceptible to the virus; in fact, nearly 60 percent of all HIV-positive people in sub-Saharan Africa are women.[5] Not only are we more likely to become infected ourselves, but we are also the caregivers. Whenever someone is sick, there's always a mother, a grandmother, a sister or an aunt close by saying, "I will care for you." As the number of people infected with HIV and AIDS sits at around thirty-three million, a woman's role as caregiver accounts for much of her time. This is valuable time she cannot spend working, nurturing and educating her children, or tending to animals and vegetables. Arguably the worst consequence of AIDS is the way it keeps people locked in the cycle of poverty.

Each night I left Bakaba Banakashi to stay with Bamaa overnight while I returned to sleep in the village. Sometimes there was not even one chair for her to sit on, and there was definitely not room for two of us to remain overnight. Every morning I woke and made the nervous journey back to the hospital, not knowing what lay ahead.

I saw so many emotions pass across Bamaa's pained eyes in what we all knew were her final days: soaring pride and an endless flow of love but also guilt and desperate sadness at the knowledge she would soon be leaving me and my siblings in the world with so much responsibility. Sensing she was close to the end, Bamaa removed her ivory bangles and asked me to look after them always. Though her wrists were so tiny, she'd been able to leave the bracelets on because her large, worker's hands prevented them from slipping off. I wear those bangles to this day. Each time I look at them or hear the sound of them clinking together, I am reminded of my sweet Bamaa and her request of me.

Bamaa took great strength in her faith; it provided her with a sense of calm in her darkest hour. The pastor visited Bamaa in the hospital when he could, and we often prayed together. This was before the rate of AIDS deaths had escalated. Today, too much of pastors' time is taken up with burying their dead to make regular visits to the sick.

Passing through the hospital corridor one day I overheard the doctor talking to a clinician. "The woman, Mrs. Kasune, is dying. We should tell the family there is no hope for her."

The clinician disagreed. "We should give the family hope that she can live. She has developed thrush in her throat and there is a drug that may help."

"No. There is no point," said the doctor.

Once again I was alone hearing painful words about my mother's health. I ran outside and sat under a tree and cried. When I finally regained my composure, I went back to Bamaa's bedside and tried to forget what I heard.

Later that day, a doctor came and spoke to us. "We believe the drug

Miconazole will clear Joyce's infections. It may save her." My family looked hopeful, optimistic even, for the first time in weeks. While my heart hoped and prayed that this one clinician was right, that the drug could save her, what I had overheard made me want to cry out, "Don't bother—she is already gone."

My family must have noticed my hesitant reaction. They looked at me, disappointed, not knowing what I had heard. They also didn't know my mother had already told me she was dying, so they sent me and Beatrice on a ten-hour roundtrip journey to buy the drug.

Miconazole is a simple antifungal drug readily available in many countries. But in Zambia in 1993, when my bamaa needed it, it could only be bought at the Konkola Mines Hospital in Chililambombwe. Even then we could only access the drug because my Aunt Erika knew people at the hospital.

Silent and forlorn, Beatrice and I made our way to the main road to hitchhike the distance. Eventually we made it to the hospital where we collected the drug before making the slow, nervous journey back to Liteta Hospital.

When we finally arrived and made our way to Bamaa's ward, something inside me told me she was gone. We heard people crying. In Africa people share their grief loudly and openly, so we knew someone had gone. Still, it could have been anyone. There were a lot of patients at this hospital and almost every day someone died. But somehow I just knew. I felt my stomach turn and I almost had to run to the bathroom. As Beatrice and I inched toward her ward, my fears were confirmed. Bamaa was gone. I never had a chance to say goodbye. And all because, like so many Africans, she did not have access to a simple fungal cream.

Joyce Mwanamusulwe, the woman who taught me so much, not by words or talking but by her deeds and everyday actions, had left this world. Beatrice and I had traveled more than ten hours in a vain attempt to save my mother, even though I had overheard the doctor say it was hopeless. I didn't get to be with my sweet bamaa as she left this world, and it is a regret that weighs on me to this day.

She died on the twenty-ninth of October, 1993, and was buried in Kasukwe village on the second of November. Outwardly I didn't cry that much at the funeral, to the surprise of many onlookers. Little did they know I had done my share of crying, and with all the responsibilities resting on my shoulders, this was a time for strength not tears. Yet deep down in my heart I was crying, broken and sorrowful. In the midst of all my sorrow, God wiped away my tears and helped me remain strong, as Bamaa wished. My older brother Kelvin cried while I comforted others. People were saying, "Who is that one? How is it that she is not crying?" People misinterpreted my strength and thought I was cold; they wondered whether Bamaa had been my real mother. But the Lord had given me the strength and courage to do what I had been asked to do.

Of course Bataa was at the funeral. People seemed to blame him for my mother's death, and I began to believe them. She had loved him so much, and he had hardly been to visit her in her sickness. He himself, though, was now looking very frail.

As for me, now it was time to take my place in the village. I had to assume my mother's role and attempt to carry out her legacy. I had made a promise to Bamaa and to myself and I was determined to keep that promise, come what may and whatever sacrifices I had to make. I would not only care for my brothers and sisters but for the other children my mother cared for and my grandparents as well. I knew what I had to do.

✤

While I tried to adjust to the lifelong, daily struggle of grieving for my bamaa, my bataa was becoming more emaciated and weak. It became clear why he had not been able to nurse my bamaa himself and why he had not taken us children to live with him. This time I knew what to expect. He too was dying. I forgave him instantly and began to spend as much time with him as I could. Bamaa Banini had died some months earlier, seemingly from the same disease, and Bataa needed help.

I remember trying to carry him on my back to the same hospital where Bamaa died, roughly nine miles from his village. He was over sixty years old by this time. I could carry him because I was strong from village life and he had lost so much weight, but he was still a tall man and his legs dangled in the dirt. I used every shortcut and narrow bush road possible to get us there. I feared people would laugh at us if we took the main road: *look at what they have become.*

The hospital treated my father with Panadol. It was as futile and ineffective as placing a small bucket at the base of the rainbowed torrents of Victoria Falls and trying to catch the flow. The virus was too vigorous and aggressive and it had simply advanced too far; his immune system was completely shattered. Just six months after my mother's death, my father too lost his battle. Now I was truly alone, an orphan and head of our household.

I had always been told my bataa died alone in the bush, and I took that literally. The image of my father lying there alone and afraid, unable to move, broke my heart. And so it came as some small relief when, on a recent trip to Zambia, I learned that Bataa had passed away in a grass hut with his brother by his side. For a man who had fathered twenty-four children and married five women throughout the course of his life, who had held a high-powered city job, to die in a mud hut in the village with just his brother by his side, saying *he died alone in the bush* makes sense. Still, after all this time I am comforted to know he was not entirely alone. On this same trip I was also taken to visit his grave for the very first time.

Death is so much more common in Africa, but does it hurt us less? I've thought about this a lot. I believe that losing your parents or anyone you truly love hurts the same no matter where you are from. Death may not surprise us as much in Africa because it visits too many of us too early and too often. We're always wary; we know the ugly head of tragedy may lurk in childbirth, in the contaminated water we drink, in the mosquitoes that bite us as we sleep, in the breast milk we have no choice but to feed our babies, in an outbreak of TB or cholera that spreads when opportunity is ripe and immunity low, in diseases much of the world has the luxury of calling preventable. But does it hurt less? I honestly don't think so.

I can still recall the pain. Even now there are times when it sneaks up on me, making me wince. I still see myself curled up in a tight ball, a sharp ache spreading from my heart, throughout my body, exhausting me. So no, I don't think it hurts less. And, as all who have loved and lost know, through the pain comes the knowledge that one trial has ended but the real burden, the burden of living with the loss, is just beginning.

For me, this was the beginning of the sugar daddy syndrome.

PART TWO

CHANGES
AND CHALLENGES

7

The Sugar Daddy Syndrome

THE MONTHS AFTER LOSING MY PARENTS were empty and confused. I was a teenager stuck in the eighth grade, and while my aunty Erika Lukoshy had agreed I could remain with her in Chililabombwe, in reality she was overwhelmed with her own responsibilities. I had to pay my own way at school and pay for my brothers and sisters, who were now living scattered among my extended family. While we all had a roof over our heads, there was simply not enough money to go around. We borrowed from where we could and lived in debt to others. This made us vulnerable. AIDS is, after all, a disease that thrives in and perpetuates poverty.

At Bamaa's funeral her employer had solemnly told me they would take care of us, that we'd promptly receive the money owed to us as her dependents. However, the money just never arrived. I traveled the expensive ten-hour trip again and again to ask for it, but there was always an excuse.

I had a friend, a boy called Terry, who wanted to help. We were students together at Chililabombwe Secondary School; Terry was two or three years ahead of me and from the Lamba tribe. Initially I was too naive to notice how much Terry liked me. Later as my eyes opened I felt I had no choice but to push Terry's feelings and my own aside.

As our friendship grew I'd catch his eyes searching to find me at any chance he could. Walking down the hall, while he was talking to his friends, when he walked by the window of my classroom—there was always Terry, beaming affectionately. He was shy, not boastful or overly confident, and in a sweet, boylike way he was romantic and intimate.

After twelfth grade, as part of a summer job while waiting for his grades, Terry went to work in the mines for a short time. While he did not make much money—his pay did not even cover the cost of traveling to work and eating lunch each day—it was the first money Terry had earned. He was so proud when he came to show me his first paycheck.

"Princess, look at this. What should I do with all this money?" I was happy and proud of him.

"Well, Terry, you should give it to your parents so they bless you and then buy yourself something." When a young person in my culture first earns money, it is customary to return some to the parents for all they have done in raising the child; it's seen that you receive blessing with this action.

"What about you?" I sensed Terry's optimism that with this little money, he might be able to provide for my family.

"Terry, you know I am okay."

I sensed disappointment in his eyes but I didn't let on. Without another word he went and bought me a wristwatch and a handbag. "I just want you to have something. I want you to be happy and educated," he told me.

He would never hint or push for sex the way so many boys did. He said he wanted us to have a future together. Terry was serious about his education and encouraged me to follow my own dreams to become a broadcaster. When I think now about that level of maturity in a schoolboy, it warms my heart.

I liked Terry, and if I'd let myself, I know I could have fallen in love with him. He would have been a wonderful, loving partner. But the truth was Terry faced some tough competition.

In the name of caring for my siblings I had secretly started to date older men, father figures who could provide for us. I was nervous and unsure of what I was doing, but I figured I didn't have the luxury of falling in love with a poor, young student. It saddens me when I look back on the choices I made in the name of survival.

Sugar daddies, as I came to call them, have a way of spoiling you; they can be more charming and sophisticated than an innocent schoolboy ever could. But Terry didn't give up easily. When he learned what I was up to, he gave me a plastic, white rose and a card that he sprayed with some kind of perfume. It was sweet of him. I smelled the rose and, even though it wasn't real, it was just as if I were holding a fresh rose in my hand. Still, I couldn't let Terry in. I fought off the feelings. As sweet as the gesture was, what help was a plastic rose to me? It just proved to me that Terry was poor, young and inexperienced and that I would have to stop my heart from falling for him.

While older men did their best to charm me, dating them wasn't all smooth sailing and romance. I remember one of the first men I dated; he told me he was single and that he would marry me. He promised he would take me shopping for nice clothes and buy me a car. I so missed the father figure in my life that I craved what this man could offer. More than the material possessions, I wanted to have someone looking out for me, providing for me and keeping me safe.

Once he took me dancing and drinking. At first I thought I was so sophisticated, but afterward I was sick for days. To make it worse, I soon found out this man was married. I was sure I was in love with him and sure he loved me back. It came as a painful, shocking lesson to realize he had lied to me. I pictured Bamaa's sweet face as she warned me of choices like this through the "Munge Munge" story. *But Bamaa,* I thought, *this is reality, not a fairy story. We have school fees to pay, food to buy.*

I forced myself to dust myself off and continue my search for a sugar daddy. In the months that followed I heard the empty promises and lies often and from many mouths. Still hopelessly naive and optimistic, I became emotionally attached to every man, every father figure I dated. It was hard to concentrate on my studies.

Little did I know I had already met the man who would go on to become my husband and the father of my two daughters. Back in 1993, after Bamaa's conversation with me as she lay dying, I had secured a role in a play at the Kamenza Theatre in Chililabombwe. Playing the role of a mother whose daughter needed disciplining, I got to wear a blue dress that made me feel so special. Rehearsals went for some months, providing a great distraction from my daily life and the fear of what might lie ahead. On stage I was happy and free.

I'd acted through primary school, but this was the first time I'd ever acted in a real theater, and the Kamenza Theater was very grand by Zambian standards. Plays were held there most weekends, but people also went just to socialize.

Walking home from school one evening along Impala Avenue, not long after the play, a white Land Cruiser painted with a "Mines Police" sign passed me and stopped. A man got out.

"Hi."

"Hi."

"I've seen you before, in the play and around town. I'd like to see you again."

At first I didn't recognize the man at all, but as we talked, I realized I had in fact seen him before. A month or so earlier my friend Sandy and I had seen this lanky man running along Impala Avenue, jumping fences, ducking and weaving, in pursuit of a thief. Sandy and I had found the sight hilarious, and we stood laughing at him as he ran. The memory made me smile, which sent the wrong message.

"Ah, now I know I have also seen you before," I said. "Did you ever catch that thief you were chasing?"

He was pleased I had seen him in action and assumed he had an admirer. "I did, and I took him to the police station."

I had to put a stop to this. From his car and uniform it was obvious this man was a policeman from the mines. In my predicament I couldn't afford to waste time with him; his salary would not be enough to support my family. I told him I couldn't see him again, yet for some reason I found myself giving him my name and contact details.

As soon as he was out of sight, I raced to Sandy's house where we laughed that the sinewy old miner we saw chasing a thief had asked me out.

"Sandy, please! He's not even a miner; he's a low-level policeman for goodness' sake! That job pays about the same as a teacher. They don't earn any money at all." We went on laughing and giggling.

Suddenly Sandy stopped laughing and became serious. "He may be a policeman but he may be your way out. You told me he was in a car. This could be good, Princess. You should think before dismissing him."

The exact timing of these events is slightly blurry, but I guess this fact demonstrates a point. There is a term in the international humanitarian community used to describe children affected by HIV and AIDS: "orphans and vulnerable children." From memory, my first meeting with Moffat happened while my parents were still alive, but they were already very unwell and unable to support us. The signs of lack of provision were already there, so I was already beginning to see sugar daddies as my only option. If we were not yet orphans, then we were definitely vulnerable, and this influenced every decision I made.

Reluctantly, I agreed to go on a date with Moffat Zulu. Our relationship progressed slowly, just going on an occasional date. But after some time I came to be infatuated with this man, who turned out to be the deputy head of the mine police of Konkola Mines in Chililabombwe. After Bamaa was gone, it was Moffat who took me to the government offices to chase Bamaa's money. He gave me money for my education and for my brothers and sisters to go to school.

But after a time, he began to place restrictions on what I could do. In particular, he forbade me to act, and reluctantly, I obeyed. Now I regret this decision, but at the time it seemed necessary.

In time I learned that Moffat was also married, but just like the other man, he told me that divorce proceedings were underway, and that his marriage was over before we met. His wife, he said, was just staying with him while he tried to find a place, and I believed him. Even so, Moffat's failed marriage weighed heavily on my heart. When the town's women discovered we were dating, they didn't help matters, calling me a marriage wrecker and greeting me with disapproving looks everywhere I went. On top of my bamaa's passing and my responsibilities, this was a lot for a schoolgirl to deal with. I tried to ignore it; Moffat had told me his wife was the problem and somehow I believed him. I was too foolish to stop and think about the fact that he had also had two other wives previous to this.

Aunt Erika was furious at this whole situation, as I was in school and not supposed to be dating. "This man is not good for you, Princess. He has married over and over again. What on earth can make you think he is good for you? Once he is done with you he will discard you too." On and on she would go, "You will reap what you will sow, Princess." And "What makes you think you are different, you silly girl? This man has married three women and one is still with him." But in addition to my vulnerability, I was a typical, defiant teenager who liked to get my own way; I was sure I knew better.

If only I had listened to Aunt Erika or seen the emerging signs. One story that clearly sticks in my head that should have rung warning bells took place after Moffat and I had been to the cinema with his niece one evening. On our way back to the car, Moffat's niece nudged me and pointed out a young boy selling peanuts on the street in the dark of night. "That's Moffat's son," she said.

She must be wrong. Why would Moffat's son be out at night? Why would he need to sell nuts for money? I was determined to get to the bottom of this strange story. Once in the safety of the car, we had to circle back past the boy, who noticed his bataa driving by and began to wave. Moffat pretended not to notice and drove on, turning his head away from the boy waving at the window.

"Who is that boy waving at?" I asked. Moffat insisted he would tell me later, but I would not hear of it. "Moffat, I know who that boy is. You go back and pick him up and take him home to his mother."

When Aunt Erika heard me crying in the garden that night, she thought I was so stupid. Furiously she warned, "If he can't look after his own children, why would he look after you and any children you might have with him?" As though I didn't have enough challenges in my life! I decided I was going to save Moffat's children. "Aunt Erika, I will rescue those children and make sure they are well cared for." Does that tell you how young and stupid I was?

You've got to give credit to older men. They have had more time to perfect stories and excuses so they can get their own way. Moffat saw the appearance of his son on the street as an opportunity to illustrate the flaws of his wife.

"See, Princess? This is the real reason I need to divorce my wife. She does not even care for our children properly. What kind of a woman is she? Surely you cannot expect me to stay with someone who does not care for her own children?" Again I believed him. Any concern I might have had for this woman was gone. *How could she do this?* My instincts to protect the young and vulnerable were so strong I decided I would remain with Moffat and take the place of the children's mother. I would become the world's greatest stepmother.

I had hoped that my young family could be self-sufficient when Bamaa's money finally came through. We were unhappy living apart and longed to be together again, so it came as a cruel blow the day Bamaa's dues arrived. It was the pitiful equivalent of three or four hundred dollars. I was heartbroken, partly because this was not enough to support my extended family and partly because this was all Bamaa had to show for the fifteen years she had worked for the government. Her salary must have been so small. She had worked so hard for so little.

While she was alive I had often been ungrateful. I wanted more: more clothes, more outings, more. I didn't understand the magnitude of her responsibility. I didn't understand how little she really had and how far she had to stretch her money. I wish Bamaa had shared with me just how little money she earned; perhaps I would not have been so demanding. I felt a burning sense of remorse.

On the other hand, things were going well with Moffat. He gave me money whenever I asked for it without seeming to want much in return. *Not bad,* I thought to myself, never stopping to think that perhaps this was the reason his children had no money. After some months, though, the painful reality of my situation came home to roost when Moffat asked, "Princess, how will you repay me for all I have done?"

I gave Moffat a look that showed I didn't understand the question.

"Of course you know how you can pay me back. Now it seems you don't have the cash; you can always pay me in kind." *Of course.* Of course this is what Moffat wanted. I soon gave in and slept with him.

At this point I must admit I had not been perfect previously. In fact, Moffat was not the first man I had slept with. Still, I was naive, and Moffat should have warned me about contraception and condoms. So at eighteen I found myself pregnant to Moffat Zulu, a man some twenty-five years my senior.

I realized my condition when I began vomiting at school. I knew it was hopeless, that I couldn't continue going to school for long. It seemed my future was over. I didn't know what to do. While it is true I was using Moffat to help me, I felt he had taken advantage of me by not warning me about contraception. He was older than me. He knew I would get pregnant. I realized how stupid I was. I had made choices and now had consequences to face.

"Princess, do you think you are the only one who has ever been in this predicament? You need to abort the baby," my friends comforted and advised when they visited me at my aunt's one evening.

"What? But how do you do that? You mean kill the baby?" I couldn't believe what I was hearing. To take a baby's life seemed too much to handle, but at the same time, I couldn't see another way out. It felt like my predicament was going from bad to worse.

"What makes you think you are the first schoolgirl to get pregnant?" my friends asked. "You have so much life ahead of you. You cannot stop school. We have all done it at some point. Don't be silly; you are in trouble. You know there is a potion we can get you. Once you drink it, you'll be fine and you can come back to school."

I finally agreed. The girls brought me a concoction of African herbs and medicines—*umunsokansoka* combined with *muhilwe,* taken from the bark of the tree.

One night it so happened that I was alone in the bedroom (usually there were three or four of us in there), so I went ahead and drank the potion that my friends had put in a little brown bottle. Deep down in my heart I felt sad. I was full of regret and shame for my actions. But somehow I summoned the courage to drink the potion, for I was in deep trouble and this seemed to be the only solution without anyone finding out. Given Aunt Erika's growing disapproval of Moffat, I could not bear to tell her.

Not too long after taking the medicine I began to feel dizzy, and then a burning sensation filled my stomach. Creeping out of my bedroom to the bathroom, I immediately began vomiting food, water and blood. It occurred to me I might die. *I deserve to die,* I thought, since I was just about to take another life. But something told me to start drinking water. Little did I know I was rehydrating myself, an act that diluted the potion and possibly saved my life.

The next morning before heading to school, my friends rushed to my aunt's house and asked me what happened.

"I drank the concoction, but I didn't see anything come out," I informed them.

"Princess, this is not a good sign. There is a myth that if you don't see the baby come out at once, you shouldn't take the mixture again. You may die," one of them said. "But maybe in your position you should try it again. You are in trouble." My friends' words provided me with no comfort. We carried on our conversation in hushed voices, hoping no one could hear us. I became convinced that I needed to drink the potion once more. I was terrified but again tried to find the courage.

I thought of little else all day. The whole experience was so painful and frightening that I wasn't sure I could go through with it again. That afternoon I walked home slowly. To my surprise, as I reached Aunty Erika's I found the little brown bottle that had contained the potion smashed all over the path. *Who could have done this?* I wondered. I sensed I was in big trouble.

As I entered the living room, I discovered my aunt was home early. Her eyes told me she knew I had been up to something. "What have you done, you silly girl? What have I been telling you all this time? Now you see the shame you have brought not only on yourself but on our entire family." *Who had told her? How did she know?*

Apparently my friends and I had not been quiet enough that morning. My young cousin Barbara had eavesdropped at the door as we talked. It was Barbara who had broken the bottle on the path and told my aunt I was pregnant. My aunt was furious. She had six children of her own and many other dependents she loved dearly. She bore her burden gladly, but it was hard for her to care for so many. While another mouth to feed would only make things more difficult, she would never think to abort a child. Barbara realized what she had done. In her sweet, young, innocent voice, she told me she would quit school and take care of the baby.

Others suggested different methods for ending the life of an unborn child—using a bicycle spoke or the stem of a kasava leaf. I rejected them all and accepted the consequences of my actions.

While I was raised a Christian, my faith was not a driving force in my life at this time. I knew God would not approve of my actions, but it was the memory of my bamaa that made me feel the greatest shame. I could not face myself in the mirror. I could not look up to the sky. I felt Bamaa would be so disappointed in me. She had such great hopes for me; she had asked me to protect her family and I had already let her down. I felt the embarrassment of the shame I had brought on our family. *I'm sorry, Bamaa.*

Rather than face the humiliation of telling the school what was happening, I simply stopped going. My form teacher, who was from Ghana, had believed in me and nurtured and encouraged me. When he noticed I was missing, he asked that I be found and brought back to school. But it was hopeless; I had decided I could not continue.

He sent my friends time and again to arrange a meeting with him. I finally agreed to meet him in a restaurant. He was a gentle man who now looked deeply concerned. "Princess, they tell me you aren't coming to school."

"No, sir. I am pregnant." Somehow I felt free. I had confessed my shameful secret.

"No, no, no, it can't be true." I could see the pain in his eyes. He had seen so many bright students drop out of school because of poverty and vulnerability. "Oh, Princess, this is such bad news. I think you need to abort the baby."

I explained that I had tried but had now accepted the baby. He told me I could go to the hospital, which I thought was illegal in Zambia.

"It is, but you can find doctors to do it for you. Talk to your aunt about it."

I knew that was pointless; my aunt would never take me. My teacher was not about to give up, though. He offered to take me himself, to pay for a proper abortion so that I could return to school. "Princess," he said, "you are supposed to be one of our candidates to become prefect of the school. You are one of our top students. This will not only be a loss to you but to the whole school community. Please reconsider."

"I'm sorry, sir. I cannot do it." Here was another person who had faith in me whom I had also let down.

"You have really broken my heart," he said as he made me promise to keep in touch so that I could return to school the following year.

I promised, but deep down I knew it wouldn't happen. At that time, girls with children couldn't go to school unless someone could be found to look after the baby. Such are the challenges facing young girls. No one would notice if a boy who impregnated a girl returned to school, but girls with babies were not allowed.

At nighttime the faces of Terry, my teacher and my friends kept coming to my mind. I had big dreams for my future, and I wasn't ready to let go.

I told Moffat I was pregnant with his child. I also told him he needed to arrange for me to go to the hospital. Outwardly he agreed. "I'll take care of it," he told me. Little did I know he was just buying time for my pregnancy to advance. He knew that soon it would be too late. The baby kept growing and growing inside me.

Moffat became set on me having the baby and on us getting married. He knew if I furthered my education and broadened my horizons I might come to my senses and bring an end to the whole relationship. For men of Moffat's generation, a beautiful, young trophy wife was quite the prized possession.

When Terry heard I was pregnant from Moffat, he wrote me a letter from college saying he wanted to marry me. I never got the letter. He came back home on holidays when I was seven months pregnant. I had already told my family who the baby's father was, but he asked me to say it was his. Sweet Terry offered to care for this child as if it were his own.

I was torn. What if Terry couldn't cope with the burden and I was left all alone? What if his parents disapproved? What if they found out Moffat was actually the father of the child? How would Terry provide for my siblings as well as my baby?

Even though my parents had their own challenges and lived separately toward the end of their lives, they never divorced. I had always been grateful that my parents weren't divorced; I thought every child had the right to grow up with a mother and father. I tended toward marrying Moffat for this reason; I myself had been looked down on by the community, and I could not bear this for my child. People could be cruel to children with no father. They were called *abana bakupula,* or bastard children.

Terry begged me. I was in such a state; I felt helpless. Terry suspected Moffat would continue seeing his former wife and that he would not make a good husband. While I now felt a strong affection for Terry and knew he would always try to make me happy, I was confused and searching for the best solution to fix my mess. Marrying Moffat seemed best in my predicament.

8

A Teenage Mother Growing in Faith

I THINK SOMETHING IS HAPPENING TO ME, AUNTY," I laughed as September dawned. I could feel the baby moving around as I had for the past couple of months, but this time it seemed to be moving downward.

"*Uoumwana,* I think it is your labor pains. The baby is coming!" said my Aunt Erika, once again in disbelief at how childish and naive I was.

"Really?" I continued laughing. I had been walking around almost the whole day shopping for my cousin. My aunt's father was also there; he accompanied me to the hospital. I could not tell you whether anyone else joined us. By this time I was delirious with the pain. I do remember Aunt Erika calling out as I made my way to the vehicle that if I remained brave through childbirth all would be fine. "You are now a big girl needing to be strong. Now you have become one of us," my aunt said.

I was at the Konkola Mine Hospital, where I had come for antifungal cream on the night Bamaa passed away. Now I was here to deliver my child. By Zambian standards, this was a well-equipped Western hospital left by the colonists and now run by the Zambian Consolidated Copper

Mines. I was lucky to have a midwife present to deliver my baby, as there were, and are still, only around twenty nurses and midwives for every ten thousand people in Zambia at the time.[1]

I was alone when my time came, with only nurses around me, as fathers were still not welcome in the delivery room. I remembered all the stories people had told me, like my aunt saying if you are brave and strong for your first child's birth, then every time you give birth it will be easy. So I pushed and pushed quietly, fearing that I would curse myself for life if I did otherwise. At about 6 a.m. when the baby actually came, I felt a sharp pain, but as soon as the nurses told me "It's a girl!" I was so happy I forgot about it.

I remember the brilliant whites of her eyes the first time the nurses showed me my baby. Her eyelashes were so long, but she looked funny because she had no eyebrows. I was happy to meet her, but I was so tired that I slept for several hours. I didn't know what I was supposed to do. When my family came to visit they found me sleeping.

"Where's the baby, Princess?"

"I don't know. The nurses put her somewhere. Please, I'm so tired. I need to sleep."

"Princess, be careful. Someone could steal her. You are a mother now. Your sleep does not matter." Aunt Erika was again shocked at how childish and unprepared for motherhood I was.

Next it was the turn of the nurses. "Princess, you haven't fed your baby. You haven't even seen her. You need to look after her. Here she is for you."

I could not believe it when I saw my beautiful baby, all freshly washed and wrapped in a blanket, here to meet her aunt and cousin for the first time. She was so precious she stole my breath away. At that moment there was no place I wanted to be more than with my baby. I was so glad we had made it.

Now that I had time to look at her properly, I saw that her skin was light and she had only a few hairs, which was unusual; African babies usually have a lot of hair when they are born. It felt ticklish the first time she sucked from my breast. *What is this little thing doing to me?* I wondered.

Moffat was told of his baby's birth and passed by while I was sleeping. I was told he was full of joy, but he did not want to wake me.

I was discharged from the hospital the next day, just two days after the baby was born. Aunty helped me care for her and taught me the dos and don'ts of caring for a baby.

As you know, this time in the life of a mother and baby, before the baby's umbilical cord drops, is steeped in tradition and superstition in our culture. I was not allowed to touch the stove or fire or perform any household chores. Giving the new mother rest is just part of the reason for the tradition. There is a belief that throughout this time the woman is unclean, and by preparing meals she may infect others. Whatever the reason, I was very glad to have the rest.

And, just like when I was born, we could only name our baby once her umbilical cord had dropped. For the first week or two of life, while we awaited the auspicious naming day, she was simply known as "Baby." While some choose the modern way and dispose of the umbilical cord without ceremony, we followed tradition and buried the former lifeline under a tree, just as my own parents had done. Moffat suggested we name the baby after my mother. I agreed, so we called this precious little child Joyce.

Moffat was full of joy and excitement about this baby, his sixth born. After just two weeks, she was already accompanying him to football games at Konkola Stadium. He was a wonderful father who just wanted to show Joyce off everywhere he went.

I, on the other hand, was exhausted. Having a baby was so much work. Joyce and I were still living with Aunt Erika, who helped me care for her, but I could not get enough rest. Joyce would cry when I was in a deep, deep sleep. Aunt Erika had to wake me, saying, "Princess, really, you have to feed your baby." My aunt was such a blessing; she helped me learn how to wash Joyce's diapers and made sure she was cared for. I simply would not have known what to do without her. In a world without books and magazines on childcare, we relied on our elders to pass on the vital information of caring for our newborns.

Apart from settling into the role of motherhood, so many other things were happening around this time. There was the question of my future with Moffat, for one. I had begun joining Moffat at the church he attended, where he was going through a period of repentance. As the mother of his child, he was ready to marry me, though I still felt unsure.

In my culture, it's customary to discuss relationships with your family, so a meeting was planned at which Moffat would ask my aunt and uncle for permission to marry me. "Princess, do you want to marry Moffat, or is it just for the child?" they wisely asked.

This was it. I had to make a decision. I still felt at a crossroads. My heart wasn't in marrying Moffat, but what were my options? Terry was now out of the picture. I had no education, no income of my own and no other prospects. It wasn't uncommon for a girl as young as me to marry. The United Nations reports that roughly 24 percent of Zambian girls between the ages of fifteen and nineteen are married, divorced or widowed.[2] In a country where women's rights are not strong, where women are not given the opportunity for education and where our main role is child rearing, the journey into womanhood often starts too early. Then there was Moffat. To say I didn't love him, even a bit, would be a lie. Despite my doubts, I was infatuated by his charms. This older man had so much power over me. I felt I could settle for a marriage of convenience with Moffat, and that would offer the best future for my child. Besides, there was a good possibility that Moffat could provide a roof for all my siblings. "I want to marry him," I said.

Reluctantly, my family gave their approval, as they felt this was probably in the best interest of my child.

As per tradition, Moffat was asked to give two hundred thousand kwacha in damages, the equivalent of roughly fifty dollars, for impreg-

nating me while I was in school. He humbly agreed to pay this while another date was set to discuss the dowry.

Now at eighteen, two months after Joyce's birth, my family gave their
blessing, and we were joined as husband and wife in the eyes of our culture. We still had not taken the final step of marriage through the British
system, which would make us eligible for joint health care and legal recognition. This required a formal marriage certificate from the court and
would take some time to organize.

It was suggested I now move back to Chililabombwe with Moffat,
who seemed to have accepted responsibility for his new young family.
That year between our traditional marriage and court marriage was
filled with more confusion, though. Living with Moffat allowed me to
get to know him better, which only filled me with more doubt. Some
nights I'd wake in a sweat as dreams of the "Munge Munge" story tor-
mented my sleep.

As people predicted, it became known around town that my new husband was continuing to see his former wife. I was hurt, embarrassed,
angry and no longer certain I could spend my life with this man. Aunt
Erika's doubts also grew by the day. She now felt the marriage was a mistake, that perhaps the official court marriage should not proceed. In fact,
my whole family now wondered if we had all made a big mistake and if I
should perhaps return to school instead.

After several more family meetings, we agreed I should move away
from Moffat and live with another uncle and aunt in Kitwe, a town some
two hours away from my husband. We hoped the move would give us the
distance required to think objectively about the second, legally binding
stage of our marriage.

As I write I realize that, from a Western perspective, the list of aunts
and uncles and relocations can be difficult to follow, as can the fact that
my siblings were split up among so many different families. This is the
extended African family system at its best. We have a saying you may
have heard: It takes a village to raise a child. This is something we firmly

believe. When AIDS first struck our continent and began claiming the lives of parents, this richness of connections served us well.

In Kitwe I was left to contemplate my future. Despite my own feelings, I kept considering the burden I would create for my family if I was not married. Even though my uncles and aunts wanted to help financially, they simply did not have the capacity.

Of course, once I moved away from Moffat, he begged for forgiveness. I think he knew the power he had over me and often used it to manipulate our relationship. He convinced me that if I forgave him I should marry him. Our spiritual awakening had begun, and during this time Moffat had given his life to the Lord. He knew he had done wrongly by me and said he was sorry.

Throughout this time I also had begun my own spiritual journey. Now that I was a mother, I craved the solace and guidance of the Lord to help me make the right decisions for my family. I needed a father in my life, and it dawned on me then that there had been a Father waiting to embrace me all along.

I took a step forward in my faith when I attended a Pentecostal crusade held by an American man visiting Kitwe; I think his name was Dr. David Newsbery. Inside the stadium the doctor preached a message of forgiveness. His words moved me and encouraged me to forgive Moffat for all that he had done. I felt that forgiving him and beginning a new life with him was the godly thing to do. Only when I was more mature in my faith did I realize that I could have forgiven Moffat yet encouraged him to return to his former wife, or forgiven him and let him be. At the time, though, all I heard was "forgive him and marry him."

Once I made my decision I was excited to recommence a life with Moffat. For all his faults, he was the father of my child, he had admitted his mistakes, and we were ready to move on. Joyce and I moved back to Chililabombwe and into Moffat's home. We soon married under British law, and I found myself happy for the first time in many years.

Moffat and I continued our journey with the Lord, and in fact, it was during this time that the church truly took hold in my life. Through the church I met some new friends, Eddie and his wife, Miriam, who introduced me to their pastor, whose name was Faith. They shared with me passages from the Bible that guided me and nurtured me. One that sticks in my mind was the Lord's words in Isaiah "though your sins are like scarlet, / they shall be as white as snow; / though they are red as crimson, / they shall be like wool" (1:18).

I could not believe there was this Jesus whom I could have a personal relationship with, who would love me even though I was a sinner, who would forgive me for all the wrong choices I had made, who would give me another chance. I was beginning to like what I heard. I was falling in love with Jesus.

Pastor Faith encouraged me to repent of my sins. One day she asked me, "Princess, have you taken the Lord as your personal Savior?" I was feeling closer to the Lord every day, but at this I was confused. I had grown up as a Christian. *Wasn't that enough?* I knew I had made mistakes in recent years—dating a married man, although I did not know that at the time, and trying to abort my child. Of these mistakes I felt a sense of deep shame. But up until recent years I thought I had been okay.

Still, Pastor Faith explained the need to repent of my sins, so on October 19, 1995, I committed my life to Jesus Christ, to have him as my Lord and Savior. This was such a big moment for me; I felt such peace knowing he was there to protect and guide me.

While I was still a novice in my faith, my calling and connection to the church grew in strength each day. Early in 1996 I attended a prayer meeting at which a man they called Prophet Zimba called me away from the crowd, claiming to have a vision for my life. "I see you standing at an airport carrying suitcases," he said. "There are flights going in different directions, all around the world. I also see the flags of many nations waving all about. But some flags are standing out stronger than others: they are the flags of Canada, Australia and America." He concentrated hard, as if looking into the distance, and continued, "And the

American flag has come to a standstill."

Interesting, I thought to myself. *What is this man talking about? I've never even been out of Zambia. Why does he think I'm going anywhere, especially to the other side of the world?* But Prophet Zimba wasn't finished: "Very soon you'll move from Chililabombwe to another town, and that's where your true ministry will begin." I didn't know what to think. I left Prophet Zimba and rejoined the crowd at the prayer meeting. *Could this be true?* Sooner or later I forgot all about it, but in the years to come I would be reminded of his vision and words.

The words of the Bible were so stimulating to me too, providing me with a source of comfort and guidance. I just could not get enough of what I read. Verses were commended to me from so many different places. One that was repeated over and over came from Jeremiah 1:5-10:

"Before I formed you in the womb I knew you,
  before you were born I set you apart;
  I appointed you as a prophet to the nations."
"Ah, Sovereign LORD," I said, "I do not know how to speak; I am only a child."
But the LORD said to me, "Do not say, 'I am only a child.' You must go to everyone I send you to and say whatever I command you. Do not be afraid of them, for I am with you and will rescue you," declares the LORD.
Then the LORD reached out his hand and touched my mouth and said to me, "Now, I have put my words in your mouth. See, today I appoint you over nations and kingdoms to uproot and tear down, to destroy and overthrow, to build and to plant."

The words had a powerful resonance. They came to me when I was gardening, doing the laundry, at the market; they followed me all around and I knew somehow they were meant for me. In Zambia, this is the way we approach the Bible. When someone hands us a verse, we take time to wonder, *What is God saying to me? What is the Bible saying to me through this verse?*

This was such a transformational time in my life. The church became my solace and my strength, while my new Christian friends became my family in Chililabombwe. With this new community of believers I was no longer ashamed. I felt accepted and forgiven. The love they showed me and that we showed to one another was amazing. For years I had searched for love in the wrong places, but now the vacuum was filled with a deep and pure love that so depicted community life represented in the Bible.

❀

Moffat and I settled into life as Mr. and Mrs. Zulu. He was still working for the mines police, and we lived in a big three-bedroom, two-bathroom house with electricity and a servant cottage. From time to time there were servants in the quarters—a maid and someone to tend the gardens. Some of my brothers and sisters moved in with us too. Once more, after so many years, life was rich and full.

Unlike many Zambian men, Moffat began to help around the home. Traditionally, if a man was seen cooking and cleaning he would become a laughingstock. So Moffat would sweep the bedroom but leave a pile of dirt in the corner of the room so no one would see him carrying it to the trash can. Some weekends he would even help with the laundry, though I could never get him to do the ironing.

All the while, our baby Joyce was growing to be a very outgoing baby. Together Moffat and I watched our daughter grow into her joyful personality. Even as a small baby she played with everyone and seemed to adore all people. Also, she was never scared of anything and would even pick up small locust insects that we call *inshonkonono* and eat them. Given the joy we felt watching her grow and from our connection to the church, the name Joy seemed appropriate for our baby girl. Soon that's what we shortened it to, and what she is known by to this day.

As it happened our period of smooth sailing didn't last for long, unfortunately. I had heard, and Moffat had reinforced, the myths that contraceptive pills give you cancer and that you cannot get pregnant while you are breastfeeding. So it came as a great surprise when, with baby Joyce just around nine months old, I found myself pregnant again.

I couldn't believe this was happening to me. First, I didn't think it was physically possible. And second, the neighborhood that already disliked me now had another reason to make fun of me. "Look, see that silly girl is having another baby," they whispered. While my growing faith and my church community eased the pain, I felt that burning sense of shame return, which caused me to make yet another decision I would soon regret.

I found the courage to say to Moffat, "Now that I am a married woman I can abort the child. I can't have another baby; everyone is laughing at me. I have heard that if you have babies close together the firstborn may die." Now that my faith has matured I cannot imagine why I believed this.

While Moffat was annoyed at first, some days later he came home with the familiar small brown bottle. The next day when he went to work, I swallowed the mixture before either of us could change our minds. For some reason I preferred to be alone when I did this. My body had the same reaction it did when I attempted to abort Joyce, and this time I was sure I would die. As I lay in pain I was once again angry at myself.

Ashamed and confused, I sent a message to one of the few women outside the church community who had befriended me. When she heard my message, she came running and counseled me not to take the concoction again, reminding me that I was a new mother and did not want to die and leave my Joy alone. She discouraged me from abortion altogether but advised that if I was adamant about my decision, as a married woman I could have a procedure at the hospital. I would have to come up with a good medical reason for it, though, and I would need my husband's permission. As soon as Moffat returned from work, I was ready with Plan B.

Moffat and I argued. I told him he was to blame for this situation; he was the reason the town was laughing at me. Moffat was deeply troubled by the whole idea and had never supported the option of abortion, not even with baby Joyce. At my demand, however, he made an appointment for a Monday morning when I was roughly three months into my pregnancy.

Still young in my faith, I didn't think about the impact of abortion, naively reasoning I would prefer to turn to the Lord for forgiveness than become a laughingstock again. When I reflect now, I see the error in my judgment as a human being and as a Christian. How many times do we take the easy road, thinking we can apologize to God and seek forgiveness, when in human form, the damage has been done?

On the Saturday prior to my scheduled abortion, the couples' meeting for our church was taking place in our home. Usually meetings included Scripture readings, testimony and prayer. However, that Saturday a visiting pastor, Pastor N'gambi from Chingola, was going to speak to our group. I was so excited. I did a lot of preparation for the visiting pastor, as this was our first time hosting the group and I wanted to make a favorable impression.

It was one of the few days when people were not on African time and everyone arrived early. When it came time for the session to start, the visiting pastor advised us that we would not be proceeding with our meeting in the normal way but rather we would commence with prayer and a movie that would form the basis of the day's discussions. I got my VCR and television ready for what I assumed would be a movie on something biblical.

To my great surprise, the movie opened with a doctor explaining the process of abortion. I sat frozen in my chair, desperately trying to hide the guilt from my face. The video described the tools and equipment used and graphically showed the process of killing and then removing an unborn baby at different stages of pregnancy. At the conclusion of the movie the doctors, who were now born-again believers, confessed regret for their part in the abortions they had performed over the years.

The images were heartbreaking. It all became too much. I sobbed as the movie played out. Until that moment, I had not fully grasped the true horror of abortion. Right then and there I was convinced that what I was trying to do was wrong and ungodly.

I tried to compose myself as the group began to discuss the issue. The theme of the discussion was that even some Christian couples find it okay to go through this process just because they are married and have made a decision as a couple. I couldn't keep my secret to myself any longer. Sobbing, I told the group I was pregnant and that I was booked for an abortion on Monday. I told them how sorry I was. At this, others in the group expressed their own regret at past terminations and attempts. The emotional pain still haunted them.

As the group departed I was left wondering if the Lord led Pastor N'gambi to show the video or if it was my husband who confided in him to help bring my petition to an end. Either way, in my heart I knew God had just shown himself to me and saved me from killing a child. When Monday came I didn't go to the hospital.

Now that the decision was made, I began to grow excited about the baby inside me. It was truly a miracle. Unlike Joy, this baby kicked so hard that I was sure it was a little boy. Joy and a baby brother suited me just fine.

As the baby grew I faced another challenge to my faith. Traditional healers recommend you take a mixture of African herbs to protect your unborn baby and its siblings if they are close in age. I had pushed my luck with the Lord enough, though, so I renounced the beliefs of the traditional healers and refused to take traditional medicine based on superstition.

Just as when I was pregnant with Joyce, I carried on my regular activities throughout my pregnancy. This time, though, when the now-familiar pains began I was not laughing. It hurt more than the first time yet I remained composed. Moffat rushed me to the Konkola Mine Hospital, and just after midnight on February 5, 1996, I gave birth to our second child, weighing 7.7 pounds, which was about a pound more than Joyce had weighed at birth. The nurse happily told me, "You have a healthy baby girl." I didn't believe her until I had a chance to see my new daughter with my own eyes. She was so different from her sister, with thick black hair that even sprouted out her delicate ears and her tiny little nose. I fell in love with her instantly. And this time I knew how to care for a baby, so I nursed her right away.

Ten days later when her umbilical cord fell off, we named our second daughter Faith Zulu after Pastor Faith, who had been so important in guiding the early stages of our walk with Christ, and after the faith that grew inside me as I carried this tiny little miracle. My cousin was particularly determined we should call her Faith.

Faith was a healthy, chubby baby. In Africa it is a great compliment to be called fat, as food is so scarce. She was a very dark-skinned baby, and her thick, dark, curly hair made her look so beautiful. I remembered my bamaa's saying, *Black is beautiful,* and looking at Faith I thought, *You've got that right, Bamaa, black is beautiful!*

One month after Faith was born, her health took a turn for the worse. She became sick and had to go to the hospital, and then was in and out of the hospital for the next seven months. At first I was terrified, as her temperature soared up to 105.8 degrees, and I wondered if I should have taken those African herbs. But then, to the surprise of those around me who began to lose hope, I prayed in the hospital for baby Faith, trusting that the Lord would look after her and protect her. And I knew she would be okay. Faith fought so hard for her life and did pull through. To this day my baby Faith is a fighter, and I often wonder if this is a result of fighting so hard to hang onto life. Her fighting spirit reminds me so much of myself that sometimes I just shake my head.

As soon as she could talk, this feisty little child would say, "I want to be called Kasune, not Faith." She insisted we name her after my bataa. "My Love, that is your grandpa's name. You are Faith." I think she knew Joyce had her grandmother's name and she wanted her grandpa's!

She also grew up wanting me all the time; whatever I did she would try to cling to me and hold me. She even wanted to sleep on the same bed with me, where she would drink from my breast throughout the night. If I was going to the market, I would ask her, "Faith, what do you want me to bring you from the market?" "I only want you," would be her reply—no lollies or candy, just her mother.

One of my greatest joys in life, then as now, is watching my daughters' personalities develop. Moffat too loved being with his tiny daughters—he loved them dearly and couldn't wait to see them when he arrived home from work each day. As the oldest child, sweet Joy was more independent. She was so relaxed with other people—her stepbrothers and stepsisters like Moffat Jr., who would put little Joy on his back, and Ethel; and my cousin Rhoda and other family members who were always there to help. I was glad of their support as I found it so hard to care for the two girls and look after the whole family. Many times, just as when I was a child, there were between eleven and sixteen of us in the house. The African village was alive and well in our home.

When I saw Joyce take her first steps in a tiny, soft, yellow jumpsuit, when I heard Faith saying her first prayers, when they cuddle me and tell me they love me, and every day of my life, I thank God for the gift of my daughters and for preventing me from taking their innocent lives away.

9

A Call to the Sick

SOMEWHERE AROUND THIS TIME Moffat came home from work with the news that he had been transferred to another town on the Copperbelt called Luanshya. Prophet Zimba's words popped into my head: "Very soon you'll move from Chililabombwe to another town and that's where your true ministry will begin." But I dismissed the words as coincidence. While I was still a new believer, I knew enough to be mindful of false prophets. Besides, the other aspect of his vision—the suitcases and the American flag—still seemed unreal.

So the Zulu family packed our bags for a life in Luanshya, where we could make a fresh start away from wagging tongues. We knew our past mistakes and had confessed them to God. At some point you have to be able to move on. It was therefore so refreshing to become part of a new community who accepted Moffat and me as the parents of two dear baby girls without questioning our past. Through our pastor back in Chililabombwe we found a new church in Luanshya, and this community embraced us as we embraced them. We soon began holding prayer meetings in our home.

In this new town and church my faith continued to grow, as did my love of the Bible. What stands out most in my memory from this time is a series of Scriptures—prophecies, I remember they called them—that people felt compelled to share with me, verses they felt had been sent for me. One day, gentle Sister Melody came to me and said,

> The words God spoke to Isaiah are standing out for you, Princess. You are meant to hear these words:

> "This is what the LORD says to his anointed,
>   to Cyrus, whose right hand I take hold of
> to subdue nations before him
>   and to strip kings of their armor,
> to open doors before him
>   so that gates will not be shut:
> I will go before you
>   and will level the mountains;
> I will break down gates of bronze
>   and cut through bars of iron.
> I will give you the treasures of darkness,
>   riches stored in secret places,
> so that you may know that I am the LORD,
>   the God of Israel, who summons you by name." (Isaiah 45:1-3)

All these words and visions from God were confusing to me as a young believer. "What do you mean, Sister?" I asked.

Looking off into the distance, she said, "Well, Sister, the Lord showed me that there will be something that is going to happen in your life that will be as big as a mountain. Of all the words it is the mountain that is standing out to me. But he is saying, 'Fear not.' He will go before you; he will clear the way so you will know it is him who has called."

I tried to make sense of what she said, but I simply had no idea what this mountain could be. I got the symbolism of the words, of course—that there was some great problem coming into my life—but again, *what could it be?* No one knew. I was still less than a year old in my faith and someone was handing me a second prophecy. This was getting to be too much.

A few months passed and then yet another prophecy was given to me. This time it was from Sister Witness: "Sister Princess, God has given you a vision." I was unsure what to think as she proceeded to give me the words from Habakkuk 2:3:

> For the revelation awaits an appointed time;
>> it speaks of the end
>> and will not prove false.
> Though it will linger, wait for it;
>> it will certainly come and will not delay.

I didn't know what to believe and what not to. *Why were all these people telling me the Lord had something for me to do?* Sister Witness tried to comfort me, saying, "Wait for it, Sister Princess. Be patient. It may take weeks, it may take months, it may take years, but it shall come to pass."

This really was becoming too much for me. *Where is this God they are speaking for?* I wondered. I tried to tell people that I was just a novice in my faith, that I didn't understand, but they persisted. With two young girls, I just wanted to get on with my ordinary life. To console myself I thought, *If it's God's will, it will be.*

One good friend I met through our Luanshya church community was named Chilufya. She was one of the few people in town close in age to me and whom I could relate to as a young friend. With three children, she had been married longer than I had, so she could also advise me on marriage and on being a mother.

Chilufya had a passion for the sick. She spent her spare time at the Luanshya Hospital, where she would pray with and encourage patients. Soon she invited me to join her. The memories of Bamaa's sickness and more recently Faith's were fresh in my mind, so I didn't much care to spend more time at the hospital. Still, I accepted Chilufya's invitation, as I wanted to see for myself what this was all about.

On my first visit I fell instantly in love with the patients at the hospital and came to draw strength and peace from talking with them. I seemed to spend most of my time with people who had little time left to live. Those who had found faith in Christ had such a peace and joy about them it was moving to see. After that first visit, I joined my new friend as often as I could. At the hospital, Chilufya went to pray with people from our neighborhood. Strangely, I left her and began to wander around on my own. I found myself drawn to people who all appeared to have a similar disease. In fact, they looked to have the same symptoms as Bamaa and Bataa in the final stages of their lives.

As time went on I felt closer and closer to these people. Somehow I thought I felt their pain and bitterness. I wanted to be there to help them sip cold water when they could no longer lift their heads on their own or to peel an orange that they could no longer peel themselves.

So much mystery and discrimination still surrounded this disease that was spreading more and more widely. By now large numbers of people had begun to die from it, and people everywhere were terrified. We never knew who it would strike next. Those who were infected were made to feel ashamed. They were often in denial about what was making them so sick. Many preferred to say they had TB or malaria. Those who remained well responded with sly glances, whispers and rumors instead of compassion and kindness. This just deepened my desire to spend time with those infected.

In one of my early visits to the hospital I met a man in the last stages of life. I knew he was close to death because he looked so much like my bamaa did at the end. But I had heard that the last sense to leave us when we're dying is our hearing, so I sat and prayed with the man, holding his cold, bony hand, hoping he could still hear that he was loved before he moved on to the final resting place. As I prayed, I overheard a group of visitors passing by say, "Why is she praying for someone who is already dead?"

Outraged that those were some of the last words this man would hear, I wanted to stop praying and slap these people. Every human being deserves dignity, no matter who they are, where they come from or how they contracted the virus. Every human being has the right to die with dignity, with someone by their bedside telling them they are loved. I pictured myself in the shoes of this dying man and felt a great sense of sadness.

Some were even shunning their own family members afflicted with the illness. A young woman I met had been abandoned by her entire family. Crying and alone, she waited to die in a smelly, dirty hospital. She had been a virgin when she married her husband, whom she loved dearly. Some years into their marriage the woman had become sick, contracting illness after illness that she just couldn't get rid of. Now it seemed that a combination of these other illnesses would claim her life.

"How could this be?" she asked. "It seems so unfair. This can't be real." I agreed; it seemed so wrong for her to be in this situation. As time went by, she became more and more open with me. So much of her pain came from her husband's abandonment. Instead of nursing her and caring for her, he simply neglected her, discarded her and left her to die in the hospital. Such a sad, empty pain filled her eyes. Her Christian faith was waning.

Throughout the days as we talked, the young woman became brighter and brighter. Each time I visited I was excited to see her again. Our relationship grew into a meaningful friendship. I gave her a brooch from home that said "Jesus Loves You." It was a little thing, but when she received the brooch it brought a radiating sunshine to her face for days. It was powerful to see how one small gesture of love and kindness changed her worldview. Just a few days later when I went to see her, she managed to say, "I have forgiven him."

"Who?" I asked in response.

"I have forgiven my husband. I feel so much peace. I have rededicated my life to the Lord."

She continued to talk about the peace she felt from forgiving her husband, and I was so happy for her. The following day I was eager to see her, to see the joy on her face once more, but as I entered the hospital I noticed the blankets missing from her bed.

Where can she be? Has she moved to another room? But as I moved closer the truth became clear. This woman whom I had seen just yesterday with the brightest, most joyful smile, wearing her little brooch that had changed her view of the world, had gone.

I was filled with a sense of loss from her death, but I also felt joy, as I sensed that I had witnessed a miracle. She was gone, out of my life, but not gone forever. I knew that her soul was at peace and she was no longer in pain.

Not every reaction to the disease was the same. Not everyone was loving and forgiving. People found it hard to understand why they should suffer, why they should die. Another patient, who chose to call himself Chibamda, which means "ghost," continually said, "There is no God. How could there be a God that watches over so much pain and suffering?" He announced his displeasure with God to anyone who would listen. This man was full of bitterness, and every time he saw me or Chilufya coming he looked away. We tried and tried to talk to him about the unconditional love of God, but he was certain he would rather go to hell than believe in a God who didn't care. He died in that state.

Sadly, Chilufya and I were among the few Christians willing to minister to people suffering from the illness. In fact, at times this disease made me ashamed to be a believer. Christians seemed comfortable praying for people with other obvious diseases like malaria, but when it came to people with this unknown disease, they couldn't get away quick enough. It seemed as if they were afraid to touch the patient. I even stopped carrying my Bible to the hospital because of how the church was behaving in those early years.

My love for the sick coupled with my outrage at the lack of empathy for the dying saw me visiting the hospital more and more often. Even without Chilufya, I went to see the patients on a regular basis.

People often asked me to pray for them. One day a man, who looked very wealthy, called me to stand by his bedside and pray for him. As time went on, he gave me the story of the life he led prior to becoming sick.

He told me he had lived the high life with many partners but now regretted this as he had to leave his family all too early.

I didn't know why he had asked me to pray for him—how did he know I would not laugh at or ridicule him?—but we became close, and when he died his daughters told me, "Our father took such strength and comfort from you. There is such a grace and courage about you. Thank you for having done this." *How could he have known how I felt about people like him?* I stopped to think for a second. I knew this was not my doing but God at work.

I did whatever it was the dying wanted and needed in their last days: I held their hands, helped them take small sips of water, prayed with them, listened to their stories and covered them with blankets when they were cold. As I left each day I was filled with joy. I loved these patients and I felt they loved me back. Seeing their smiles in the midst of all they endured gave me a great sense of joy. Sometimes I would come back to find them gone, but I wasn't sad that they had died; instead I was overjoyed. For the most part I had helped them die in peace. I came to learn what compassion really means.

These were some of the most precious moments of my life—being there with people as they leave this world. I cannot explain the joy and the peace this brought me. I learned that there is one power we all share if we choose to exercise it: the power of a simple word or an act of kindness.

It wasn't long before a nurse at the hospital noticed how much time I spent in the wards. In addition to being a nurse, she was involved with the humanitarian organization Care International, and she shared that she too was a believer. "I think you have a calling in your life," she said. "I see the way you care for and bring such peace to our patients, when few others care."

She lent me a book with a pink cover that she said would explain the cause of this illness. "It is a virus called HIV," she told me. Something in me stirred with that book in my hand. I couldn't wait to know more. I raced home to begin reading.

10

I Have to Know

IT WAS A BASIC BOOK BUT IT TOLD ME all I needed to know about this illness. When you first contract it, it's called the Human Immunodeficiency Virus, or HIV, the book said. But by the time a person becomes sick and dies, the virus has progressed to a stage called Acquired Immune Deficiency Syndrome, commonly shortened to AIDS. According to the book, it was a new disease first identified only in the early 1980s, for which there was no known cure.

The pink-covered book began by describing the ways HIV is transmitted: primarily through sexual activity and blood transfusions but also—frighteningly—from a mother to her child. It showed photographs of a person looking healthy and then, in the next shot, the same person wasting away, pale and weak with big burnlike blotches on their skin that fill with fluid. From this pink book I also learned that it is not AIDS that kills you. Rather, the virus weakens your immune system so you become vulnerable to other sicknesses—opportunistic infections that become the killers.

So many things became clear with this book in my hand. This virus must be the reason so many people were dying in the hospitals, cities and villages. In fact, the book said HIV had already taken hold across Africa, where a combination of factors meant this pathogen could spread like wildfire before we even knew it existed: few people had access to television, literacy levels were low, governments could not afford broad-scale advertising education campaigns; cultural practices like polygamy did not help and then there was our health system—powerless against the rising tide of infection. The virus spread across the world, hitting gay communities in the developed world.

As I read about and saw photographs of the symptoms I was witnessing firsthand every day, it also became chillingly clear that this was the illness that had taken Bamaa, Bataa and baby Linda. I stopped for a moment to wonder who had brought this disease into my family home. The truth was, it didn't matter. They were all gone now.

It was now 1997, and here I was learning about the virus for the very first time. I did not even know it had a name. But the book was telling me it was first identified in Africa sixteen years ago. *Why don't more people know about this?* I wondered. There was a killer in our midst and information just was not getting through. I remembered that there was a doctor called Mannasseh Phiri who had recently begun to talk about the mystery illness on television, but most people just turned the TV off when his program came on. *From now on,* I vowed, *I will watch that program all the time and encourage everyone I know to do the same. People have to be warned. We have to find a way.*

As I reached the end of the book, I began to wonder about my own health. "I have to know whether I have this virus," I said out loud to myself. While it wasn't common practice, I now knew it was possible to test your HIV status, and I was in possession of three critical pieces of information that meant I had to know whether I was infected with the virus: First, two of Moffat's three previous wives had by this time died from a disease no one could put a name to, and I had just learned it was possible they had died from AIDS. At this time I had been married to Moffat for three years. Second, the book taught me that HIV is primarily a sexually transmitted disease. I had to be at some risk. But it was the third and final fact that terrified me: the virus could spread from mother to child either during pregnancy, delivery or while breastfeeding. *I had to know.*

My eyes widened further as another alarming thought came to mind. I remembered seeing spots on Moffat's back when we were first together. The spots had reappeared from time to time ever since. When I had asked Moffat what they were, he said that when he was young he had eaten fish that caused these blotches. But come to think of it, he was often drinking antibiotics. Should I have been more curious? I was young and naive and had no reason to think I might be living with a blood-born potential killer.

The very next day I woke up nervous and excited. Having decided to walk the roughly two miles to the Luanshya Mine Hospital to be tested, I fed Joy and Faith their porridge and left them with their stepbrothers and stepsisters. We were fortunate to live near one of the few hospitals in all of Zambia that could test for HIV.

I found myself walking quickly as I couldn't wait to get to the hospital. I had barely slept that night, haunted by the book and by the knowledge that the virus that likely claimed my parents might also be inside me. More important, I might unwittingly have passed the virus to my precious girls. After all, Faith had been sick as a baby. Again, images of baby Linda's skeletal body flashed before my eyes. But there was something else, something at the time I could not explain, some force that was pushing me to know.

At the hospital, after a nurse took my weight and blood pressure, our family doctor, Dr. Tembo, came out into the corridor and called me into his room.

"Hello, Mrs. Zulu. What can I do for you today?" Dr. Tembo was a friendly, gentle man whom I, as the mother of two young daughters, had come to know well.

"Hello, Dr. Tembo. It is lovely to see you. I am just fine, thank you. I am here to know my HIV status," I told him. I was proud that I knew this terminology and certain Dr. Tembo would applaud me for my initiative. Instead he was dismayed, "Your HIV status? Mrs. Zulu, you are a married woman. You look healthy, your husband looks healthy, and your children look healthy. What could make you think you may have this virus?"

"Doctor, this does not mean I am not infected. You simply cannot tell from looking at a person. I have been reading about this disease. I need to know for myself and my daughters." I was dumbfounded that even a medical doctor would suggest you could know a person's HIV status from looking at them. But I was even more dumbfounded at what came next.

"Unfortunately, Mrs. Zulu, you cannot find out so easily. Your husband must give you permission."

"Doctor, surely not. What kind of rule is this?"

"I am afraid it is the policy for the whole country, and it is not likely to change. Besides, Mrs. Zulu, if you knew you had this virus, what would you do?"

He clearly wasn't able to test me but I didn't give up that easily. "Doctor, I have to know."

Anger was building inside me. While I had to remain respectful to Dr. Tembo, the policy seemed crazy. I didn't know anything about human rights, but something at my core told me this was wrong. *How could a woman be denied of her right to test for HIV, to know her own health?* This was absurd.

I committed then and there to learning my own status and also fighting for the right for other women to test. I just couldn't get my head around the fact that we needed our husband's permission to find out our status. There was a growing, angry voice inside me that could not be silenced. I knew I had to fight.

I told Dr. Tembo I would be back and I would be tested. "I am sorry. That's just the way things are," he emphasized. Dr. Tembo was used to seeing me as a meek mother. He had not seen this side of me before, the side that refused to stand by and allow such an injustice to go unchallenged.

I left, shaking my head as I waited for Moffat to return from work.

When he came home I told him I had been reading about HIV and AIDS. "Moffat, now that I know about the virus, I have to know whether I have it, and I need your permission."

Moffat was shocked. "What? What is this nonsense? Why do you need to know such things?"

"Moffat, I just have to know. You have been married before and I was not a virgin when I met you. It's possible we are infected, and what about Joy and Faith who I breastfed?" We argued, with our exchange of words ending the same way it had begun: Moffat angrily denied me permission to be tested.

"You know I will do it and you will allow it," I pleaded.

But Moffat stood firm; he was not about to change his mind. I felt betrayed. *Surely I should be able to learn about my own health.* The thought kept repeating in my mind. I also thought of all the women in my country who didn't stand a chance: First, they had never heard of this disease. Second, there were only a few places in the whole country where they could be tested. Third, for most Zambians testing costs more than three days' wages for them. And the final straw was that they needed their husband's permission. Or was the final straw that there was no treatment and no cure available? I could not get over just how many forces were shortening people's lives unnecessarily. A need to fight this injustice stirred deep within me.

But I knew I needed to be wise about this. Fighting with Moffat wasn't going to get me anywhere. I needed to use my best skills in diplomacy to change Moffat's mind. I had discovered Moffat was most receptive during our evening prayers, so as we prayed together I prayed out loud for my husband's heart to soften and for him to allow my test.

When my prayers didn't succeed I turned to persistence. The first thing I would say to Moffat when he came in the door after a day at work was, "Have you written my letter yet?" From August to November, I never let up. Moffat had seen signs of my spirit before, but nothing like this. He must have questioned his decision to take on a young wife.

Finally, the Lord answered my prayers. On December 19, 1997, Moffat came home from work and grunted that he would take me to the hospital. Miraculously, he wanted to know his HIV status as well.

I could not resist shouting, "Jesus is Lord!" as I jumped up and down, excited at this development. "Thank you, thank you, thank you, Moffat. Let's go tomorrow. I will call the hospital now." Before Moffat had a chance to change his mind, I made our appointments. Without him knowing I made an appointment for Joy and Faith too.

The following morning I woke excited, ready to drop another bombshell on my battle-weary husband. "Moffat, I thought we would bring the children with us. We should know their status too."

The look on his face was part hurt, part annoyed, "No. I said I would come with you but these girls are not coming. I will hear no more of this nonsense. There will be no argument over my children." I understood why Moffat was reluctant to test Joy and Faith, who by now were three and almost two years, respectively. Great stigma surrounded this disease, and here I was dragging my children into it. They would be the subject of ridicule if they were found to be HIV-positive, and besides, there was no known cure and no treatment available. But I was obsessed with the need to know. While the doctor said nothing could be done to help the sick, I knew that knowledge was power. If they were positive and I didn't know, they would certainly waste away and die. If I knew, I could learn how to keep my babies healthy. There was a chance they would be okay. They had to be. I wasn't scared for my own status but I was terrified for my daughters. In the end, I had my way, and Joy and Faith came to be tested.

At the hospital, I faced more opposition. The nurse taking the blood that would determine my fate asked, "Why are you doing this? Can't you just leave it alone? Even as nurses we don't want to know."

The nurse taking Moffat's blood joined in: "Even if you knew your status, what could you do?" Moffat nodded his head in agreement with the nurse as he said, "Finally, someone is making some sense."

The nurses didn't help by adding, "We hear about some medication in faraway countries like America, but you can never have that expensive medication here in Zambia. Here, there is nothing left to do but die. There is simply no reason for you to know."

Enough of this talk, I thought. *I believe in a God who is greater than the whole universe. He is the Lord who grants health. He is Jehovah Rapha.* I told the group, "If there is nothing Western medicine can do for me, I will take it to the Lord in prayer."

Our results were to be available one week from testing. And so, on the second of January, 1998, just four days before my twenty-second birthday, Moffat and I were set to learn our results. Moffat was going to meet me at the hospital in the middle of his shift. As I left the house, my praying partner Mrs. Banda called to me, "Good morning. Where are you all off to this fine day?"

I thought it was time I told her what was going on. "Mrs. Banda, Moffat and I are going to see the doctor to learn our HIV status. I am excited."

"That incurable disease?" she asked, shocked. *So Mrs. Banda had heard of HIV?*

"Yes, I am excited. It's so important. I have to know. I will let you know when I come back," I shouted as I set off on my life-changing journey.

Moffat met me at the Luanshya Mine Hospital as he agreed he would, his head hanging like someone soaked from the rains. It was as though his fear was now becoming a reality. As for me, I felt ready.

Before Moffat and I were to learn our own status, Dr. Tembo was going to give us the results for Joy and Faith.

"I have your results, Mr. and Mrs. Zulu."

At this point I looked at Moffat tenderly, my anger forgotten. His head was still bowed.

"The test results say that your daughters, Joy and Faith, have tested negative for HIV."

I took a big deep breath, a sigh of relief. *Thank you, Jesus.* Dr. Tembo paused for a moment and then said, "Yes, this is very good news, but you have to bring them back two months from now, and then in another two and another two after that, just to be certain."

A wave of emotion—gratitude, and a love so deep—engulfed me on hearing this news. As a parent, your number-one job is to protect your children from harm. For months I feared I had failed them, and now I rejoiced in the news that they were okay. The only similar feeling I have known is the joy I felt when I gave birth to my girls; all the worry, pain and apprehension washed away the first time I looked in their eyes. That's how it felt when Dr. Tembo gave me the great news.

At the same time, though, my heart went out to the mothers who are not so lucky. Along with their sadness they would feel such a sense of shame and failure, loss of dignity. As the sickness progressed through their own body, they would also face the heartache of nursing their own baby to its death. Around two thousand infants are born with HIV every day. Each year, more than half a million children under the age of 15 die of AIDS, most having acquired HIV from their mothers.[1] Nearly two million live with the virus.

For a moment or two I hoped beyond hope that, since Joy and Faith were HIV-negative, Moffat and I were too. But you know that was not the case. You know that on learning my status it felt like the roof split open so that a great, bright shaft of light could enter the room, envelop my body and enrich my heart. This was God at work. "Praise God, praise God, praise God," my heart wanted to shout. Please don't read into this that I felt joyful. This was not happy news. At the time HIV was seen as a death sentence. Moffat and I would be leaving our children alone in the world as my parents had done. I feared for my girls. Yet still I felt a sense of calm, of destiny, and this made me strong.

I will level the mountains; I will break down gates of bronze and cut through bars of iron. I will give you the treasures of darkness, riches stored in secret places, so that you may know that I am the LORD, the God of Israel, who summons you by name. This was it, I knew. This was my mountain.

11

I Shall Not Die Before I Am Dead

Sitting there in Dr. Tembo's room, I found it hard to believe he didn't have at least some sort of practical advice for us.

"So, what next, Doctor?" I asked him enthusiastically.

"Well . . . there is nothing that can be done."

"But Dr. Tembo, are you sure? What about eating healthy diets, exercising and living positively? In our sexual life as husband and wife shouldn't we use condoms so we don't reinfect each other?" I was doing my best to recite everything I had learned from my pink-covered book.

As though a positive HIV diagnosis was not harsh enough news for one day, now Moffat Zulu's young wife was telling him that he would need to wear a condom. He became outraged. "You heard the doctor. We are both infected. What are you talking about condoms? You are my wife," he quipped.

"Dr. Tembo, I read that the virus may mutate and reinfect us further. Doctor, what about eating pumpkin leaves, cassava leaves, bean leaves and foods which are high in iron? What extra proteins do we need?"

"Oh, yes, of course, those things may help. And yes, a balanced diet is a healthy option," the doctor said, seeming more defeated than convinced. While he may have believed a healthy diet would be beneficial, kind Dr. Tembo worked on the frontline of a disease that was by now claiming lives all around him. He was being responsible, not giving us false hope when, to the best of his medical knowledge, Moffat and I would be dead in six months' time. I could not tell him I felt safe in the knowledge that this disease was my calling.

When I arrived back at the house that afternoon I locked myself in the living room to pray. What else could I do? I knew all sorts of Scripture about healing that I used when I visited the sick in the hospital, but every time I opened my mouth to ask for healing I felt like an invisible hand had tied my tongue and I could not speak. Instead, I remembered my need to shout "Praise God!" and when, instead of praying for lenience, I spoke praise, the words flowed like a river, peaceful and joyful. The burden was lifted. Instead of asking "Why me?" I found power and strength from praising God in the midst of my affliction. The Scripture that came to me was Psalm 118:17-18: "I will not die but live, / and will proclaim what the LORD has done." *Yes, that is it,* I thought. *That is how I shall live my life; I shall not die before I am dead.* I became determined to testify about God's goodness and about people living with HIV.

When Moffat returned home that night he called me to his side, saying, "Have you done as I asked and kept the news to yourself?"

"No. How could I keep it quiet, Moffat? I told Mrs. Banda, so she could pray for us, as well as my cousin Barbara." I decided not to mention that I had also told the man who drove me home.

"I don't understand you," he scolded. "How can you tell other people? We will become the laughingstock of the community." I knew Moffat was grasping at straws when he continued, "Anyway, the doctor's test results may be wrong."

I jumped in quickly. "Moffat, I feel strongly that this is my calling. This is the mission God has for me. I think I have been called to speak on this issue."

He looked at me, both serious and confused, "Don't you bring God into this. This will make you look shameful to other people."

I was not giving up. "If this disease is what it is, the symptoms will catch up with us and we'll have nowhere to hide. It's like being pregnant; sooner or later it just becomes obvious to everyone."

"What nonsense. Who knows whether the doctor was telling the truth? Maybe the machines and the tests were wrong." I could tell in Moffat's eyes he was becoming serious. You could feel the tension in the room. "Princess, you need to keep this to yourself. If you don't, you know the consequences. I will make you go back to the village, and you will have no one to blame but yourself."

Of course I knew what that meant. Going back to the village meant I would lose custody of my children. I had no work and no income of my own. If Moffat took me to court, the girls would be taken from me. I understand that in many Western countries, when there is a dispute over custody, the courts tend to side with the mother, but in Zambia the opposite is true; custody is more often awarded to a father. My children were my reason for my living, my daily sunshine. To think I might not be there as their mother broke my heart. But something inside tore at my heart even more than being apart from my own children, and it made me feel strong. I knew it had to be God. Where else could I get this strength in the midst of my challenges, in the midst of an incurable disease and threats from my husband? I knew what I had been called to do even though I might have to suffer painful consequences.

"Moffat, I can't explain to you, I feel this is my calling. This is my mission. I want to tell people to protect themselves."

Moffat got a look in his eye, a look that began to frighten me. "You will do as I say and keep this to yourself."

Tension had already begun to build in our marriage, and this was only making it worse. Moffat had sounded the warning loud and clear, but with the numbers of those sick and dying rising by the day, and with a clear call to act, I felt I had no choice but to disobey him.

PART THREE

A WARRIOR PRINCESS

EMERGES

12

A Fountain of Life

From this point forward a constant tension brewed in my relationship with Moffat. Not all days were bad and not all days were rosy, but it was always there. Sometimes a look or an event would trigger a spike in hostilities, but other times it just simmered away in the background. Moffat had taken the news of his HIV diagnosis hard, and I am sure this affected his demeanor much of the time. We continued to argue about keeping our diagnosis private, with him insisting that I not speak out.

From outward appearances we were a happy couple, and indeed there was much that was positive in our lives. We were believers and parents. Our relationships with our children and with Christ filled the void. We knew it was important to set a good example in the community, so we immersed ourselves in our faith and in raising our daughters. I also pondered ways to care for the local children, many of whom were now being orphaned. It was becoming more and more common to see local children living with aunts and uncles and elderly relatives. I knew how they felt. Even the love of extended family cannot replace having your parents to hold you, love you and raise you. These children were being robbed of their childhoods and, in many cases, their chance to go to school. When I thought of how vulnerable these children were and all the challenges that lay ahead of them, it broke my heart.

One Saturday, I sat on the sofa at our home, half asleep. Joy and Faith were playing around me, and Moffat was reading a newspaper. The sun was streaming through the window, and for once I sat quietly, watching the little girls I love more than life itself. *What can we do to help the orphans?* I wondered to myself. As I sat there I began to daydream of a place where children could be children, where they could laugh and learn and play. I must have dozed off, but the dream continued. I could hear the children singing, learning the alphabet and their multiplication table; I saw them smiling, saw hope returning to their eyes. *How will I do it? Where will I begin?* The questions flowed through my dream as though I were in conversation with someone. When I woke, the dream was so clear that I knew I needed to act on it.

The feeling grew stronger and stronger in me as I sat in the sun's warm rays. I thought about what Jesus would expect of us. Our Lord modeled love, compassion and mercy for others. It didn't make sense to me that those impacted by HIV and AIDS were left out, forgotten. *How can it be that we talk about love but cannot care for the least of these?* I wondered to myself. *This is not Christlike.* It was clear the children needed practical help.

I became a believer in the first place because I was shown love by the church community; they loved me and they loved one another, the community of believers. They also shared everything, and I wanted to be part of them. This Jesus they loved was not absent; he dwelt among them. He was speaking through them. I said to myself, *Lord, here I am, use me.* This was my call and a way of showing my love to my Lord like James 1:27 calls us to do: "Religion that God our Father accepts as pure and faultless is this: to look after orphans and widows in their distress and to keep oneself from being polluted by the world."

In my days of school we learned about Nelson Mandela, the great hero of Africa. I remember that he said, "Education is the most powerful weapon which you can use to change the world." With all these thoughts and dreams rushing through my head, it became clear I should start a school for orphans. *A school. I like it,* I thought as I sat silently with my eyes still closed and my family close by.

To make it real, the school needed a name. Wanting to think of the perfect name, I turned to the only book I knew, the Bible. As I flipped through its pages, the words came to me: Fountain of Life.

While the thought was so clear in my mind, I wanted to share the idea with Moffat. When I saw him putting his newspaper down I said to him, "Moffat, you know I've been thinking about the orphans and how we can help them. Well, I'd really like to start a school for orphans." I watched his face and waited for his reaction. "A school, hmmm. Okay. But how will you do this?"

I continued, "Well, we'll just start one day at a time with the little resources we have. Maybe instead of sending Joy and Faith to another school, we can homeschool them and use their school fees to start our school."

Whatever his faults, when it came to children, Moffat would do anything to help. His tender side shone through as he said that he too was troubled by the orphans all around us. Right away he jumped on board. "I like it a lot. I will do anything I can to support your idea."

I was so excited to receive my husband's blessing that I hugged him. "Thank you," I said.

"And hopefully this will get you away from this crazy idea of disclosing your status," came his reply. I did not say another word.

I was excited beyond belief. Moffat had given the school his blessing. My own circumstances and my lack of education had made me vulnerable. I had a tenth-grade education when I lost my bamaa, but many of the children I wanted to reach had lost their parents when they were as young as four or five. I wondered what would become of them, what would become of my country, who would be our future leaders, doctors, teachers when one in three children grows up an orphan.[1] How could I sit by and not help?

Money to run the school would be a problem. I had a little to get me started, but Moffat's salary was certainly not enough to support a whole school. A wild idea for funding came to me: start two schools—one a private school parents would pay for their children to attend and a second school for the orphans. The money made from the first could fund the second. Joy could simply attend the private school, as could Faith when her turn came. In my mind, then, the money problem had been overcome, but there were two other key problems with my plan: I was not a teacher and I had nowhere to run my school.

Moffat soon agreed to use our home at 25 Lantana Avenue, Luanshya, to establish the two schools: Fountain of Life Private School and Fountain of Life Ministries Community School for orphans. When I say I had little starting money, I mean that I really had very little starting money—roughly fifty thousand kwacha, the equivalent of ten dollars, which was supposed to be for maintaining my home and buying food for my family. It had now become my only budget for books and pencils for students.

I made posters to advertise: "Fountain of Life Ministries—A community school for children who have lost one or both parents and those who cannot afford to be in school. No uniforms or shoes needed." Over the course of the next week, a group of friends and I spread out to hang our posters all across the different neighborhoods, sticking them to trees, lampposts, bus stops and any other available surface.

Everywhere I went I stopped and told people, "Please send your children to Fountain of Life. If you know anyone who needs help, please send them." I figured I would have to tell a lot of people to get the twenty students I hoped for. I would soon learn I underestimated the demand.

In the years after Zambia achieved independence in 1964, we were not experienced in running the British style of government we inherited nor the copper mines on which our economy depended. When global copper prices fell, our inexperienced government borrowed excessive sums from international money lenders like the IMF and World Bank. In an effort to inspire structural reform of our country, conditions were placed on our borrowings. No more than 5 percent of our GDP could be spent on civil servants—doctors, nurses, teachers. They also introduced a "user pays" system for education, encouraging belt tightening for a people much too poor to own belts.[2] When destitute families must choose between the immediate need of hunger and the long-term need for education, a child's future will always suffer.

While only five children enrolled for my private school, including Joy, Fountain of Life Ministries Community School was a different story altogether. The day classes were to start I woke in a mixture of anticipation and excitement. Before I had even taken a bath, I made my way to the bedroom window to open the curtains. To my great surprise, there were around one hundred people standing outside my house, waiting for school to begin.

Oh my goodness, what have I done? I asked myself in disbelief.

I had only wanted twenty students, but before me stood children of all different heights, shapes and sizes. How would I teach them all? I retreated from the window and sat down at the kitchen table with my head in my hands until I found the courage to face the group.

Once outside I studied the sea of desperate faces. Some of the children had been brought by grandparents, uncles, destitute mothers whose husbands had died. Other children—some as young as six—had walked barefoot and alone.

I introduced myself to the guardians and thanked them for coming. My heart pounded as I gave them the sad news. "I am so thankful you brought these children, but I am so sorry. I just don't think I can teach so many. I just wanted to do something small in my home to help up to twenty children."

The magnitude of the problem struck me. Just as I was responsible for so many dependents, so too were others in our community. Today I know there is an expression for the children who stood before me, some of the poorest in the world. They have become known as serial orphans. Until thirty or so years ago, the concept of an orphan was unfamiliar to our culture, as there was always a village to care for our children. But serial orphans are those children whose parents have died and who are sent to live with an aunt, who then passes away, followed by a second relative who subsequently dies. That child, along with their siblings, is passed around and around until they end up with, in most cases, an elderly grandparent or, even worse, alone. Every three seconds of every single day a child loses a parent to AIDS. Another one of AIDS's cruel tricks is that it takes young adults, the sexually active, the most productive members of society—the parents, the doctors, the nurses, the teachers. It leaves behind the most vulnerable members of our community—the children and the elderly.

One woman standing outside my house found the courage to speak up. She choked back tears as she said, "Princess, please help us. We really need this. We cannot afford regular schools. If you don't take them in, who knows what will happen to these children? The boys may go on the streets, they may end up selling charcoal or turning to crime. Please just take them so at least their minds can be occupied and they may have a chance of a future. Without this school they have nothing."

Another joined in, "We cannot afford the school fees in government schools, let alone the uniforms and shoes they demand. Your ad said you will teach children with no shoes, and you will teach them for free."

As they spoke a poster on the door of the room that was to become my office inside the house caught my eye: "With God all things are possible." There it was—the truth; what could I say? So, with a few pencils and crayons and just five dollars left, I enrolled over sixty students at Fountain of Life Ministries Community School, trusting what I knew so well: that God would equip me.

I studied every night to prepare my lessons. Then every morning I woke up and commenced classes in my private school, which had to be taught separately and meet a very high standard to justify the fees I was charging. Joy was there, and often Faith came too to keep her company, until she was old enough to be enrolled herself for preschool. They had to learn to call me "Mum" at home and "Teacher" or "Mrs. Zulu" in class.

Once the private-school students had started their activities, I would run outside to the carport to the precious group of orphans in their dusty, tattered clothes, barefoot, sitting straight-backed and eager to learn. Back and forth I went all day long, from one school to the other, trying to make sure all children had the chance to learn. As tiring as it was, the Lord gave me grace and wisdom, for he is faithful to equip us with everything we need to accomplish the task he has called us to.

Many of the students at Fountain of Life Ministries Community School had not experienced school before. Some of the orphans were ten years old but only had the knowledge of much younger children. By midmorning, many of the children were tired and weak because they had walked far. In addition, by that point many had not yet eaten for the day.

We didn't have much food, but what we had was shared. Each day we prepared a basic meal of *nshima* and bean sauce and sometimes *kapenta* for the orphans at lunchtime.

Running the schools was an undertaking for the whole family. My stepchildren, David, White, Moffat Jr. and Ethel, helped clean the house to get it ready for school each day. Moffat Sr. dug a well so we could have access to water, and my brother Muyani and other dependents Elvis and Rhoda would fetch enough water from the well to get us through the day, while others helped with cooking and cleaning bowls.

I soon began to suffer from exhaustion. One particular morning I was so tired I simply washed my face quickly and skipped my full bath before class. The community school children normally made such a noise when they arrived, but on this particular day they were quiet. I wondered what was going on.

As I wearily made my way out to the garage-classroom, I could hear my students praying. I wasn't sure who was speaking, but I stopped to listen, still out of sight: "Lord, bless Aunty Princess for all she has done for us. If you ever bless Aunty Princess then we'll be blessed as well. Please bless her so that we may be blessed."

The power of their precious words just grabbed me. I stood motion-
less and cried for those children. When they finished their prayers, I
gathered my strength and promised myself to do all in my power to make
a difference for the children of Africa and for the children of the world.
Their words remind me that there's always a child crying, if only we can
hear their cry.

There is a painful sadness unique to young children who have lost
their parents. They long for the nightmare to end—to return to a time
of play, to the comfort of their mothers' arms, to being thrown high in
the air by their fathers—but their joy, their innocence and their childhood will never return.

Within a year or so, student numbers grew to more than ninety. This
placed a real strain on our finances and made our living environment
very cramped. I put word out to the community that we needed helped,
and they responded. Strangers came by each day to help us cook and
clean. I made more posters and ads, this time asking for food, clothes and
money to support Fountain of Life. The community joined in to help.
Many of these people became great friends to me and an extended family
to the students. It was no longer just my dream, but the dream and the
achievement of the community.

When word spread of what we could offer the orphans, the community school continued to grow. Sadly, the private school that was supposed to fund it never grew. Its numbers dwindled from five to three,
and eventually it closed altogether. So the community school was never
well resourced; the children had to sit in the dirt to learn, but they were
just so eager to be taught that none of them seemed to mind.

While running the school made me so tired, I can't describe the joy I
felt when I would walk out into the sunshine to see my family and friends
cooking for the orphans, sharing their stories and helping them grow. At
lunchtime we all played together on our few swings and slide, and we ran
around and sang. While to this day I miss my parents dearly, helping
these children slowly began healing the scars left by their loss.

As time went by we were able to pay a few teachers, which enabled me to become more of a director of the school. My primary concern was fundraising, as the school seemed to grow on a daily basis. I started approaching companies and anyone who could help. The first company that came to our aid was Colgate. They couldn't donate money, but they came to Fountain of Life and taught the students to brush their teeth. They also gave all students toothbrushes and toothpaste to take home. This was the first toothbrush some of these children had ever used. Until that time they had only brushed their teeth with their second finger, rubbing salt or ashes from the fire into their teeth and gums. Or they would use a chewed, frayed mango stem covered in salt.

Watching them giggle and smile as the white toothpaste frothed in their mouths and covered their faces was a precious sight; it's still fixed firmly in my memory. Most of us would not think twice about toothpaste. But for these destitute orphans, their toothbrush and toothpaste became some of their most treasured possessions.

The teachers and I all knew we were experiencing something great with these orphans. God cares for every child. All children are precious in his sight. He is the father of the fatherless and cares for the children regardless of where they are. He is the fountain of life.

Hitchhiking with Truck Drivers

WHILE THE SCHOOL WAS SUPPORTING LOCAL ORPHANS, it was not stopping the spread of the virus. I still needed to find a way to help keep people from becoming infected. Children growing up with two living parents was a much better option than educating orphans. It seemed more helpful to put a fence at the top of the cliff to protect children from falling than have an ambulance at the bottom waiting to catch them. I realized that, if I was to succeed, I needed to get the message through to our men.

There were a number of reasons for this. I now knew that biologically and otherwise, women are more susceptible to the virus. Physiologically, it is easier for the virus to transfer from a man to a woman than from a woman to a man. To exacerbate this, inequality, poverty, lack of education, lesser physical strength and cultural practices combine to place women in a vulnerable position. Condoms are widely available now, but around the time of this story, they were not. While their availability was a challenge, women's powerlessness to insist on their usage was as great a challenge.

I am not trying to portray women as completely innocent. But statistics do show that in Zambia, men are more likely than women to have multiple partners. Sometimes this is due to polygamous marriages considered legitimate by our custom. Sixteen percent of all Zambian women live in polygamous marriages.[1] In other cases it's due to the fragility of our economy and the fact that men are forced to spend long periods away from home working. Indeed, it is now known that the key groups of men who travel for work—drivers, soldiers, traders and miners—have played a key role in the spread of the virus in southern Africa.[2] With inadequate transport systems and no great need to travel, most of the rest of the population remains in one place for much of the time, unaware a deadly virus may soon come knocking on their door.

During my hospital visits, which had by this time become few and far between due to the commitments of Fountain of Life, I had heard the same story over and over. Women lay dying with stories of husbands returning home just a few times a year, in many cases bringing the most unwanted traveler, the killer virus, with them. Tragically, in too many cases it does not take long before the virus spreads not only to the wife but also to any future children.

So one day as I sat down after Fountain of Life activities, I found myself wondering, and not for the first time, *How can I reach them? How can I change the behavior of men? There must be a way.* I pondered the problems of my country, the circumstances that lead to promiscuity and whether there were any clear occupations to target in my landlocked country. The image of Africa as a woman, with cars and trucks spreading cells of the virus through her body, had returned to me, and I knew this had to be part of the solution. As I thought about the number of times I had been propositioned hitchhiking, bingo! An idea came to mind.

I ran to my friend Chilufya's home, desperate to share my idea with her. "Chilufya, I've got it, I have an idea. I need you in on this with me. Truck drivers are a part of this problem, and I know how we can reach them." Chilufya looked intrigued and was trying to anticipate what I would say next. "We can pretend to be commercial sex workers, hitch-hike with the drivers and then educate them about the virus once we're on our way." Chilufya's face fell. She was used to my wild ideas, but this seemed to be too much for my friend.

"Chilufya, think about it. We live in a landlocked country. All goods for import and export must travel by road. With no computer systems, drivers are forced to stay at the border for days. It's here they cause the most trouble, but if they can, they will pick up a girl along the way to take to the next border town with them."

"Princess, I know this is true, but what does it have to do with us?"

"I need company just in case someone we know catches us and won-ders what we are up to." I knew I would have a hard time trying to con-vince a friend of Moffat's or someone from our church that I was only pretending to be a commercial sex worker. "Besides, Chilufya, it will be safer if there are two of us."

Chilufya's reaction wasn't what I'd hoped for. "Princess, you are a married woman—we are married women—and Christians, for that matter. How can we do such a thing? What will people think of us? You are right; they will conclude that we are being promiscuous. I think you should forget about this idea. It will only put us in trouble if our husbands find out. Please, let's forget about this thing and leave it alone."

"But Chilufya"—by now I was pleading—"there are people dying of AIDS every day. As Christians we are called to respond with compassion and yet we aren't. Shouldn't we care more about those people who are infected and dying than those people who might judge us?"

My daily struggle was that as Christians we care about judgment and people not getting to heaven; true, we need to care about people's souls and eternal life. But we should also care about their lives while they're on earth and work to protect people now. Whatever I said, though, I just couldn't talk Chilufya into my plan, so I left her alone.

On the way home from Chilufya's house, disappointed and lonely, I pon-dered our discussion. Putting myself in her situation, I could see that Chi-

Iufya was right. She had reason to fear as this could jeopardize her marriage.

I tried to let it go—for the sake of my own marriage as well as to be at peace. While Moffat found solace in his faith and in his daughters, his mood was growing darker as he became increasingly bitter over his HIV status and jealous and suspicious of me, wanting to know where I was at all times. Moffat was not a violent man by nature, but as his temper grew more volatile, I often wondered what he was capable of.

The idea wouldn't leave me. Educating the trucker drivers had grown into a need, a burden that had to be met. I had to find the strength and courage to go this alone.

The morning of my first planned hitchhiking mission I behaved like a perfect wife so Moffat would not suspect a thing. I had waited for the school holidays so I had no responsibilities for Fountain of Life. After I woke, showered and dressed in my African clothes, I prepared a hot breakfast of sweet potato and ground-nut sauce for my husband and then waved goodbye as he set off for work. Leaving the children with some of our extended family, I gave them instructions on what to prepare for dinner, so it would appear I had been home all day. I now had eight clear hours ahead of me.

When I was sure the coast was clear, I left the house carrying a plastic bag full of the items that would become my secret weapon in the fight against AIDS and headed for the gate that welcomes you to Luanshya. Looking to make sure no one was watching, I then jumped into the bushes by the side of the road. A few minutes later I looked like someone else altogether in tight jeans, a short blue silk *shaba* tank top that showed my belly, high heels and red lipstick. The transformation was empowering but also a little frightening. I'm not sure if it's something I should be proud of, but I passed easily as a commercial sex worker!

I stood still for a few moments, hidden from view, wondering whether I really had the courage to proceed. But I thought about how many girls would be saved if just one trucker changed his behavior—and, if it wasn't too late, how his wife and children would be saved too. *What if I could*

change two drivers, or ten, or a hundred? Those feelings of intense hope helped
me forget the risks. My fears forgotten, I was no longer scared. This was
something beyond my own doing. There was a greater power driving me
on. *Let the mission begin,* I thought.

Drivers didn't seem able to resist my voluptuous African figure and
curves. Their big rigs would be charging down the road, and then I would
hear the sound of those giant big brakes kicking in. I would climb up into
the cabin and away we went. Each time I got a lift, the conversation went
something like this:

"Hey, my dear. Where you going?" the driver would say.

"I'm going to the next town," I would respond.

"Well how 'bout that? I'm going to the next town too. Jump in. I will
give you a ride. What's your name, sweet girl?"

For some reason I always used Doreen as an alias, or occasionally Doris;
who can say why?

"Well, Doreen, why don't you come along with me to the border
post? We can have more time together there."

"Sure, I'm not in a hurry. Let's go for a ride."

It never took long for the driver to get suggestive in *that* way, which
was my cue to switch gears.

"Sir, I have to tell you, I'm on a mission. I am sorry I actually cannot
take you up on your offer."

"What are you talking about?" the driver would ask indignantly.

"I just got into your truck to tell you about a disease called AIDS."

If he had heard of AIDS, the driver would respond with something
like, "Do I look promiscuous to you? That disease doesn't concern me. It
is for people who are promiscuous and who sleep with prostitutes."

I would choose my words carefully. These men were usually older
than me, and our culture insists we show respect. I also knew that the
wrong approach would shut down a driver's willingness to listen. "Please,
sir. Even the girls you pick up on the street—they may look healthy but
they still can be infected with the disease. No one is immune or bullet-

proof to this disease, sir." Once I had their attention I would continue. "If a girl is HIV-positive and you have unprotected sex, the chances of you becoming infected are high."

"Who do you know who has this virus?" the drivers would often ask.

At this point, I would quickly reach into my bag of tricks and pull out my own HIV results. "I do, sir. Could you have guessed if I didn't tell you?"

One driver, I remember, nearly caused an accident. He was changing gears and the shock was too much.

"But you look so healthy. I can't believe it."

"That is the secret weapon of this virus, sir. You can never tell who has it. Please, do be careful at all times. Of course, girls won't tell you if they are HIV-positive. They need the money. Many may not even be aware they are infected. But this will not stop the virus from spreading to you and it will not stop you taking it home to your wife and even your unborn children. Please," I pleaded, "I ask you to try and be faithful, and if you can't, please always wear a condom."

I knew even the hardest of men would hate the knowledge that they could pass the virus to their children, so this seemed like a diplomatic avenue to pursue. "Not only do I have the virus myself, it took both my parents while I was still a teenager. Do you know how vulnerable that makes a child? Do you want this for your own children?"

Responses from drivers varied. Some still believed they were at no risk from the virus. Their excuses and justification for their behavior flowed thick and fast. Sadly, some of my favorites were, "The girls at the border just force us. They disturb us by knocking on our truck doors while we are sleeping. We're only giving them what they want—we help each other out." And, "They dress so seductively; they encourage us. What can a man do? Sometimes I am away from my wife for several months. Am I not a man?"

But other drivers took this as a time for reflection. They thanked me for sharing my lesson with them. I knew their behavior would change, at

least for that day. Human beings, we can be such creatures of habit; I just
prayed the drivers' old habits didn't return.

Depending on the driver and their responsiveness to our conversation, I would also introduce them to my faith and encourage them to
develop a closer relationship with God. When this part of our conversation was well received I was truly happy, as I had the chance to protect
life on earth as well as share about everlasting life.

Some days the drivers would drop me in Ndola and other days I'd ask
them to take me to the nearby mine town of Kitwe, where my Aunt Erika
happened to live. Once or twice, when Moffat was away for work, I asked
drivers to take me all the way to the border. The first time I reached the
border of Congo, the area called Kasumbalesa, I could not believe my eyes.

The reality of young girls and women living through desperate times
means there's always a gathering of commercial sex workers waiting for
weary drivers at African border towns. Sadly, many are just young girls,
often orphans themselves, trying to put food on their tables or make some
money to pay for their education fees, uniforms and shoes. As I looked in
the eyes of these girls I saw that they carry deep shame from their actions,
but necessity forces them to play a hand they would rather not. As someone who has been in a vulnerable position, I know how this feels. The girls
have a tragic saying that conveys their reality and shows how inextricably
AIDS is linked to poverty: "AIDS may kill me in months or years, but
hunger will kill me and my family tomorrow." This is what extreme poverty does to people; it robs them of the ability to think long-term. I knew
desperation would see these girls return again and again, regardless of
what I said, unless the drivers were willing to change their behavior.

Such girls are known as commercial sex workers, but I struggle with
that title. Many of them are just teenagers, and will charge as little as
fifty thousand kwacha or ten dollars per "turn" with a driver. That fee is
likely to be halved or dropped as low as one dollar if the girl wants to use
a condom to protect both herself and the driver from an incurable, deadly
disease.[3] *What is commercial about this transaction?* one may ask.

The implications of this behavior are staggering. On noticing a rise in the number of commercial sex workers contracting AIDS as far back as the late 1980s, a researcher named Job Bwayo at the University of Nairobi decided to test some women. Groups of prostitutes he screened tested as high as 80 percent for HIV. Then, curious about their clients, he began to test truck drivers in 1989, again with frightening results: 36 percent of the Ugandan drivers were positive, 19 percent of the Kenyans and 51 percent of the Rwandans.[4] Today long-haul truckers have an HIV-infection rate that is roughly twice that of the general population.[5]

Fighting AIDS among commercial sex workers is an example of how the response can be hampered by politics and ideology. The challenge is that buying sex is illegal and considered immoral, yet in countries the world over, it continues to happen. But knowing it happens, conservative policy-makers and humanitarian agencies won't fund AIDS prevention programs for these girls. They deem any strategy targeting commercial sex workers as an endorsement of their work. The result is that many initiatives designed to help these young women find a new income—say sewing clothes or making crafts—never gets funding, trapping the girls in their horrible existence. What sense does that make, either from a disease-control perspective or a moral standpoint? Didn't Jesus work among the prostitutes? Didn't he bless them and allow them to wash his feet? What gives us the right to sit in judgment of the people Jesus blessed?

An inspiring African female leader, Graca Machel, wife of the great Nelson Mandela, whom I was blessed to meet at a conference in Thailand when she chaired a panel on which I spoke, was interviewed by an international journalist named Stephanie Nolen for her book *28: Stories of AIDS in Africa*. It is an extraordinary book that I implore you to read. Mrs. Machel was interviewed around the death of Nelson Mandela's son Makgatho Mandela from AIDS, the virus that killed Mrs. Machel's own brother-in-law Boaventura Machel six years earlier. Mrs. Machel's interview is compelling, but one quote in particular captured my attention and helps explain the difficulties around tackling AIDS amidst commercial sex workers. She says tackling AIDS "brings up the ugliest part of us as human beings." The fact that AIDS is, in many cases, transmitted sexually, "warps the response that might have been made had HIV been spread by mosquitos or sneezing rather than sex."[6] With my own eyes I have seen this to be true. When we decide HIV is too difficult and confrontational to discuss, we allow its deadly march to continue.

The more I rode with the drivers the more necessary it seemed to continue. Every day I was alarmed by some new behavior or attitude I uncovered. To me it was a matter of life and death. Every day I believed that if I changed the behavior of one driver, one life might be saved—one girl or mother. That seemed to me what making a difference was all about.

On a good day I worked as hard as I could to get in three trips before hurrying back to change in the bushes so I could beat Moffat home from work. I always made sure I had a story up my sleeve in case I mistimed my journey. My undercover activities created inner turmoil for me. I knew it was un-Christian to lie to my husband; I risked harming my marriage and losing my daughters, in addition to risking my reputation as a Christian. Yet my conscience told me walking away would also be the wrong thing to do.

Every single minute of every single day one child dies from AIDS-related illnesses, and one more is infected. This virus had killed my parents and my sister, and in the years to come it would also claim my brother Kelvin. I was surrounded by orphans who had lost their parents and whose world was crumbling. AIDS was crippling my country, yet some wouldn't even believe the disease existed. It was clear to me I was following my calling; I had a chance to show kindness and compassion, so I took the risks.

Meeting Dr. Phiri

Friday, July 28, 2000, is a date I remember clearly. The winter sun shone high in the vast blue sky, gently warming all in its path—typical for Zambia at that time of year. It was a day where anything seemed possible.

A truck driver had dropped me in Ndola where I planned to educate the staff at a Zambian electricity company (who didn't know I was coming) on how to protect themselves against the virus. In addition to my hitchhiking, for the past year or so I had been visiting large companies, asking if I could educate their employees about HIV and AIDS. Initially I conducted these activities during the school holidays, but once Fountain of Life had some paid teachers I could even go during school terms.

Some days I hitchhiked *and* visited companies. These days were truly exhausting. I'd head out in the morning and ask the truck drivers to drop me in Ndola, the nearest large town, where I'd try to find a company who'd let me in. Each time I presented myself at a company's door I made sure I was wearing a beautiful African outfit made from a colorful *shiterge* fabric and head wrap so that I looked older and wiser than my years. On the days when I combined this with my hitchhiking, I had so many outfit changes it was hard to keep up!

I had been buoyed to continue my work with companies when the Ndola branch of our postal service, Zampost, had become the first company to let me in many months earlier. The Zampost manager seemed to surprise himself that day when he said, "While we can't pay you, you will be welcome to speak." Before he could change his mind, I thanked him and told him it was in the best interest of Zampost if everyone from the top leaders all the way down heard what I had to say.

I began by showing the assembled Zampost workers a book containing some very graphic pictures of people in the last stages of AIDS. The book depicted both men and women in whom the virus had progressed to AIDS, displaying symptoms from various opportunistic infections such as candidiasis, mycobacteria infection, herpes simplex, cytomegalovirus, cryptococcosis and pulmonary tuberculosis, and malignancies such as Kaposi's sarcoma, non–Hodgkin's lymphoma and more. I told the assembled staff that AIDS itself is not the killer but rather these opportunistic infections. The pictures I showed them were like an atlas of AIDS—a world tour of pain and suffering. Many of the workers could not look for long.

"If this is what sleeping with women can do, I will never sleep with a woman again!" remarked one male worker, trying to lighten the mood. Of course, my purpose was not to create fear. Fear only stays with us a short while; sooner or later we forget. We need another motivator to bring about long-term behavioral change and transformation. Accurate education, reinforced again and again, was what would create lasting changes to behavior. I knew I had to use every bit of knowledge I possessed if I was to get these workers to listen. Again, though, since I was a woman and they were older, respected men, many of them in senior roles, I had to show great respect and diplomacy, particularly discussing such delicate matters.

I told them that directors, executives and people who earn more money are greater targets for young girls. In saying this I also had a hidden agenda: that all workers be treated equally. Workers in blue-collar roles often faced the greatest discrimination, as they were often, for some reason of innate prejudice, thought more likely to be infected. I didn't want the ordinary workers to think they were immune, however, so I qualified my statement by saying, "While the girls may target your managers, the virus itself does not know if you wear a tie or work in a mine. The virus does not discriminate and we are all equally vulnerable."

Finally I shared my own story of how I was living with HIV, and that the virus had killed my mother, father and baby sister. Many didn't believe me until they saw my test results with their own eyes. Somehow the virus seemed more real to people once they saw a piece of paper showing a positive result. The questions flowed once I disclosed my own status. Quite clearly they had never heard from someone who was openly living with the virus. I encouraged people to learn their status for themselves. "Knowledge is power," I told the group.

"Princess, you are a married woman," someone said. "What is the status of your husband?" As hard as it was for me to keep it to myself, I told the group everyone had the right to discuss their own status and that it was not my place to discuss my husband. "By the way," I added, "if you ever see me with my husband, please do not tell him I have been here to speak as I am here against his wish." I hoped to delay Moffat learning of my activities for as long as I could.

In the early days of my secret activities, such as when I returned from Zampost, I imagined I'd make a great spy or actress, as Moffat remained oblivious. By July 28, however, he was growing suspicious about my absences, even though it was plausible I was out fundraising or sourcing supplies for the school. These days I had to exercise great caution, especially since speaking to companies put me more in the public eye.

Once the Zampost workers understood the gravity of the HIV pandemic they became hungry for information. The questions continued for over an hour, and I was more than happy to provide as much information as I could. These people had never had the chance to openly ask questions about the disease that was claiming the lives of their coworkers, friends and family. They realized that with knowledge they could protect themselves and those they love. When the session ended, the managers thanked me and the workers gave me a long round of applause. I was overjoyed that a difference had been made in at least one workplace, and I was inspired to continue.

Speaking at Zampost opened the door for me to share at other companies. Soon after my Zampost engagement, a friend invited me to speak at a business workshop for Standard and Chartered Bank. Again the response was overwhelming. In fact, the desire for knowledge was so great that they scrapped some of their planned business discussions so that my time could be extended. They then invited me to come back the next day to speak to the next bank branch attending the workshop. Of course I jumped at the chance. Dr. Tembo had given me six months to live and I had well and truly exceeded this. I felt like I was on borrowed time. My time to make an impact was running out. Standard and Chartered Bank, along with BP, became two of the frontrunners leading the charge to create awareness and provide treatment for workers.

✼

Not all companies were as progressive when it came to HIV and AIDS. Just a little earlier, sometime in the year 2000, Moffat had lost his senior job with the mine police, and we had a strong feeling it was related to his HIV status. The doctors of the Konkola Mine Hospital had prescribed a particular medication for Moffat, the cost of which he had reclaimed from his employer, as company policy allowed. The medication was a treatment for some kind of opportunistic infection related to HIV and therefore more expensive than most other medications on the market. He had heard an allegation that the mine management had accessed his medical records at the hospital (their hospital) to investigate what this expensive treatment was for, although of course it was illegal for them to do so. Shortly after submitting his medical expense claim, Moffat was told that the mines were restructuring their police division and he was no longer required.

Termination on account of an employee's HIV status was and still is illegal, but it is difficult to prove, as discrimination is silent and subtle and evidence of it is hard to come by. We felt that this was what had happened to my bataa, and now, more than ten years later, we suspected this was also the reason for Moffat's termination. We will never know for sure—but perhaps my husband had sound reasons for wanting to keep his HIV status quiet.

Moffat's job loss had a number of repercussions. From a financial point of view, life became more difficult. Work in the region was scarce, so Moffat had little choice but to accept a basic job in Kitwe, the next mine town, some forty-five minutes to an hour away depending on the condition of the bus, and indeed the road, you took there. It was a far more junior role than Moffat was qualified to do and, like so many African men, he was forced to stay away from home during the week, arriving home again each Friday night or Saturday.

There were some upsides to Moffat being away during the week. It afforded me more freedom to educate truckers and workplaces about HIV and AIDS. And frankly, it was nice to have some space between us. By this time, our marriage was in trouble. Moffat was now continually angry and suspicious, accusing me of all sorts of things. We both desperately wanted our relationship to succeed and had begun seeing our pastor for counseling in the hope that it could be restored. Being a Christian made it easier to forgive and overlook differences, so I continued to hope there would never come a time when we had to part.

With Moffat still in Kitwe on this particular July Friday, I took myself to the offices of one of our electrical power companies, and asked to see someone senior. A man came down the stairs looking puzzled. I was used to this look.

Undeterred I said, "Hello, sir, my name is Princess Kasune Zulu. I am very pleased to meet you. Can I please have some time to speak to your employees?"

He peered down over the end of his glasses, partly amused and partly frustrated, indicating that he didn't have time to waste. "About what, young lady? And what qualifications do you have?"

I responded meekly, "About HIV and AIDS, sir. Potentially it can kill many of your workers. While I have no formal qualifications, I . . ." I was about to tell him my story when he gruffly cut me off and went on to explain, "We have our own nurse. She speaks to our employees about health matters." With that, he was gone. I stood with my mouth open, trying to hold my shoulders high so as not to show my embarrassment in front of the receptionist.

I had a list of four other companies to visit that day, but sadly I was turned away by all of them. So far the day had been completely unsuccessful by every measure possible. Disappointed and very hungry, I went about buying some food for my family and the school.

I had decided to go home via the Ndola prison, where inmates grew a large vegetable garden and sold its produce to fund the operation of the poor, squalid jail. Unlike Bamaa, I was not much of a gardener, and we needed some spinach and vegetables to maintain the iron in our blood and to help our children and the children of Fountain of Life grow.

As I walked toward the prison I felt deflated from the day's rejections. Some days it all became too much; I couldn't understand it. People were dying. *Surely their employers should do everything in their power to protect them. People need to be given a chance,* I thought. I found myself talking out loud to the Lord, making three requests: "Lord, will you please take away this burden? Or else just help my husband and people accept my cause. If you can't do this, then just let me die. I am so torn between feeling that this is what I am meant to do yet every door is shut. My husband is angry with me, companies will not open their doors to me. I am tired, Lord."

Upon arriving at the big prison gates I was told the garden was closed and I couldn't buy my spinach. *When will this day end?* I wondered. I was so disappointed and exhausted. It had taken me longer than normal to hitchhike to Ndola, and I had been rejected by five companies. I just wanted to be at home with my children like a regular mum, preparing a meal and getting my little girls ready for bed. Now I would have to go home empty-handed. If Moffat happened to be home, it would be hard to explain my absence. After all, it was getting late.

My feet throbbed and ached as I had squashed them into high heels to impress the companies I visited. To make matters worse, I had just missed a bus and there wasn't another due for some time to come. While I was fed up with hitchhiking for the day, it was the only chance I had to get home to Luanshya before Moffat arrived from his week in Kitwe. Even then I would be pushing my luck. I was beginning to panic.

Standing by the side of the main road out of Ndola, I waved my hands furiously at every passing vehicle to indicate my desperation. Cars and trucks passed me by, which was unusual. By this point I had my shoes in my hand, but I was not the only barefoot Zambian woman hitchhiking. My bare feet were unlikely to be the reason drivers failed to stop. Realizing I was in a bad position, I moved locations and then jumped and waved my shoes at the oncoming traffic. Still no one stopped.

I was so desperate to get home I would have been happy if a man riding an elephant stopped to give me a ride. But as it happens, a lovely, brand new, green Toyota Camry—so different from the rusty cars most commonly seen on Zambian roads those days—slowed down and then stopped.

I was caught off guard as the driver of this executive-looking car asked, "I saw your desperation. Is everything okay? Where are you going?" With my head leaning in the window, I saw that the inside of the car, like the outside, was beautiful. It smelled more fresh and clean than any other car I had ever come across. I got in, trying to put my shoes back on as I did so, and worrying that I would make the seats dusty and sweaty. Not daring to sit back on the plush gray leather, I perched myself on the edge.

As if trying to ease my obvious discomfort, the driver calmly said, "I stopped for you for two reasons. First, I am so impressed to see a young woman wearing such beautiful African clothes. So few young women do these days. It is really wonderful to see. Second, it was desperation that made me stop. What is your name? Are you okay?"

I told him my name and added that I was just in a hurry to get home. Then I added, "I love wearing my African clothes. I even designed this outfit myself."

"Is that right? What do you do, Princess?" he asked in reply.

I could tell he was an important man with a very high-level job. Feeling embarrassed, I thought for a moment and coined a new term to describe what I thought I did: "I am a freelance AIDS activist."

"A freelance AIDS activist? I have never heard of such a job before," came his surprised reply. I agreed I might be the only one in the country. I had actually never heard of this title before, but I so wanted to sound professional, and I knew *freelance* was the term used for journalists who worked for themselves—so *why not?*

"How interesting. Me, I am Mannasseh Phiri," was all he said next.

We drove along for a few minutes in silence, and I began to wonder, *Just who is this man driving me?* Nice car, smart-looking man . . . Mannasseh Phiri is his name . . . I turned to steal a glance at his face and noticed him wearing the red ribbon that symbolizes an interest in HIV and AIDS. Suddenly it dawned on me—*could it possibly be?* "Are you Dr. Mannasseh Phiri, the doctor on television?"

"Why, yes I am," he replied, so calmly.

Dr. Mannasseh Phiri was the famous doctor with the television program *Your Health Matters* on HIV and AIDS and other health issues, the one I had begun to watch after reading the pink book on the virus. Of all the people in the world to stop and pick me up! I could not believe this was happening!

"Dr. Mannasseh, I am HIV-positive. That is why I do what I do. I like to educate people about HIV and AIDS through sharing my story. That is why I called myself a freelance AIDS activist."

"HIV-positive and a freelance AIDS activist?" He sounded genuinely surprised as he continued, "You are amazing. I am so happy to meet you, Princess Zulu. You are God-sent."

Dr. Phiri sighed, explaining that he was not in the habit of collecting hitchhikers but that I looked so desperate he thought I must be in trouble. What a blessing indeed that he happened to stop for me.

He went on to explain that just last week he had returned from the Twelfth International AIDS Conference in Durban, South Africa. He had returned feeling somewhat despondent because nothing new had come out of the conference. He had nothing concrete to offer his patients and other Zambians dying from AIDS. Dr. Phiri explained that on the long drive he had been thinking of the friends, family members and patients he had counseled as they lost their battle with the virus. Not one would ever speak openly about their condition.

The conference addressed the very topic of encouraging people who are HIV-positive to accept and speak openly about their status. A statement was also signed by over five thousand scientists and physicians, including eleven Nobel-prize winners from fifty countries and five continents; the paper, called the Durban Declaration, confirmed the link between HIV and AIDS.[1]

Dr. Phiri told me, "I would love us Zambians to talk more openly about this. We have to be more open about this disease. It is simply claiming too many lives for us to remain silent." He asked whether I had heard his weekly radio program on Radio Icengelo (Radio Light) the previous Sunday night. I said I hadn't. He explained, "I appealed for someone living with the virus to come on the show. I am looking for someone who is open and unafraid—like you. That's why I say you are God sent." There was a slight change in the tone of his voice as he continued. "I have an idea. Would you mind coming on my radio program this coming Sunday night? I believe this would help a lot of Zambians. We really need to break the silence, and we need someone like you who is brave enough to proudly disclose their positive HIV status, to show that it is not the end of the world but just the beginning of a new world of living with HIV and AIDS."

My heart was skipping with joy as I tried to comprehend what my famous driver was asking. "Definitely, Doctor. I would be honored. I have so much to say and it's so hard to get people to hear me." Dr. Phiri told me more about his radio program and encouraged me to come to the Radio Icengelo studio on Sunday at 9 p.m., just two days away.

He dropped me off as close to home as he could, apologizing that he had to rush to Kitwe to take over as the doctor on call for the night. I had about a thirty minutes' walk to my house, but I didn't care. Finally I would have the chance to tell my story! I couldn't wait until Sunday night. *Dr. Phiri is God-sent too,* I thought. On Sunday I would tell him I had always wanted to be a broadcaster. Given all that had happened in my life, just appearing on his program as a guest seemed like a dream come true. Once again I knew that God was continuing to work in miraculous ways.

Feeling free as a bird I ran, with my shoes in hand and the pain in my feet long-forgotten. The sun was setting and the air was cooling. Memories rushed through my mind: "One Zambia, One Nation. Here is the latest news with Maureen Nkandu"; Bataa trying to hurry me out of the bathroom; my family calling me "The Reporter."

Was it possible my dreams were returning? *Yes! See, this is my calling. This is what I am meant to do; it is meant to be.* Skipping and singing, I waved my arms about in the air. The doctor's invitation had renewed my spirit and made me excited to go on. Forget about dying now; I was full of life and hope. The Lord had answered my prayers.

As I came closer to home, however, reality set in. *Moffat.* I was afraid I was in trouble. As it turned out, I was right to be worried.

15

Trouble in the House

Deep down I knew one day I would be caught. You can't tell so many people your HIV status without it coming back home. I had vowed to get as far as I could, to reach as many people as possible before the news reached my husband—and when that day came, I would simply have to deal with the consequences.

Moffat was an intelligent man and a policeman by profession. His suspicion had peaked at this time. Though he didn't know what I was doing, he could sense I was being mischievous. He must have been tying himself in knots trying to imagine what I was up to with him away five days at a time. Each time he arrived home for the weekend I could see his mind ticking, trying to guess my crimes as he searched the house for evidence.

I had become frightened of him. I knew I wasn't sharp enough to outwit my suspicious husband if he chose to interrogate me when I was exhausted and vulnerable. And the reality was, I was beyond tired; hitchhiking, running a school, raising my two daughters and caring for my dependents was hard work.

Walking up to the house that Friday, July 28, I could see that the lights were all on, but that was normal since the children and other family members had been home all day. It wasn't until I walked in the front door and heard his voice that my fears were confirmed. *He's home.* Moffat had come home earlier that Friday.

Despite my exhaustion and anxiety about Moffat, the elation of being invited on the radio still whirred through my body, severely clouding my judgment. I was a little nervous but a lot more blasé than I should have been. "Hello Moffat, how was your week?" I asked smiling, oblivious to the trouble that lay ahead.

What I did not know was that there had been a visitor to the house that day. A man named Mulenga had stopped by under circumstances that looked suspicious to Moffat. The truth about Mulenga was that he, his wife and his child had all been sick. To me it was clear they had AIDS, though they may not have recognized the truth themselves. I had counseled them through their sickness until Mulenga's wife died.

Now the wife's family wanted to follow an ancient but common Zambian tradition which, in Bemba, is called *ukumuwamya pakumupyanika,* or sexual cleansing. It is believed that when you lose a husband or wife, the spirit of the dead spouse remains with you until you are sexually cleansed. The family was encouraging Mulenga to marry his dead wife's young sister so that all evil spirits in him as a result of his wife's death would be cured and the couple's baby would have a mother and father again and the two families would remain united.

I was deeply disturbed by this, as it was likely Mulenga would pass the virus on to the new wife, and the cycle would go on. These are sensitive cultural discussions, but somehow I had created a relationship where this man was willing to hear me. I was doing all I could to discourage Mulenga from marrying his wife's sister, including visiting his home several times recently to see how he was doing. I had missed him each time, however, so on the most recent visit I left a note that read, "Hi Mulenga, I have been by your home several times but have not found you in. I would very much like to see you. Princess." It was under this pretext, and with this note in his hand, that Mulenga came upon my husband that afternoon.

Moffat's chest was heaving in and out, and his face had a look of barely controlled anger on it. *Is this the moment I have been waiting for?* I wondered. *Has someone reported my hitchhiking?*

I proceeded, more boldly than I felt. "Moffat, I went to shop in Ndola today"—though I carried no shopping bags—"the garden at the prison was closed and I could not catch a bus home. I think there was some kind of a shortage, so I decided to hitchhike, as I wanted to get home as quickly as possible. You'll never guess what happened as I traveled . . ."

"You tell me what happened." He sat there with his eyes firmly fixed on me, breathing deeply, his nostrils flaring.

"You know Dr. Mannasseh Phiri from the television program," I said, choosing my words carefully. "He sensed I was in trouble when he saw me on the roadside and so he gave me a lift home. He also has a radio program that he invited me to be on. I told him I would love to." Moffat looked troubled so I added, "You can come too, you know."

"I see," Moffat said without a hint of emotion in his voice. "And what would you talk about on this radio program?"

"Oh, I will just be sharing my testimony around my HIV status." He looked troubled so I added, "And of course what God has done for our family in the midst of this situation. That way, not only can we talk about HIV, we can talk about our faith as well. He told me there is a need for Zambians to be encouraged to test to know their status. I am excited, Moffat."

There it was. And I did it myself. It was like all hell was starting to break loose.

"You. Woman. You have all sorts of tricks. You just never listen to me, do you? Haven't I told you not to go around telling people this nonsense?"

"Yes but this is on the radio, and you know I have always wanted to be a broadcaster . . ."

I now made sure I was standing close to the door in case I had to make a quick exit. Moffat had still never been physically violent; I think he made a promise to himself never to hit me, but now I wasn't so sure that promise could hold up. He was stronger than I was, so if he hit me, I could be in real trouble.

His whole head was shaking in disbelief. "Now it is Dr. Phiri. A few hours ago your boyfriend came around. You thought you were safe while I was away, didn't you? Your boyfriend told me you have been calling to his home and missing him. He even showed me a note, written in your very own handwriting. Well he's back in town now and you can visit him any time you like. What has gotten into you? Must I hear these things in my own house?"

Moffat loved me dearly, almost to a fault. He was acutely aware of our age difference and was naturally suspicious of the affections of men my own age. And now Mulenga was knocking on the door of his house. My boyfriend? *My God. How will I answer these accusations?*

In the heat of the moment I thought I came up with a plausible reason for visiting Mulenga. My church ministry had been growing and included accompanying other church members to people's homes to encourage them in the Word of God. This seemed like a safe part of the story to explain, so I simply told Moffat that I had been ministering the Word of God to a sick family, even before his wife had died. Moffat took a minute to digest what I had said.

As for the radio show, I insisted I would go that coming Sunday evening. I reminded Moffat I had always wanted to be on the radio. I also told him that sharing my story on HIV and AIDS was my calling and that to deny me to speak on the radio program was to deny God's provision. At this point, my husband's anger was like a volcano about to erupt.

"Princess, you have gone too far. Something was telling me you were doing things against my will and now I have the evidence." Moffat was fond of using police terms.

Somehow I found the nerve to stand up to him, reminding him that

I was not a suspect under interrogation. I should have known better, though. Every word I said only made him angrier. With much banging of doors and stamping of feet we argued all night and throughout the following day. Moffat declared, "you have lost your mind" and that, being a married Christian woman, I needed to obey my husband. He said that the fundamental role of a wife was to be submissive. So on top of his anger, he felt embarrassed and insulted by my disobedience to him. Moffat also felt that I had failed to live out my Christian values. In his eyes I had broken my vow of obedience to the laws of marriage and to the laws of the church.

Around 9 p.m. on Saturday, more than twenty-four hours after our fighting began, Moffat apparently had had enough. "You have really gone too far, woman," he said. "You need counseling. You will come with me now," he shouted with authority. Moffat escorted me out of our home and to the home of our pastor where he knocked on the door, waking the pastor and his wife. We were invited into their home where Moffat told them that Mulenga came looking for me and that I had no proper explanation for this story.

"Surely, Pastor, if she was sharing the gospel with this man it should be in the company of others, not alone in his home?" *So my excuse didn't satisfy him,* I thought to myself. "Next she arrives home after dark telling me she hitchhiked with a doctor and plans to go on his radio program to tell the whole world about her HIV-positive status. Can you believe it, Pastor?"

The Pastor looked at me, concerned. "Are all of these allegations true, Mrs. Zulu?"

"Yes, Pastor." I didn't know what to say, but I figured I was in enough trouble and it was best to be brief. The pastor did not seem surprised at Moffat's disclosure of our HIV status. I wondered if Moffat had told him already, in confidence.

My husband continued. "She is supposed to be a Christian woman who knows to be submissive to her husband at all times. She insists I wear a condom and yet I am her husband. She discloses her status to the world when I have told her not to. To make matters worse, my friends spotted this crazy woman drunk at the station last night."

Drunk at the station? Well, this last story was definitely not true. Someone must have mistaken another woman for me. I thought about defending myself, but decided against it. Instead, I laughed to myself. *Thank goodness no one saw me riding in trucks!*

The pastor was getting serious now as he asked me to explain myself. "Mrs. Zulu, what is this all about?" I looked the pastor and his wife in the eye and spoke from my heart. "Fighting AIDS is my calling, my purpose, Pastor."

"Now Sister Princess. Do you think, as a leader in the church, you are setting a good example if you are disobeying your husband?"

"No, Pastor."

"Then why do you want to go against your husband's will and go public with your HIV status?"

"People are dying, Pastor, can't you see? And what are we all called to do as Christians? The Bible calls on us to respond with compassion, to do something about it."

Moffat jumped in, "This is not coming from the Lord. This is the work of the devil."

There was a short period of silence as the pastor thought about the right action to take. When he spoke, his words crushed me: "Princess, I feel the Spirit is telling me you have to be excommunicated from the church in accordance with the power that is given to me by my office."

I felt like I had been punched in the chest. I had told this man of God that I felt my calling was coming from the Lord, and this was the response I got. And, while I had been accused of things I hadn't really done, telling the whole story would only make things worse.

I was confused and conflicted as well. *Could it be that I was the one in the wrong?* In my eyes I was answering the whisper that I had heard from God, and making painful and necessary sacrifices to follow my calling, but now this man of God said I wasn't being obedient to God. Even though I didn't know how things would play out, I trusted that if it was God who had given me this whisper he would level the mountains for me to answer his call.

Just before midnight the meeting came to a close. Moffat was calm and silent on our way home, walking the walk of the victor who has won but also trying to stifle the spring in his step, since his victory came at the expense of another. As for me, I walked ten steps behind, my voice lowered to a sob, a stabbing pain in my chest. The tears flowed freely but I tried to cry silently so as not to attract the attention of our neighbors. I was completely shattered. My pastor, the one man I felt should have helped me, had turned his back, and now I was all alone.

When we reached home, I let my grief pour freely, no longer concerned for who might hear. In our darkened room Moffat asked me to join him in bed, but I could not bring myself to share a bed with this man. Instead I lay down on the hard wooden floor, where I turned to God for solace. *Why must I go through this? Am I in the wrong?*

The pastor had said my excommunication had come from above, and I could not argue with the Spirit. Yet I felt such pain and confusion that a man of God would say such a thing. I consoled myself with the knowledge that church leaders are human and make mistakes. But on July 29, 2000, I could not muster such understanding—not for the pastor and not for Moffat, who tossed and turned, sleeplessly. I could tell he felt remorse. He asked me again to come to bed, but I was not ready for such a conciliatory gesture. I remained on the floor without even a blanket and continued to weep.

The soft light of dawn found me still sobbing on the cold floor where I continued my conversation with God. *Lord, I pray with the dying as they leave this world, I sacrifice my household budget to care for the orphans, and I fight to protect people against a killer disease. I do all these things in your name and to your glory and yet the church turns its back on me? How can this be?*

The prayer that had been growing in my heart emerged once more, stronger and clearer this time: *Lord, I believe you have called me for this work and I must answer your call. I cannot live in this world and not do what you have planned for me. My life would be hopeless and meaningless. I don't want to see another child infected; I don't want to see another woman unable to protect herself. If I must live on this earth and not do your work, Lord, I ask you to take my life right now because I cannot go on like this. Or Lord, if I am mistaken and this calling is not from you, please take this burden away from me and let me live quietly. Finally Lord, if this is your will and it is you who has called me, please allow me to do your work; make my husband understand and support me and make your church understand me.* Even in my darkest hour I knew the time would come when the church would call me back. If not the church, who? The church has such a platform; it can reach so many. As far as I was concerned the world was waiting for the church to rise up at such a time as this.

I must have eventually cried myself to sleep as I woke on the hard wooden floor to Moffat preparing to take Joy and Faith to church. I, of course, was to stay at home since I was now excommunicated.

While I felt abandoned by my own church, my faith did not abandon me. Indeed, my faith was all I had to sustain me. In my desperation I recalled Daniel praying to God in prayer and petition, in fasting, and in sackcloth and ashes. I said out loud, "Okay, Lord, I will bring both my heart and a sackcloth before you as a sign that I am desperate right now."

With everyone at church the house was empty. I made my way to the kitchen where we had empty bags used to store 110 pounds of cornmeal. I took one of the big bags and cut a hole for my neck and one for each arm and then put it on. There was no ash in the house, and I realized if I started burning firewood to create ash I would have to wait a long time for the ashes to cool lest I burn myself. So instead, I smeared some cornmeal on my body. Then I went back into the bedroom and prayed like Daniel, in my sackcloth and cornmeal, and assured myself that God was in control. *Lord, I am not perfect but I am desperate. I need you right now. Take me as I am. Here before you I confess my own sinfulness, I confess that I have turned away from your commandments.*

After church Moffat dropped the children off at home and headed back to one of the cell meetings held after each service. Joy, curious as to why her mother was not at church, came to find me, only to discover me bent down on the floor praying in my sack. Naturally amused, the girls asked, "Mama, why do you have white cornmeal on your face?" Joy in particular was old enough to know this sort of behavior would normally be associated with madness, rather than being something their bamaa would do. I could see the awkwardness on Joy's face as she asked again, "Mama, why are you wearing a sack?"

I didn't know how to explain other than to say, "I am praying to God."

"Why do you have to pray in a sack with cornmeal on your face?" her innocent voice questioned.

Not knowing how to explain to a child, all I could say was that this was how they used to pray in the old times when they were desperate for God's help. Children being children, they let me be and went out to play.

I was not going to leave the Lord's presence until I had an answer. Time went so fast that day; it must have been around 3 p.m. when suddenly I felt an unusual strength come over me, almost like I was being lifted up. I also heard a voice in my ear saying, *Get up. Your time of crying is over.*

I obeyed, and went into the bathroom where I saw myself in the mirror. My eyes were puffed and red from almost twelve hours of crying before the Lord, and there was cornmeal smeared across my face. I smiled.

I had been so weak, but now I was overjoyed and filled with an inner strength. I removed my cornmeal sack and showered, singing songs of praise to God. Refreshed and dressed, I set off to find Moffat.

It was now four o'clock, and I was supposed to meet Mannasseh Phiri at five for the broadcast. Even though Moffat had banned me from attending, I was definitely going on the radio that night, and out of courtesy I felt compelled to tell him. I was now ready to do all it took.

I rushed to the cell meeting Moffat was attending. The host encouraged me to join the group, but I knew better. Excommunication as I understood it meant not participating in any church-related activities. There wasn't time to explain any of this so I simply said, "I cannot explain now. Please just do me a favor and find my husband."

Moffat's face stiffened when he saw me. He could not believe his eyes. "What are you up to now? What brings you here?"

"Moffat, I am going to the radio program on Radio Icengelo. I didn't want to go without telling you."

"I told you 'No'!" Moffat was furious. "When will you listen to me? Why are you here, you defiant, stubborn woman? Even being excommunicated from the church hasn't done anything to stop you."

Now I was losing it. "Moffat, I am so tired of this. If being a Christian means staying quiet, and if watching people die is the way to get to heaven, then I would rather go to hell."

"How do you think you will get there? You don't even have money to get to Kitwe, and I will not give you any. If you go against my wish, I am warning you, do not come back to my house, for you will find you are not welcome. Your bags will be packed at the door waiting for you."

I had passed the point of no return. "Then let me find my bags packed. I am going anyway." I knew my husband was serious, but I was ready to obey the voice I had heard.

16

The Making of a Broadcaster

TIME WAS TIGHT. I ran as fast as I could along the East Drive toward the bus stop. When I think back now, I smile at the memory of me racing along in a long, flowing, green-and-lime dress called a *booboo dress*. Married women didn't normally run like that, and I am not a graceful runner, but I was beyond caring. I had to make the bus to Radio Icengelo. Moffat wasn't quite right—I had a little money, just enough to cover the fare.

Here was my neighbor Mrs. Banda again. "Where are you off to this time, dear?"

"I'll be on the radio. Make sure you listen to Radio Icengelo tonight," I shouted as I ran on by.

"Reeeally? What will you be talking about?" her voice trailed after me.

"Just listeeen Mrs. Bandaaaaaa. I'm sorry I have to run!"

I made it just in time for the last minibus from Luanshya to Kitwe, which I crammed into like the last sardine in a can. Zambia's blue and white minibuses are renowned for being mechanically unsound, unreliable and often dangerously overcrowded; some of the seats are usually removed to cram in extra passengers. It was not uncommon to hear of nasty fatal accidents involving these buses, and I avoided them whenever possible, but this time it seemed my only option.

While the broadcast didn't commence until nine o'clock, I had agreed to meet Dr. Phiri at five at Aunty Erika's house so he could brief me in detail for the program. That hour had long since passed, though, and I had no way of getting in touch with the doctor. My aunt did not have a phone, so I could not even call him once I got to her house. The one place I knew in Kitwe that would definitely have a phone was the Edinburgh Hotel. I'd make my way there and beg to use their phone, as I had only enough money for the bus fare. By this point it was 8 p.m. I could still make it in time for the show.

When the bus reached the stop closest to the hotel in Kitwe, I ran, huffing and puffing, into the lobby where I blurted to the unsuspecting receptionist, "Please, I need your help to make an important call. I believe this man will pay you for the phone call when he arrives. I am supposed to be on his radio program tonight."

Dr. Mannasseh Phiri made his way straight to the hotel to collect me. He never asked me why I had not made it on time, and I had no desire to share the story. He was a mature, wise man in his fifties, and he must have sensed I had a hard time getting there.

As we pulled into the station I could barely contain myself. Radio Icengelo means "light," and the station is a Christian community station run by the Ndola diocese of the Catholic Church and services the entire Copperbelt region. With no time for a formal briefing, we went straight into the studio where Dr. Phiri spoke first on-air. He explained that tonight, in place of the regular program on child survival, he had a special guest who would focus on a matter that greatly affects children. He referred back to the previous week when he had appealed for someone to come forward and be his guest. As if God had answered his prayers he had a very special guest. "I know you'll all enjoy listening to Princess Kasune Zulu."

My head was spinning. This was my dream, to be a broadcaster. *I made it! In a few minutes I will be on air and thousands of people will hear my message.* Though it was a simple studio I was dazzled by my environment, fascinated by the knobs and dials, the meters, wires, microphones, headphones. I imagined myself back in my childhood bathroom. *Here is the latest news with Maureen Nkandu.* Seated in the studio chair, I tried to compose myself.

When my turn came to talk I spoke so fast, trying to cram in every single fact, every piece of information I could think of about HIV and AIDS, everything from my life and faith that might prevent people from contracting the virus, or that might help those infected to live more positively. I spoke of abstaining from sex, faithfulness, of healthy diets, home-grown vegetables, eating more protein and iron, testing, condoms. I gave it all I could, speaking so quickly knowing this might be my only time on-air. I fully expected when I returned to Moffat that my bags would be packed for a life in the village, without my children. Besides, it was now two-and-a-half years since I had tested. Surely my time on earth was nearly up?

When the show opened up for questions, the phones rang like crazy. It was clear that people were listening from across the entire Copperbelt and that they had understood my message. Nothing had prepared me for on-air question time. It was not like speaking to groups of workers. Broadcasting is a delicate skill, and I was a layperson; I didn't want to make a mistake. When I didn't know the answer to a question, though, it was great to have the benefit of a medical doctor and an AIDS activist there to back me up.

Calling a radio station gave people anonymity, so they spoke more freely, and asked a range of questions. I never knew what question was coming next.

One caller, for example, asked, "Can I catch HIV from kissing my girlfriend?"

"This is very unlikely. There is no evidence to show HIV can be transmitted through kissing. There have certainly not been any recorded cases of this. It might be a problem if the two people have cuts in their mouth or gum disease."

Hidden safely out in the ether, callers didn't feel the need to ask for information "for a friend." At last they had a safe place to call—and they were hungry for knowledge.

"I share a house with someone who is HIV-positive," another caller explained. "Should I ask them to move out?"

"No, no, no. This is the time we need each other most. You have to exchange a significant amount of body fluids to contract the virus. Usually this happens through unprotected intercourse, through contaminated blood transfusions or in mother-to-child transfers during birth or breastfeeding. Living in the same house, eating from the same plates, using the same toilet are all perfectly safe. Even if a mosquito bit your HIV-positive housemate and then bit you, there would be no transfer of the virus."

And so it went. There was no way we could get through all the calls. People's hunger for information was so evident. When the program finished, I was on a high. My heart was racing as Dr. Phiri drove me back to Aunt Erika's where I was to spend the night. The doctor had given his cell number out on-air, though, and it rang all the way home. In between calls, he told me he was heartened with the response. In all his years of broadcasting, this was one of the best responses he had ever received to a program.

As he dropped me off at my aunt's place, Dr. Phiri invited me back onto his radio program the following week. "The response tonight was so powerful, a follow-up program is important. The listeners absolutely loved you," he said. Even though I didn't know where I would be living or what would be happening to me by that time, without hesitating I said "Yes, I would love to. I will be back, Doctor."

How I wished Bamaa and Bataa were there to see this day. It was a dream come true to know that there was a purpose to it all and I did not just delay them in the bathroom for no reason. Here I was with a chance to fight the disease that killed them—a chance to protect other families from such pain. Even though I knew there was a chance I was going to have to return to the village to live, I went to bed very happy that night.

Princess Kasune Zulu the broadcaster had arrived.

Early the next morning there was a knock at the door. I was nervous. Moffat had arrived, and he summoned me, my aunty and my cousin together. I could barely sit still, for I knew what lay ahead—Moffat was going to tell my family all that I had done. But still, I was ready to face what came.

"Did you hear her on the radio, Aunty?" he asked gruffly.

"Yes, Moffat. She was great. She was so brave and so open," Aunty Erika responded, unaware of Moffat's motives.

"I'm going to divorce her for that. She had been warned. This woman is unsubmissive, untaught and uncultured." In Zambian culture being called uncultured is the ultimate insult if told to a married woman's family. It means they did a poor job of raising the girl to be a dutiful wife.

"What?" Aunt Erika asked. "Princess, have you been unsubmissive to your husband? He is your husband. You are married. Why would you go against your husband's wish to do such a thing? Now look at the consequences you bring on yourself and your family. Where will you go if you are divorced?"

"If I have to go to the village, I will go, for there is nothing I can do to reverse my situation," I responded humbly. Aunt Erika would have taken my side, but she was a traditional woman; she could not believe these words. "But Princess, you will lose your children."

"They are my children. I will always see them."

"Why are you doing this? Why can't you just let it be?" she asked as Moffat sat silently.

"I want to protect women and children. I want to protect the women in villages, the women like my bamaa. Yes, as women we want to give our total selves to our husbands, but should it be at the expense of our own life? Should a woman stay in a relationship if she suspects her husband is cheating? She must protect herself. When women die early they are taken from their children. How many women have died? They never had the chance to live and protect their children. I have been there and I know how painful this is. I am determined to make a difference. If this means losing my husband, then this is the way it has to be."

"Princess, please listen to your husband—don't go back on the radio next week."

Moffat had lost the rage he showed just days before, but he remained firm in his convictions. "Princess, I am chasing you away. You are embarrassing me. You are doing this radio program at night with another man. You are not behaving like a Zambian married woman when you go out against the will of your husband at this late time."·There was no way to resolve this amicably. I insisted on continuing my work and Moffat continued to assert that it was wrong for me to do so.

I caught the bus home that day while Moffat remained in Kitwe for work. When I arrived home, Joy and Faith ran to me, full of excitement. "Mummy, mummy, we heard you on the radio. You are famous."

There and then my heart broke. My girls didn't understand HIV and AIDS. At their tender ages, they just thought their mummy was a celebrity. Even though I had asked them to listen and they had heard me disclose my status on-air, I knew they didn't truly understand. Tears welled in my eyes, but I fought to hold them back in front of my children.

"Yes, my babies, I know it was good, but do you know what AIDS is all about?"

Right there, alone with my children, was the first time I talked to them about AIDS. "It's a disease that's killing millions of people." They didn't even understand the concept of death, and while they seemed so young to learn, I felt it was important.

I simplified my language as much as possible. "It is the disease that killed your grandmother and grandfather. HIV and AIDS is taking lots of mummies and daddies. That is why your mummy wants to speak out. Hopefully this will help and protect people."

"But Mummy, do you have this disease as well? Does this mean that you will die too?"

"I do, girls, but Mummy is healthy and we are going to pray that Mum lives a very long time."

"Okay Mummy, we will pray for you."

And off they ran to play. I knew they still didn't fully understand, but from that day forward I committed to talking openly to my children about AIDS, even though they were so young. I also talked to my step-children and other dependents who were older now and more immediately at risk. Whatever age children are, it is the responsibility of the adults who protect them to find a language they can understand.

With Moffat in Kitwe for the week, I had some time to figure things out. Could I really go back and live in the village? He seemed adamant about me leaving. Should I try to take the girls or would it be better for them to stay with their father? He did love them dearly, and they'd be better off in a nice city home than in the village—I could not bear to be without them and yet this was even more important to me. While these thoughts played out in my mind, I didn't think for one second that I should change my decision and refrain from going on the radio. It was too important. Radio enabled me to fulfill my mission to reach as many people as possible, far better than trudging the streets of Ndola or hitchhiking with trucks. It was clear I was meant to continue. I'd just have to trust God to make it all work out for the best.

At home in Luanshya my radio appearance was the talk of the town. People wondered why I would bring such shame on myself and my family once again. I heard the whispers, "She may just be lying to make some money. She doesn't look sick at all." People did not believe I was HIV-positive. "Look at her; she is fatter than all of us. It must be for the money." Again I tried to block out their voices and keep my head held high.

Later that week my faith was rewarded, because what happened next was something of a miracle. The phone rang. It was Moffat calling from Kitwe. *Here we go*, I thought to myself. But through the crackly line my husband said something that almost made me fall off my chair. "Princess, I would like to come to the radio station with you on Sunday."

"Really?" I was confused. *What was he up to?* This was unbelievable. Could it be my prayer was answered? It was hard to tell from his tone of voice just what was going through my husband's mind.

When the day came for my second broadcast, Moffat met me at Radio Icengelo. A new kindness appeared in his eyes now that he had had time to reflect on his actions. Before we went upstairs to the studio, he told Dr. Phiri that he also wanted to speak on-air.

When his turn came, Moffat tenderly began to say he now felt that, as an older man, he had taken advantage of me as a young girl, and he regretted this. He encouraged other men to treat young girls with more respect, to consider their futures. He even opened up on-air about his HIV status. I didn't know what to do with myself. This was God at work.

I was so proud of Moffat that day. He had been through a lot, being HIV-positive and losing his job. Then he had the added challenge of such an outspoken wife, one of only a few young women in Zambia at the time who wanted to publicly share their HIV status. Most Zambian women are reserved and are content just to remain at home with their husband and children, yet somehow God had given Moffat me. I could not believe how his thinking had changed in just one week. I was proud of him and of us.

The audience's response to Moffat and me together was even more overwhelming than the week before. Listeners called in asking for us to have our own regular radio program. "Please, Doctor, consider this," they said. "This couple makes such a great impact talking about this illness. We need to hear their message. This is important."

Dr. Phiri agreed wholeheartedly. He had also been thinking I should have my own program, and now he realized that to have an HIV-positive married couple would be such a boost to the fight. Off-air he asked, "Princess, Moffat, would you like to do what the people have asked? Would you be able to handle a show together if I get you an hour of air-time each week?" He was wise enough to ask us together, knowing that Moffat would have trouble saying no in this forum.

As hoped, Moffat gave his blessing, but he told me he felt I should do this alone. I wanted to jump for joy. Here I was, an HIV-positive orphan who grew up in a village, a mother of two, a freelance AIDS activist about to become a real, regular broadcaster. It was not long ago that I was a young woman who thought all her hopes and dreams were lost. I could not stop thinking about my personal verse that had carried me through the days, Psalm 118:17: "I will not die but live, and will proclaim what the LORD has done." *I did not die in six months, and I will not die in six months,* I told myself happily.

"Now hold on, hold on." Dr Phiri tried to stop me from becoming too excited before the decision was 100 percent solid. He told me he would do all he could to encourage the station to give me the time slot, but he couldn't make any promises. I'd also need training. It wouldn't be easy. Still, his words didn't dampen my excitement—nothing could. I knew the show would come through, so we all sat down together to try to think of names. Somehow we came up with *Positive Living*. It sounded perfect! I could feel my eyes and face glowing at the thought, *Positive Living*. After the stress of the week I felt so elated that I jumped around the studio. My joy was mirrored by the doctor. This was what he had been waiting for—someone to admit their status, which would lead to greater awareness among people, breaking the silence that lead to stigma and discrimination. He beamed with pride.

With issues between Moffat and me seemingly resolved, the children and I left our big home in Luanshya and followed him to live in Kitwe. This time the home was much more humble, as Moffat's new job paid only a small salary. Still, now we were back together as a family and living just a short bus ride from Radio Icengelo. We had to leave the school behind, but we left it in good, loving hands.

The following week, with Dr. Phiri's help, the radio station agreed to give me a time slot, which was all I needed to get started. At some point my program would require some funding, but at least we were on our way. Once again, I was in business, this time with my husband's blessing. I knew Dr. Phiri was truly God-sent.

17

"You're Listening to Positive Living*"*

THE WEEK OF THE FIRST *POSITIVE LIVING* broadcast was one of the most exciting weeks of my life. I could not believe my dream had come true! I thought about it every waking minute and dreamed about it in my sleep. The whole week I was filled with a nervous excitement that made me want to laugh.

Though I had no experience hosting a radio program, by God's grace I found myself equipped for the challenge. My feet twitched under the desk as Dr. Phiri taught me to switch on all the dials and announce, "Hello and a warm welcome to *Positive Living* radio program. I'm your host, Princess Kasune Zulu, and I am HIV-positive."

The doctor was an inspiring teacher who insisted from the start that I should learn to become a broadcaster in my own right. He graciously coached me in the tools of his craft, saying, "Princess, we have no technicians here. As broadcasters we are on our own. Once you learn here, you can broadcast anywhere." He gently encouraged me, saying with practice and patience I would make a wonderful broadcaster. The doctor saw potential in me that he was willing to nurture, and the skills and wisdom he taught me applied not only in broadcasting, but also in my broader speaking life. In these ways, Dr. Mannasseh Phiri became my first true mentor. He saw potential in me; I guess he saw the diamond in the rough.

While the doctor is quite famous in Zambia, he was always humble, never arrogant. He believes he can learn as much from others as they can learn from him. He always remains indebted to his audience, however large or small. "Be respectful of your listeners at all times," he taught me during my first week. "If you accidentally make a noise, or some sounds interrupt your transmission, apologize to your listeners. You are only here because of your listeners." In addition, Dr. Phiri impressed on me that, as a broadcaster, I must be at the station for every one of my programs, come rain, hail or shine.

While the program was confirmed as a regular feature and there were months ahead to impart knowledge, I continued to speak too quickly. I still wanted to tell every single listener every single thing I knew that might protect or help them. During my second week Dr. Phiri helped me in this too, teaching me to slow down and speak clearly to my listeners. My message would be better understood if I slowed down, he explained.

As intimidating and scary as it all was, I just loved the experience. I took great pride in learning the technical skills of receiving listeners' calls, putting callers on hold and holding private conversations with people while I played music on-air. Again, when we opened up the lines for phone calls, the response was staggering. It brought me great joy to answer the questions of people just like me, to help them feel normal and loved again.

Just hours before my third broadcast, the doctor dropped a bombshell when he called me and said, "Princess, I have faith in you. You will be just fine on your own this week. I'll be at home listening. You're already a strong broadcaster but I'll note any mistakes you make so you can keep learning. I know you'll be fine." And so, I was on my own.

Here I was, hosting my first solo radio program. Just as the doctor had predicted, the show went according to plan. By the end I thought I had only made a few mistakes, but still I waited eagerly for feedback from my mentor. I had just bought my first cell phone, and one of the first calls I received was the doctor saying, "Well done." His words meant the world to me.

In the lead-up to World AIDS Day of 2001 there was an advertisement in the newspaper for an award regarding positive broadcasting around HIV and AIDS. I decided I wanted to enter and asked the doctor whether he thought I would be a good candidate, hoping secretly he would help me. "Princess, you should definitely enter," he said. "You have my blessing but you do not need my help. You have come this far on your own. The success is in your hands." With that, I wrote a letter and sent it to the American Embassy along with the tape of my first solo broadcast.

By this point, life was so busy and full that December 1, World AIDS Day, came and went without me giving a thought to the awards. I didn't really believe I had a chance to win, so I was genuinely surprised when a friend called the next day to tell me I had won something in Lusaka. Apparently my name was printed in the newspaper.

I had to find a paper to see for myself, so I checked with my neighbors and the local shops until I tracked down a newspaper for December 1. And can you believe it, there it was. My name, *Princess Kasune Zulu,* printed in the newspaper! It said I was one of the winners of the Most Outstanding Broadcaster Award. Rosemary Nkonkola had won the first prize. Rosemary was a veteran reporter who I greatly respected, so I was honored to be considered alongside her. I was even more honored when I learned she won with a tape of an interview we did together! Her prize was a trip to America, and while I really wished I had won that too, Rosemary deserved it for her absolute dedication.

The American Embassy, who sponsored the award, had no way of contacting me, and as a result, I'd missed the grand award presentation in Lusaka. When I found out, I was so upset. But little did I know, God was up to something. David Dunn, America's ambassador to Zambia at that time, was planning a trip to the Copperbelt, and it was decided he should personally present me with my prize at the studios of our national broadcaster, ZNBC, in Kitwe.

The day I was to meet with Ambassador Dunn was also the day of a scheduled *Positive Living* broadcast—and it was one of the few times in my life when I was truly sick. I had contracted a very severe dose of what I suspected to be malaria, but Dr. Phiri's words about a broadcaster being there for her program *come rain, hail or shine* moved me to honor my commitment.

I took my mentor's words too far. Of course he would have preferred me to be in the hospital instead of the studio had he known how sick I was. But as a young, enthusiastic broadcaster I felt so much was at stake, especially on the day when I was supposed to meet his Excellency. I could not miss it.

Seeing how sick I was, my friends Brian and Betty took me to the station where I broadcast *Positive Living* shivering and dizzy. If you have never had malaria, here is a glimpse of what it's like: You start off feeling tired. Soon a bitter or sour taste fills your mouth—a sure sign of malaria. Whatever you eat develops this horrible taste. The longer you go untreated, the worse the symptoms become. Chills develop, alternating with a high fever and muscle spasms as you lose more and more energy as you become fatigued.

As I continued my broadcast that day I became desperately tired and weak and my head pounded. I would speak for a little while and then play some music, which gave me the chance to sleep for a few songs. My neck could barely hold my head up, and my arms felt like lead weights over which I had no control. Looking worried, Brian and Betty just watched through the studio window. They begged me to stop.

I made it through the program and went on to meet his Excellency, David Dunn. I looked and felt terrible, but I tried to mask my pain with a smile. Ambassador Dunn presented me with my plaque and said he wished I had come to Lusaka. By this stage my skin had become hot and clammy and feverish, and I was guessing my face, along with the whites of my eyes, had developed a yellowish tinge. Still, I refused to tell him I was sick. Instead I talked to him about Fountain of Life, and he encouraged me to write to USAID for funding for what he described as "such a noble cause."

I had wished so deeply to be at the meeting in Lusaka, but had I gone I would never have had the chance to really get to know Ambassador Dunn. I so enjoyed meeting him, and he has since become a respected friend and supporter of my work in Zambia.

With my official duties of the day finished, my friends rushed me to the hospital, where I was admitted right away. As anyone who has lived in a malaria-affected region knows, if you don't get treatment for malaria very quickly, it gets worse. While entirely preventable, malaria remains a killer, claiming around one million lives each year, mostly those of pregnant women and children in sub-Saharan Africa.[1] Malaria is a major cause of anemia, low birth weight, premature birth and infant mortality. Malaria is responsible for 60 percent of all miscarriages. In severe cases a young child can die the very day she or he is bitten by an infected mosquito. And while it has been with us since ancient times, we have found no vaccine. Malaria still threatens over half the world's population in 109 high-risk countries.[2] But perhaps the greatest frustration with malaria is how relatively easy it is to prevent; a $6.40 malaria net and a $7.50 biannual spraying of a home go a long way in preventing a person from infection.[3]

Contracting malaria while HIV-positive is particularly troublesome. I guess you'd call it a double whammy! The malaria can aggravate the HIV, while the HIV decreases your body's response to standard malaria treatments.[4] Urgent treatment is critical. Unfortunately, my attack was a severe one, and the diagnosis borderline: there was a chance the malaria could reach the brain, and this is not good.

I lay on the thin hospital bed desperately ill and praying, "I will not die before I am dead," willing myself to get better. On hearing my prayer, the doctors thought my malaria had already become cerebral and that I was delirious. I remained in the hospital for a week, but I knew it would take more than a bout of malaria to finish me just when my dreams were coming true.

People couldn't believe it when, lying there stricken with malaria and HIV and now living on borrowed time, I said my dreams were coming true. But somehow HIV had become a blessing in disguise that was indeed making my dreams a reality. The virus showed me it is possible to turn any situation around, that depending on how you choose to respond to life's challenges, your curse can become your blessing. I was determined that I would not break down but break through.

Once out of the hospital, blessings continued. Through winning the award and my growing recognition for *Positive Living* I became known in Zambia's circles of broadcasting. The Kitwe branch of ZNBC liked my work, so they invited me to move my program to their station, which had a much greater reach. It wasn't long before *Positive Living* was aired nationally on ZNBC with sponsorship from UNICEF through an organization known as CHEP, the Copperbelt Health Education Program, and from international humanitarian organization Oxfam.

But it didn't end there. People's need for information was so great that soon there was demand for broadcasts in languages other than English. A grandmother wrote into ZNBC saying that both her children had died from the virus, as well as five out of six grandchildren. The sixth was not well. Friends had told her my program could help, but she couldn't understand the program in English and asked for it to be broadcast in other languages. Soon *Positive Living* could be heard in seven native languages, plus English. We were also surprised to learn that we reached across the borders of Tanzania, Malawi and Zimbabwe when listeners from these countries called in and wrote letters.

The ZNBC studios were much better equipped; I even had the luxury of producers and technicians. Each week the show was announced with, "You are listening to *Positive Living*. This is a program where you and I can share our ideas, concerns and experiences about HIV and AIDS. Remember HIV concerns all of us, and now join your host, Princess Kasune Zulu." Following this announcement came *Positive Living*'s signature tune, a track by Norman Brown. Then at the end of each show, we opened the lines and took listener questions. We also provided contact information in case people wanted to write in or email questions and suggestions.

I recently came across some old *Positive Living* scripts that have survived the test of time. One was for a show titled "HIV and Treatment," a topic that in time would become my passion. Another script that survived was, to my amazement, a program when Dr. Phiri was my guest. The program went on to discuss the history of HIV, achievements made, treatment options and what still needed to be done.

Other topics included malaria, HIV and AIDS, women in the fight against HIV and AIDS, the role of men, the role of nongovernment organizations, the response of the National AIDS Council, traditional healers and HIV, prevention of mother-to-child transmission, the church in the fight, HIV in workplaces, TB and AIDS, AIDS prevention, and transmission.

One week *Positive Living* hosted an interfaith panel of religious leaders that included a pastor, a Hindu leader, the leader of the Baha'i faith and a Muslim leader. It was powerful to hear each of these religious men and women confess that they were once in denial over HIV and AIDS. They had thought it didn't affect them, but now they realized their members were dying. In addition, caring for the sick and hosting several funerals a week had increased their workloads. They now recognized the critical role that every religion, every faith, has to play in responding to the HIV virus.

There was nothing more exciting for me than people from different faiths coming together to respond to what some social commentators were calling the greatest challenge to face humankind. This is what I had been longing for. At the time of my excommunication I remembered thinking that the church would call me back, though it may take weeks or even years. This was the time I had been waiting for. The words of Ezekiel pressed on my heart. I felt that the church was being called upon as the watchman, with a responsibility to sound the trumpet and warn its people against this dreadful disease (see Ezekiel 33:3). If as a church we choose to keep quiet, then we must be held accountable. The church is called to walk with those who mourn, to come alongside those in pain, to stand alongside those who suffer. Every faith has scripture or teaching that talks about caring for the poor, defending the oppressed and being a voice for those who have no voice. In Hinduism, Judaism, Islam and Buddhism, how fascinating and encouraging it is that each one of us is called to respond with love and compassion to the least of these. That is what compassion is all about.

As members of Jesus' body we each have a mandate to do what our leader would have done. Each one of us is born with a purpose and an assignment. We are the voice, we are the hands and feet Jesus is counting on. Every religion, every faith group, needs to join hands and embrace their role in responding to HIV and AIDS and its underlying causes.

So this day of my interfaith panel was very joyful for me; not only did I feel encouraged by the faith groups, but it seemed to also herald a new role for the church in Zambia in the time of HIV. Around this time, the response of the church in Zambia and across southern Africa gained momentum. As it began to assume its role as watchman, I was invited to speak in many churches. Slowly but surely, the church understood it needed to embrace what is among it, for the virus was already seated in its pews and preaching from its pulpits. I am pleased to say that today, pastors of all faiths are part of the fight.

Positive Living continued to grow in popularity as I grew as a broadcaster. Of the many stories that captured my heart, one in particular stays with me. A listener asked to meet me, sounding greatly troubled. Once at the studio, she asked to be directed to Princess from *Positive Living*. When the office staff pointed me out she became frustrated, "No, not that young girl. I am here to meet Princess the broadcaster," she said.

Once convinced of my identity, we sat down in a private place together, she broke down and cried, sharing that she too was HIV-positive.

At fifty-five years old, though, she had assumed we were a similar age. "Princess, I did not know that you would be so young. I have contemplated taking my life. I simply didn't know how I could go on in this world being HIV-positive. But here you are, so young, with so much wisdom and such grace. You have so much living ahead of you, so much to look forward to, so much to lose. If you can live positively, then I can live positively too."

Listening to people's stories and sharing my own made me grow in strength and spirit. I refused to become a victim. Indeed, I kept hold of the sayings that reinforced my health: "Anything that does not destroy you only makes you stronger." "I shall not break down, but I shall break through," I said to myself, almost on a daily basis. I also began to deliver these messages of hope to my audience. HIV may have taken away my parents and my sister, but the virus had come into my life as a calling. I only grew in my resolve to make a difference and leave a legacy behind, living one day at a time as positively as I could. Continually I remind myself HIV is only a visitor in my body.

I continued to be struck by the power of radio, a medium that allows listeners to disclose their hopes and fears in anonymity, yet to the benefit of a vast audience. The UN has pointed out that, in Africa, though many people do not have access to clean water, somehow most people have a radio. Even if their radio is old, with cords hanging everywhere and a coat hanger for an aerial, people find a way to make it work. I remember my own grandfather putting a calabash around an old two-band radio to form a speaker so that we could listen to it. Indeed, in a country like Zambia, with poor infrastructure and little access to television and newspapers, where over seventy languages are spoken, radio is a powerful weapon to educate, inform and encourage.

Joy and Faith continued to listen to their bamaa on the radio. *Positive Living* inspired them to take action of their own. One of the proudest days of my life was when they told me they had a song they wanted to perform on *Positive Living*.

"A song? Really? How about you sing it for me?" I encouraged them.

There was a popular song in Zambia at the time to educate people about HIV and AIDS, and the girls had adapted it for me for the show. Here they were, my little girls, by now about five and six, trying to understand the implications of the virus that was sweeping their country and taking their bamaa away from home so often. They began their song: "Willy, Willy, don't be silly, HIV and AIDS is real. Fathers and mothers, don't be silly, HIV and AIDS is real. Uncles and aunties, don't be silly, HIV and AIDS is real. Boys and girls don't be silly . . ."

So my little girls had come up with this song to speak to people in their own way about AIDS. I was just so proud of them as I said, "Yes, I would be delighted for you to sing your song on my show."

As it happened I had a slot where I didn't have a guest, and it worked perfectly for little Joy and Faith to remain in the studio as my guests. "My girls," I said to them, "this is a long radio program and you would need to stay at the station with me for the whole time. Do you think you can answer a few questions as well?"

They were excited by this prospect, so they came with me to the station to perform their song. As they nervously began, my heart just burst with pride. After they finished a couple of renditions of the song, I asked them, "What makes HIV become a deadly disease?"

"Well, there's no medicine and you get it playing with boys," they answered.

Of course, the audience response to the girls surpassed anything we had seen before.

Moffat and I were in awe of our beautiful daughters. They taught me not to underestimate the abilities of children and how they learn from watching us. On hearing Joy and Faith, Dr. Phiri now wanted the whole Zulu family to appear on his television show, and we agreed to do so. I figured that, together, we had a real chance to change behavior on a wide scale.

Our family's first television appearance on ZNBC's *Your Health Matters* captured the hearts and minds of Zambia. It was powerful for a married couple to go public in this way with their positive HIV status, especially those days. But we were not just limiting our conversation to adults; Moffat, Joy, Faith and I were encouraging Zambians to have conversations about HIV and AIDS with children. We knew it could make a difference if parents spoke to their children when they were young. We have a Bemba proverb, *imiti ikula—empanga,* "the tree one day grows into a forest," meaning the children are our future and we must protect them as it is our responsibility to see that they grow.

The other benefit television had over radio was that people could see us; they could see Moffat and me looking healthy, with no visible symptoms of the disease. This helped to break down the myth that you can know a person's HIV status by looking at them. Our family was soon invited to speak and sing for groups in churches and halls all around the country.

I was conscious of the fact that I may not be around to see Joy and Faith grow into adulthood, but seeing the way in which they responded to HIV and AIDS gave me some comfort that they would always be okay. In my situation, I am sure it would be every parent's dream to see the message sink in to their children; you want to know that they will not repeat your mistakes. As I watched Joy and Faith perform again and again, I was full of amazement and pride. I am forever thankful to God that he found me worthy to be their mother—such an amazing and humbling gift.

18

My Vision for the World

I RARELY LEAVE HOME WITHOUT TWO ACCESSORIES. One is Bamaa's set of ivory bracelets and the other is a red ribbon pinned somewhere on my clothing. One day in 2001 this red ribbon sparked the attention of a man who was visiting Kitwe's ZNBC studios on business. This stranger introduced himself and inquired about my knowledge of the red-ribbon campaign. When I told him the ribbon indicated my awareness of HIV and AIDS and my care for people living with the virus, he seemed genuinely interested. I continued explaining that the red ribbon was not tied in a knot but instead folded in a loop, with one side crossing the other. This symbolizes hope, a journey, progression, the fact that AIDS cannot stop us, that we will keep fighting and we will stop it.

The man, who appeared to be educated, seemed impressed with my knowledge and carried on the conversation. When I asked him who he worked for, he answered, "World Vision." I had heard the name before; I thought I had seen them on television once, giving out wheelchairs in a community, and I had heard their ad on the radio: "World Vision Zambia, where we believe every child should have life in all its fullness. At

World Vision we know you and I can turn the tide against HIV and AIDS, break the silence, stop the stigma and stop the discrimination by talking feely about HIV and AIDS." They seemed to be some sort of humanitarian organization helping Zambians, in particular children and those with HIV and AIDS. I was immediately intrigued, and wondered if this man might be able to help the orphans and vulnerable children at Fountain of Life.

"Interesting," I said. "You're with World Vision and I have a vision for the world! I'd love to have your card so I can meet with you to talk more about my work."

"Well, you are different, young lady," said the man with genuine curiosity.

"I promise, it's strictly business," I answered, worried he might question my intention. After all, it is highly unusual in our culture for a young woman to be so forward, initiating conversation with an unfamiliar man who is older than herself.

Fordson Kafweku was the name on the card. It continued, *Area Manager, Zamtan Area Development Program, World Vision.* Though I was unsure exactly what this meant, Fordson Kafweku encouraged me to call to arrange a time to meet with him.

I called him soon after, and we set up a time and place for our meeting. Fountain of Life was still operating back in Luanshya, but the school continued to struggle for funds. I waited for our meeting with anticipation, hoping World Vision would be able to help the students. When the appointed time arrived I told Fordson all about the school that was then caring for around sixty children. I also told Fordson that my husband and I had funded the school with our own meager resources but that this was becoming difficult.

Funding the school had indeed become a great challenge now that Moffat was earning a reduced salary. But with a heart for children, we continued to make the school needs a priority. Generously Moffat had agreed for our home at 25 Lantana Drive to continue as a base for Fountain of Life. People thought he was crazy, but we both thought this was the right thing to do. Somewhere we had heard Mother Teresa's saying, "It is a poverty to decide that a child must die so that you may live as you wish," and we felt these words to be true.

In addition to Fountain of Life, I told Fordson about my HIV status and *Positive Living,* and how I wanted to break the silence and fight for change for those in need. Fordson paced the floor as he listened. He told me he admired my courage and joy. "You know what?" he said as his face came alive. "I have an idea. Maybe you can work with us."

"Really?" I said, shocked. I never saw it coming. I've always felt I had a vision for the world, and here I was being asked to work for World Vision! It made sense given our financial predicament. And, while I was disappointed that there was no direct offer to help the children at Fountain of Life, I reasoned that working and earning a salary would expose me to more knowledge and opportunities, and some of the money could go to the school.

Fordson then told me the name of the man who could make this happen: Dr. Nimo, in Lusaka. Dr. Nimo would have to ensure there was a vacancy I could fill, but he was a very good man, Fordson told me, with a passion for those living with HIV and AIDS.

A part of me wondered why Fordson would want to hire me just from meeting me so briefly. He assured me by explaining, "I think your story fits so well with what World Vision does. It is so rare to meet someone who will admit to being HIV-positive. I am sure Dr. Nimo will do what he can to make it happen."

I had the feeling that people who worked for World Vision were educated, and I was not. *Would they really hire me?* I wondered later. But I held my head high, clinging to the conviction so strong in my heart that God had given me a vision for the world, and that if he willed it, it would happen. After all, he is the God of possibilities.

To my disappointment, it took some time for a decision to be made. I continued doing some voluntary work with CHEP, who were still funding *Positive Living*. Though I had been working independently for some years now, at CHEP I began to learn about broader approaches and policies that would affect the lives of many. While I was not formally educated in HIV and AIDS, I was on a journey to develop meaningful and practical knowledge about all aspects of the virus, both within CHEP and outside it.

At CHEP we worked under a principle called GIPA, or Greater Involvement of People Living with HIV and AIDS, which states, "People living with HIV understand each other's situation better than anyone and are often best placed to counsel one another and to represent their needs in decision- and policy-making forums."[1] This idea came out of the United States in 1983, and at the Paris AIDS Summit in 1994 forty-two countries declared GIPA to be critical to ethical and effective national responses to the epidemic. This was my first taste of HIV policy, and I found it fascinating.

I continued my learning, reading everything I could lay my hands on in the CHEP library. I also collaborated with some friends and local doctors to develop an organization with the long-winded title of African Extended Family System Support for Orphans and Vulnerable Children (AFEFSSOVC). The organization's mandate was to reduce the impact of the virus on street kids, and we had received good funding from Irish Aid to continue. This all had further enhanced my knowledge and given me a deeper understanding of how organizations work. I felt that in addition to serving the community, this knowledge was preparing me for an eventual role with World Vision.

Throughout this time I continued to speak to Fordson, and on one occasion I even accompanied Dr. Nimo to the Zamtan Area Development Program, along with a doctor from the United States. That day I learned that Zamtan is a shanty compound, home to seventeen thousand people living in corrugated iron or, occasionally, cheap brick dwellings. The township began as an illegal settling area—not suitable land to be inhabited. But the population mushroomed as a result of the now defunct

Zambia-Tanzania Road Services. When the company collapsed the workers were left without any means of survival. Many did not even have money to get them back to their villages, so many simply began squatting on this hostile land.

Over time, the squatters were joined by their families and friends, but no infrastructure followed. They lived in squalid conditions with inadequate sanitation, unsafe drinking water, constant food shortages, and no access to education for their children or proper medical facilities and care. Twenty-five percent of Zamtan's population was under the age of five.

For years the people of Zamtan remained trapped in a dusty, destitute, overcrowded no-man's land. The city of Kitwe was just eight miles away. You could see its skyline from parts of the Zamtan compound, as well as the smoke from the Copper Smelter where some residents worked, yet Zamtan's residents enjoyed none of the benefits of city life. Nor did they enjoy the benefits of rural life, for they were crowded together, in most cases without land for farming. Mentally they were trapped with the expectations of an urban lifestyle that they were powerless to achieve—peri-urban dwellers, they were called.

I could see the immense challenges for myself. Most of the residents of this shantytown were among the 87 percent[2] of my country's population who eke out a living below the World Bank's 2008 revised poverty line of $1.25 a day. If the thought crosses your mind that $1.25 may go further in Zambia, think again. The World Bank adjusts this figure so that it reflects daily total consumption of goods and services comparable to the amount of goods and services that can be bought in the United States for $1.25.[3] Extreme poverty only exists in the developing world. Indeed living in extreme poverty means that households cannot meet basic needs for survival. They are chronically hungry, unable to access health care, lack the amenities of safe drinking water and sanitation, cannot afford education for some or all of the children, and perhaps lack rudimentary shelter—a roof to keep the rain out of the hut, a chimney to remove the smoke from the fire—and basic articles of clothing, such as shoes. These were the people of Zamtan.[4]

It was explained to me that World Vision, along with other international humanitarian agencies like Oxfam, Care, Save the Children, various UN agencies, the Red Cross, Medicines Sans Frontiers, together with faith-based groups and local agencies, work with the poorest communities in the poorest countries of the world. In the case of Zamtan, with funding from people in the United States, World Vision had begun by asking community members what support they needed. Not surprisingly, the list included access to fresh water, sanitation and education. Through World Vision, the people of Zamtan were also learning community leadership, development of businesses through microenterprise loans and, in the one end of Zamtan that had a little more land, sustainable agriculture practices.

World Vision's aim is to build each community's own capacity and gradually phase out services after a period of time—maybe ten or fifteen years, depending on a community—leaving the community stronger and self-sufficient, with community members responsible for leadership. The various humanitarian organizations work together on different projects, and when there is a crisis—a food shortage or natural disaster—each specializes in a different essential service: providing water, sanitation or medical supplies. However, the work of humanitarian organizations was being seriously eroded by the virus, which was stripping away years of progress, taking society's most productive members.

This particular day, the children performed skits for Dr. Nimo and the American, to thank them for the opportunities of sponsorship and education. I later learned that performing skits and plays is one of the most meaningful ways for people with little or no means to express their thanks. Such performances, we discovered, can also be a powerful tool for educating people.

Countries with resources, whose people have access to televisions or regularly read newspapers, can launch broad, government-funded advertising campaigns to educate their people. Australia's shocking Grim Reaper HIV and AIDS campaign in 1987 was world-famous for its ability to frighten the country into realizing that every single person was at risk.[5] So successful was the campaign and its associated public-health campaigns that less than fifteen thousand people in that country today are infected with the virus.[6] I understand at the time of this writing that as people in many developed countries have grown complacent again, the German government is about to launch a shocking new advertising campaign showing Hitler as the face of AIDS. But in a poor, congested community where radio was the only media widely available, and the few media programs on the virus were still largely ignored, educative plays performed by community members would become one of our best weapons against HIV and AIDS.

While I didn't have an official role with World Vision, Dr. Nimo asked me to share something with the community. I thought it important to speak to them directly about the need for all of us to change behavior to prevent HIV and AIDS, and it was important for them to see someone speaking publicly about their own HIV-positive status. While I knew my message would be confronting, I felt I needed to be strong and firm. Speaking first to the men, I told them the days of multiple partners were gone and warned them that they could never predict just who would have the virus, pointing to myself as an example. Then I encouraged the women to speak up and protect themselves. Both the men and women in the audience seemed to receive my message well, but once again I knew it would take more than one round of applause to bring about real behavioral change.

As we traveled around the compound, Dr. Nimo told me how impressed he was with my presentation. "You would make a great addition to my team," he continued, adding that he was trying everything in his power to make that happen.

His role was to identify ways to spread the message on HIV and AIDS to all Zambians, not just those inside the compound. Two of the key groups, he went on to tell me, were long-haul truck drivers and commercial sex workers at border posts. He called this a "crossborder initiative" and described the challenges and collaboration required to work with drivers who traveled from one country to another. Certain countries and borders were more problematic than others, since some countries paid drivers in American dollars, currency treasured by girls trying to eke out a living.[7]

I can't tell you how proud I was to share my hitchhiking story with Dr. Nimo, as it seemed this was my own version of a crossborder initiative. My pride came from knowing that even as an uneducated young girl, God had put me on the right path with sound strategies to protect women. Imagine me creating the same initiatives that medical doctors and other nongovernment organizations were embarking on! Once again God had orchestrated an incredible path. I knew that if I had to work, working with World Vision would be a perfect place to start. If nothing else, I was once again filled with passion and energy for what I was doing. There are a few landmarks in any life journey that keep you going and encourage you to not lose sight of your goal; my first trip to Zamtan compound was definitely one of those.

Dr. Nimo and Fordson still had to work hard to secure a position for me. From time to time they would call me and encourage me not to give up. It was good I maintained my faith in the duo, because if my memory serves me right, it was during this time (around the end of May in 2001), before my formal appointment, that Moffat came home from his new Kitwe job with a whole new sadness written across his face. "Princess, they have let me go from my job again."

I was almost dismissive of Moffat's news as I had so much faith in God. "Moffat, it's okay, we'll be okay," I tried to reassure my husband. "Just because that door has closed, it doesn't mean another door won't open. We will have another good job very soon." I knew Moffat was greatly troubled but, being so sure things would work out, I did not know what to say or how to encourage and comfort him.

It's difficult to look back on life and explore what you would change. I realize now that I was not always attentive to Moffat's own plight. He had not taken the HIV diagnosis as well as I had—and who could blame him? He was in a different position than I was; he was a man with a lot at stake and a family to provide for. I myself had never been counseled to handle my condition, but somehow God had prepared me. Moffat, on the other hand, had not experienced this type of preparation. I did what I had to, but at times I could definitely have been more sympathetic to Moffat's concerns.

Despite my reassurance, Moffat looked so forlorn with his head hung low. Part of his sadness came from knowing he would not be able to fulfill his role as provider for his wife and children; we would really struggle to pay the rent, and the school would be in jeopardy. But it was more than that. This was the second job Moffat had lost since revealing he was HIV-positive. At my encouragement he had disclosed his status, but this had caused anxiety for some workers who were still misinformed and therefore afraid of catching the virus while at work. He was overqualified for his job and a meticulous worker, so his dismissal was unlikely to be because of poor performance. Our best guess was that the company had laid Moffat off to allay the fears of other workers, or to avoid having to care for him if he grew sick.

Sometime the following year, I read in the newspaper that up to 30 percent of the workforce at Anglogold, a South African mining giant, was infected with the virus. Because of this, Anglogold had begun providing treatment to workers, which was set to increase the cost of production by four to six dollars for every single ounce of gold produced by Anglogold. More importantly, the story continued, with a workforce of forty thousand at risk, each ounce of gold would cost an additional nine dollars to produce if treatment was not provided.[8] This was what we were up against—an epidemic so widespread it could add to the cost of gold around the world! It is likely that in the small mine where Moffat worked we were also up against an employer who was not as progressive as Anglogold—who still found it easier to retrench than protect and support its workers.

Not long after Moffat's second layoff, I received a phone call from Dr.

Nimo asking whether he might visit my family with a team from America that included a World Vision senior official named Ken Casey, a man who would come to appear at other key moments in my life. When the day came, they arrived in a big entourage of four-by-four vehicles. It was such an honor to welcome this group into our humble home.

We all crammed into our little living room in Chimwemwe township in Kitwe. My family, including Joy and Faith, were excited to welcome our guests; Joy, unafraid, quickly climbed onto the lap of the *muzuungu-kaonde,* a term used by locals to describe a white person. After introductions I was asked to share my story, which I did happily. As I finished, Ken said to Dr. Nimo, "God is at work in this house"; the doctor concurred. "I am glad you have been singing this young lady's song so loudly, Doctor," Ken continued. "I can certainly see why."

Then Ken turned to me. "Princess, one day I hope you will have the chance to share your story in America." There it was again, that word: *America.* I tried not to get too excited. For now neither Moffat nor I even had a job. It seemed unlikely we were going anywhere.

Late in September I let my excitement out, dancing, singing and jumping around the house when, true to their word, World Vision Zambia sent me my first-ever written job offer. My salary was to be about one million kwacha—roughly three hundred dollars—which was more than the salary from the job Moffat lost, but still nowhere near the amount he earned with the mines police. Moffat and I ran to show the letter to our pastors, who prayed for my success in the role. The celebrations continued to the next Sunday's service, when my job was announced to the entire church and we testified about the greatness of the Lord. To some the job might not have seemed like a big deal, but to us it was God answering our prayers, for we were just about to run out of money.

With my first day of official duties fast approaching, it was clear I needed a new business wardrobe. One morning I made my way to the bend-down, or thrift store, so called because of the sight of people bent over searching through piles of clothes. After a day's perusing, I found a beautiful collection of office-looking outfits. These I proudly took home and washed and ironed so carefully that even Bataa would be proud. I wish he was there to see his Princess. It would have been my turn to say *Sandebota*—do I look smart?

When the day came for me to report for duty I learned that I was to educate the vast Zamtan communities about HIV and AIDS. To an extent, I was prepared for this role, but I was relieved there were many people around who could support me. I began by traveling into the Zamtan community three or four days a week and just listened to people's problems. The more I listened, the more I learned and the more I loved my work. I saw not only the problems and desperation of the people but also the great joy and hope. The work was immensely fulfilling as it allowed me to spend time with all sectors of the community, understanding the unique challenges of each.

At Zamtan Primary School we started AIDS clubs to get the message through to students before they reached adolescence. The hormone-charged years of a young person's life present a real window of vulnerability, particularly in such an overcrowded, undereducated community that provided few opportunities in the way of entertainment or employment. It was important to start AIDS education long before the danger time hit, as none of the families could afford treatment; indeed, infection would mean a very short life.

With the blessing of the headmaster and teachers, we would speak to the whole school at assemblies, held outside in the morning sun as there was no hall big enough to accommodate the entire group. My most powerful weapons continued to be looking healthy and being willing to disclose my positive HIV status and putting a name and a face to this disease. I really captured the students' attention as, once again, I met with the belief that only people who were wasting away and dying were infected.

After an assembly we'd break into smaller groups where student questions could be answered. Sometimes I'd work with young boys, other times with sixth- and seventh-grade girls whose bodies had be-

gun to develop. In poor communities such as Zamtan, children and
adolescents may be in primary school up until the age of fifteen or even
beyond. In some cases I was the first person to talk with them about the
birds and the bees. I'd encourage them to say no when the time came,
and, where it was obvious the girls were already sexually active, I tread
carefully on the message of protection. I didn't want to encourage sexual activity, but I also didn't want to put the girls at further risk by
pretending it didn't happen.

We'd start AIDS clubs, generally initiatives targeted at secondary
schools; however, Zamtan as yet featured no secondary school, so our
activities were restricted to older primary students and informal gather-
ings of teenagers and young people not in school. Those young people
who felt able to become activists and educators in their own right became
the head of an AIDS club, charged with the responsibility of speaking to
other students. If the leaders came across teenagers who were already
sexually active, they would encourage them to become secondary virgins, or restored virgins, meaning that while they may have had sex in
the past, they committed to wait until marriage from this point forward.
The concept of secondary virginity has taken off. Excitingly, in Zamtan
and beyond, the raft of education initiatives targeted at young people has
contributed to a fall in the number of young people infected. There is
hope for the next generation.

Running the AIDS clubs gave young leaders a real sense of pride and
purpose. Over time I watched previously shy, passive, uneducated young
people transform into impressive young adults with powerful communi-
cation, assertiveness and persuasion skills. These young people proved
they just needed training, someone to believe in them and a chance to
shine to turn the tide on this virus. Surely we owe them that.

On other days at Zamtan I'd talk to women attending the medical
clinic with their young children. We'd talk about the potential risks of
breastfeeding children and the importance of knowing your status. I
encouraged them to get tested, but at that time I knew this was un-

likely as they'd have to travel into the town, and the cost of the test and travel was still prohibitive. Some of the women were victims of domestic violence; others had husbands who had cheated on them. In many ways these women, without education or an income of their own, were powerless. Their vulnerability and likelihood of becoming infected moves me to this day.

The work was plentiful and rewarding. One of my favorite tasks was speaking to groups of people who were already infected. They were clearly ill, and mainly clients of a home-based care program run by the Catholic Church. I'd start by saying, "I am one of you." But I had to be careful not to appear to patronize, because I had a good job and a nice home and, until recently, a husband who had supported me financially. Few of this group had formal education and even fewer had ever worked in paid employment. It was obvious that people there had lived tough lives.

The group was made up of people of all ages who would meet each week inside a large shipping container that served as a meeting room. Many would only admit to having TB, and this much was already clear as they coughed their way through our sessions. Some were already clearly dying but didn't seem to understand or chose to remain in denial.

It was only years later that I realized what a vulnerable position I placed myself in inside that shipping container, with my own weakened immune system. I loved these people and drew great strength from their spirit and will to live. I loved watching their worldviews change the more time we spent together.

Though the people I interacted with for my job were so poor and the need seemingly endless, my work always energized rather than drained me. I was reconnecting with people, and Zamtan's people had that Zambian villagelike joy about them that I'd been isolated from ever since I'd been living in city houses again. Each day we sang and danced and were happy to be alive. That is what I had missed—singing and dancing in the midst of our affliction, that ability to feel joy that makes me proud to be African.

I'm proud to say that today, thanks to the sheer persistence of people who work there and the spirit and determination of residents, people in the Zamtan community talk openly about HIV. In fact, stigma and discrimination have dramatically lessened, and the rate of HIV is declining.

Another of my proud achievements during this time was educating my fellow staff. It can be easy for an organization working with HIV to assume their staff are being cared for and educated or that they don't themselves possess discriminatory attitudes. For me it was critical to educate staff and encourage them to know their own status.

I tried to make HIV a lighter subject, too, to talk and laugh about it. When I walked into a room I'd say, "Are you talking about me because I'm HIV-positive?" "Princess, you can't say that!" my workmates would respond, but I wanted to give them the freedom to laugh, to face this disease head-on. Similarly, if I made a mistake or if I was in a bad mood, I joked, "It's the virus that's causing it!" Initially people were embarrassed; "Princess, you are too much," they would tell me. But eventually, "It's the virus" became adopted as a mantra for the entire office. After a while, people became comfortable enough to be tested themselves, and those who were HIV-positive felt safe admitting their status, or at least confiding in me. As they embraced me and we became comfortable laughing with each other, AIDS went from something hidden and secret to a topic that was discussed freely and openly.

While I loved my work in the Zamtan communities, as time went by I was asked to relocate to the head office in Lusaka where my responsibilities and horizons continued to expand. My colleagues and I now had responsibility for fighting HIV and AIDS across many parts of Zambia, around twenty-one Area Development Programs. I became part of World Vision's global response, the HOPE Initiative, which aims to prevent transmission of the virus and provides care for those affected—particularly the children—in addition to advocating on their behalf. We spent our time training pastors, church leaders and teachers, and traveling to the various communities across the country. I take my hat off to the people who work in these communities every day. Roads and infrastructure are so poor and regions so sparsely populated that field staff might walk for three hours through deep sands in scorching heat to visit a household of orphans.

In the central head office I learned more about the broader policies to fight poverty, provide safe drinking water and educate people. In an effort to help people lift themselves from poverty, World Vision did things like give families some pigs, goats and chickens. Once they bred, surplus stock could be sold or given away. These simple strategies of income generation grew a self-reliant people. This was such an empowering period of growth that continued to prepare me for what lay ahead.

PART FOUR

THE AMERICAN FLAG
STANDS STILL

19

Coming to America

M Y SECOND "KEN CASEY MOMENT" came just six months or so after his visit to my home. Mr. Casey mentioned my story should be heard in America, and lo and behold, now he was inviting me to his homeland. He wanted me to speak at a forum on HIV and AIDS where I would address a large group of pastors and World Vision donors. I could not believe my ears. *This is my calling, my destiny!* Mentally I began to prepare.

At some point I began to think about the fact that I was going to visit the land that millions of my fellow Africans had been sent to during the days of slavery. I had learned about this period in school, but to be honest, I hadn't thought about it much since. Now I felt inadequately prepared to visit the land where these people, with whom I had so much in common, were now living. Though I didn't have much time before setting off for America, I knew I had to find out more more before I left, so I embarked on the bumpy five-hour bus ride to Kasukwe Village in Chibombo to visit my bamaa's parents, Enock and Selina Bulaya.

The news that I was going to Amelica, as older Zambians call the

United States, had already reached my grandparents, so there was much excitement when we greeted each other. That night we sat on reed mats, talking by the warm, calming light of the fire. "Kaapa," I said to my grandfather, "as you know I have been invited to visit the country called 'America' for my work. I need you to tell me what you remember about slavery from your perspective."

Over the years, Ba Khapa and I had talked about many things, but we had never discussed slavery. I could see on his kind, lined old face that the mention of this word reopened some painful scars, but he gathered himself and began to speak. "It happened in many different ways, my dear. Where I lived, many slave traders came, some disguised as missionaries and some disguised as traders, so of course we trusted them at first." This much I remembered from school.

Full of sorrow and shame he continued, "Our people were in on it too. We are just as guilty as the foreigners: our village chiefs, family members, poor and simple folk, strangers, the weak or desperate would work with the white people and send their own into slavery. They traded gun powder, white cotton, food, materials, anything, for their people, for their brothers, their sisters." This fact clearly still pained my grandfather so many years later. He seemed to have trouble believing his own people could be so traitorous.

Ba Khapa went on to recite how it happened. "She fetches water each day at 5 p.m.," the African would tell the *muzungy*, or white man, to give him the best time to catch a person alone, out of sight, where nobody would hear her scream. Pain flickered across his eyes as he steeled himself to continue.

"Sure enough, off your mother, your aunty, your cousin would go to fetch water, just as she did at 5 p.m. every single day. But this time, she would not return. Her family would worry—*this was not like her.* They would go to the well—*had she fallen in?* They would search among friends and family; they would call her name, over and over again. For some days they would sit and look into the distance, watching and awaiting her return until they finally accepted the truth. That is how it happened so often, to so many people. One moment they were here, the next they were gone."

I tried to comprehend the pain as Ba Khapa told me a relative of his was taken in this way. He never saw her again. I was captivated by my grandfather's emotion, his ability to remember such a different, painful time. This was not just the stuff of school books. It was the real history of my country, the continent of Africa. Now I had learned that it also affected my own family.

Ba Khapa paused, staring at the fire. His mind had found its way back to another time. I could tell this was hard for him, but he also seemed to find healing in sharing the words. "As time went by," he continued on, "you would notice folk who were poor suddenly had wealth and material items they had no means to afford. You knew someone had paid dearly for those shiny new wares. The scars have never healed." Then he shifted gears to give me his final words on the subject: "When you go to America remember these are your relatives. If they are older like me, treat them as your grandfather. If they are your mother's age, treat them as your mother. If they are young, treat them as your children."

The conversation with my grandfather had a powerful impact on me. I already knew this trip was important, but it now took on a whole new significance. What Ba Khapa didn't tell me and what I was horrified to later learn was that the slave trade existed in different parts of the world for more than one thousand years. Africans were not just sent to America but to the U.K. and throughout parts of Europe, and many were indentured within their own continent to work for local masters. Some countries paid minimal wages, but people were still taken against their will. As many as twenty million Africans were taken as slaves.[1]

Baffled by our history, I put my mind to preparing for my departure and my presentation. The forum was titled "The Hidden Faces of AIDS: The Widows and the Orphans," a topic I was comfortable with. I was so excited to have the chance to deliver two addresses offering hope for those infected with and affected by the virus. The first address was at a breakfast for pastors and the second, major address would be to a group of hundreds of major donors and church leaders.

While I had begun speaking around Zambia and once in Namibia, I enjoyed it very much, this was a very different opportunity, a powerful chance to speak in a place called New York, in the midst of people with the money and power to make a difference. I thought long and hard about what to say. Should I prepare a speech, or should I, as I had always done, speak from my heart without notes?

My wise mentor, Dr. Mannasseh Phiri, confirmed for me, "Make no mistake, Princess. Your power comes when you speak from your heart. You live with this virus every day. The opportunity before you makes you one of just a few in this whole continent with the courage and the chance to speak directly into the hearts of those on the other side of the world, those who can make a difference."

My brother Muyani also helped to ease my nerves: "Don't you remember all the things Bataa told you? Look at you, and how your carry yourself. You are special. America will love you. Always be proud of your country and your tribe and you will do great things."

I wanted to look great for the occasion, so I had my hair braided nicely before the trip and selected my most stylish African outfits for our two-week visit. I say *our* visit because Moffat had been invited to join me. Unfortunately, tensions were growing in our relationship once again. Unable to find another job, Moffat now relied on me for income, and this ate at his pride. His self-worth diminished as he could not even meet what to his mind was his most basic duty, to provide for his family. Our marital situation was shaky, making me uncomfortable about Moffat joining me, but we put our differences aside and accepted Dr. Phiri's counsel that this trip may revive our marriage. We had become role models to the community, and us separating would send a bad message.

❧

When I first saw New York City from my airplane window I had déjà

vu, though obviously I had never been there before. Zambia's tallest building, Findeco House in Lusaka, is around twenty-two stories tall, and few
others even come close to that, even to this day. Now I was flying over mile
after mile of very, very tall buildings that could be clearly seen from the air.
Even from high up in the sky the difference was staggering. My excitement
was overwhelming. I felt like a kid flying a kite.

We were met at the airport by a colleague who was sent to help us
to our hotel. For this I was thankful, as both Moffat and I were in a
daze. I was captured by the built-up beauty of this place. Riding through
the streets in a New York taxi, I tried to make sense of it all, of my sur-
roundings, of this dreamlike world, while trying to maintain my composure. I literally had trouble believing my eyes and felt as though I
were sleepwalking.

There was traffic everywhere; it seemed like more cars and people were
packed into this city than were in the whole of Zambia. Yellow taxis like
the one we rode in tooted their horns, ducking in and out of the traffic.
People shouted, sirens wailed, and trains sounded their horns, all against
the backdrop of the magnificent, majestic buildings that reached for the
heavens. Roads and train tracks crisscrossed under and over each other. At
that point, I imagined the whole of America was like New York City.

We arrived at the Sheraton Manhattan Hotel at Times Square, where
the conference was to be held and where we were to stay. As the taxi
stopped and the driver opened the trunk, which back home we call "the
boot," men in suits and hats reached in and tried to take our bags. I didn't
know what was going on. *Surely they couldn't be thieves?* They were well
dressed, all in matching outfits, but sure enough, they wanted our bags.
I thought even New York's *thieves* must be more developed than ours to
be wearing such immaculate, matching outfits! I looked to Moffat for
help as I leapt out, terrified, and tried to protect my bag. *What would I
wear to deliver my address?* I thought frantically. Sensing my apprehension,
one of the men gently explained, "No, it's okay. We're porters. We take
your bags safely to your room for you, so you don't have to carry them.

It's safe. We're employed by the Sheraton."

Still nervous, we nevertheless left our bags with them and headed toward the hotel door to check in. The door, however, proved to be our next obstacle. It was more like many doors, joined together and spinning around and around on their own, like they were trying to beat me up. Amazing! You have to time your entry so you move in between two of these shiny, spinning doors that empty you inside the hotel. I was glad I had spent so much time jumping rope at school; it is the closest experience I can describe to judging the timing.

Inside were more surprises, the first of which was the most stunningly beautiful room I had ever seen. The dark red carpet was so deep and soft it felt like my feet would sink all the way in. I could not believe I was to stay in this hotel, which looked like a palace from a fairy tale—far, far grander than those our village chiefs live in. As I waited for our paperwork to be completed, I gingerly took a few steps toward a glass cabinet that had stunning jewelry for sale inside it. One necklace on display cost *four thousand* dollars. *One person can spend four thousand dollars on a necklace?* I wondered, shocked. *How much money must they have?* The average Zambian would have to work for ten whole years to earn enough money to buy one necklace. My head was racing as if I had spent a whole hour spinning on a merry-go-round.

We traveled up in the elevator to our room, and the surprises continued there. When we walked into our room, the lights came on to reveal the biggest bed I had ever seen, covered in more pillows than you can imagine. Luxurious curtains hung in the windows, and more deep carpet—which I just had to feel with my bare feet—covered the floor.

I was hungry and tired from our trip. We had been told that, because it was our first night and we had traveled for over eighteen hours, we should just order food in our room. *Food in our room?* One simple phone call was all it took; just minutes later, there stood a waiter at our door with a table on wheels.

I had ordered chicken and Moffat, beef. When we removed the lids on the plates, my heart sank. They knew it was only Moffat and me in the room, yet they brought enough food for an entire family. *How could it be that there is so much on one side of the world and so little on the other?* I lay on the bed crying and confused until Moffat finally made me eat. "The reason we are here is so you can speak to the American people of the children's suffering," he reminded me. "If you don't eat, this will weaken you and you will not have energy to speak. There is no point in us being here if you are too weak to speak." These were the truest words my husband ever spoke to me.

But still, questions pounded through my head. I was angry at Zambia's leaders and the other leaders of Africa. *My politicians have traveled here before me. How can they sleep at night while we live in such poverty? How much of our lot is due to their corruption? As a human being, how could you choose to benefit yourself while your people suffer, when clearly a better standard of living is possible? How could you not want more for your people?* Africa is a land of so many natural resources and untapped potential, and yet we lag so far behind. I knew that not all Americans were ordering room service for dinner, but it gave me an idea of just what was possible in a country that functions properly. Surely, after all these years, we could have made more progress than we had. *If I was a politician,* I thought to myself, *I would not rest until I had done all in my power to create a better standard of living for my people.*

My thoughts shifted from my people to those in the West. *Do they know what is happening on the other side of the world?* I wondered. *If they knew how people lived every minute, every second, without shelter and without food, would it cause them to act or would they remain still? Maybe no one has ever told them. Or maybe they need to hear it not just once but again and again, until they are moved to action.*

I knew right there and then that the Lord had brought me here to bring the two worlds together. And I knew that, the next morning when I delivered my first presentation, I would speak with all of my voice to whomever had an ear to listen. *We each have only one life,* I said to myself. *Surely we can do one thing or touch one life before we leave this world. Let's fight to leave a footprint or at least some mark that is ours.* Now I was ready to fight.

There is great power in knowing that in our time on earth we made a difference.

When I woke the next day, I had recovered from my crying. Instead of being angry with the world and everyone in it, I had turned my anger into motivation. I spoke briefly at the breakfast session for pastors, but I was most excited for the main event.

It was a serious event, I could tell, when the time arrived. The guests were seated in a very large, grand room. They were mainly men and mainly pastors and major donors from across America and Canada. I was glad I'd had an opportunity to present at the earlier breakfast, as I was now feeling comfortable.

Canon Gideon Byamugisha from Uganda, one of the first clerics to admit his positive HIV status, spoke first. Gentle and soft-spoken, the reverend is one of the most gracious men I have ever encountered. His kind manner made his message all the more powerful. He explained that as a member of the clergy and a born-again Christian family, many people had interpreted his HIV infection as a sign of his previous or current sexual immorality before or within marriage. But the Reverend Canon explained that "not all sexual saints are HIV-negative . . . not all sexual sinners are HIV-positive." The Reverend continued, "In HIV it is not a matter of whether the sex was sinful, unlawful, unfaithful or whether it was lawful, faithful and acceptable in a particular faith context. Rather it is a matter of whether it was 'safe' from the risk of exposure to HIV or 'unsafe.'" He spoke philosophically using an analogy of safe and unsafe water: "Getting typhoid from drinking contaminated water does not necessairly mean the patient stole the water!" Generally it was assumed that people contracted HIV through promiscuity, yet here was a respected member of the clergy standing before us in his robe and red collar, urging leaders to stop "using AIDS to control their congregations but rather to use their congregations to control AIDS."

Now it was my turn. The Zambian office had filmed me in the field, at the radio station and with my family, and that footage was played here to set the scene. As the video ended, I made my way up to the stage and took a deep breath. Then I told this big room full of people my story. I wish now that I had written notes of what I said, so I could recall my exact words. Perhaps hindsight makes me more eloquent and compelling, but to the best of my memory, though, here are the points I made.

I told them women are more commonly infected with the virus in Africa, but that we have the determination to live long. I spoke of my own walk with my mother and father, watching them die. I spoke of the plight of Africa's orphans—how, if orphans are not supported, they face the same plight as their parents and end up dying too young. Then I told them of my own HIV status.

"These people with HIV in Africa are people just like me," I reminded them. "We are not statistics. We are sons, we are daughters, we are mothers, we are fathers, we are teachers, we are doctors, and yet on a daily basis this disease is killing us. But me, I told them, I shall not die before I am dead but live and proclaim the word of God."

One of the vital measures of the progression of AIDS through a patient's body is their CD4 count. CD4 cells are "helpful" cells in the blood, and a healthy person has around a thousand per cubic millimeter.[2] Here I told the audience, "My own CD4 count has dropped to ninety-two and I am not on treatment, but I am not dead. I am a walking miracle. Like any person I deserve dignity and respect. With treatment I can live a long life, to care for my daughters, put them through school. Without me around, my daughters would most likely suffer my fate in years to come. It may look like a hopeless situation but there is hope."

"If 20 percent of my population is HIV-positive,[3] this means 80 percent of it is not. This is the hope of my country. So many more are negative than positive, and we need to keep it this way," I pleaded with them. "The healthy need your support just as much as the sick, for they carry the burden of caring for the sick and keeping our country running. I have come here to personalize HIV for you all. I want you to look at me and to remember me and those who are just like me every time you think of HIV and AIDS. We are real people with dreams and goals. HIV is not just about statistics. Will you stand beside us, will you pray with us, will you support the children in their distress?"

In conclusion, I stated the importance of the church getting involved. "I was once excommunicated from the church. Now the church in Africa and around the world needs to awaken. If the church doesn't have compassion for those living with HIV and AIDS, who will? If one brother, one sister, is sick, regardless of where they are or who they are, we are all affected in one way or another." This virus knows no borders. It is no respecter of persons.

Looking out across the sea of people I wondered whether they had been asked to wear black and white suits just for me. I had noticed this while I spoke, but as I concluded and they rose to their feet for a standing ovation, the effect was dramatic, like a giant flock of eagles taking off in flight. In their ebony and ivory suits, they all went up at once.

I remained calm but deep down I was so excited! They had received my message well. How I wished someone from my continent was there to see me. I had been given a standing ovation once before in Namibia, but this one will always be my most memorable. I felt like jumping and singing. I had represented my country, my bamaa and bataa, and my continent well. I was sure that more than one person in this room would be compelled to act. People were still standing as I reached my seat; they were clearly moved.

After my talk, Stephen Lewis, special UN envoy for Africa, gave a powerful speech. He pointed out that if AIDS were happening at this rate in the Western world we would have responded. This was a racial issue, he stated, asserting that color had played an important role in the world's response. I marveled at these radical words that came from a white Canadian man saying that no one hears the cries of Africa. I was energized to know this man from another culture was in our corner.

The forum was a resounding success. At the end a commitment was made from all in the room to dedicate more resources, more energy and more passion to fighting the virus and caring for those left in its wake.

People came to introduce themselves and to congratulate me before they finally left to go about their daily business.

At the luncheon held after the forum for speakers and dignitaries, Reverend Gideon said to me, "My sister, you do me proud." When I smiled and thanked him, Moffat pulled me aside, accusing me of flirting. My heart was broken. I so wanted him to be proud. How could he steal my joy on this day?

I refused to show my hurt, and I tried to block the painful words from my head. *If the virus has not crushed my spirit, I will not let this man,* I reassured myself. I am sure Moffat had thought he married a young, vulnerable woman, but the tables had turned. Now the vulnerable woman was growing in power, and it shocked his world.

While I was talking with people and worrying about Moffat, a stranger who was strongly moved by my words was putting in place a plan that would change the course of my trip and indeed the course of my life. This stranger, who was both a bishop and a medical doctor, was busy telling World Vision's American staff that with a CD4 count of ninety-two my health was in grave danger. I could not return to Zambia this way, he said. He wanted to fund my treatment at a hospital in his hometown, Chicago. To that end the Chicago staff were happy to accommodate us, so it was arranged, still unbeknown to us, that Moffat and I should travel to Chicago.

Moffat and I remained oblivious to this until a little later when an unknown African American man, tall like my father, approached us. He was dark and well built, and he spoke with such forceful authority. "Your health is critical," he said. "I am going to make sure you have treatment. If I can help two more people in this world it will be you and your husband. My wife is not here but I will tell my family about you, and if we cannot help you as a family my church family will help you. For this, you will need to come to my hospital in Chicago, where you will receive the very best of care." He told me his name: "I am Bishop Horace E. Smith."

"Bishop Horace E. Smith, are you sure?" I was just overwhelmed. "Thank you, sir." Knowing treatment in Zambia cost three million kwacha, or up to fifteen hundred dollars per month, I hoped Bishop Horace E. Smith knew what he was getting himself into. I didn't know a single Zambian who could afford this treatment.

What I did know from my reading and my work was that once you start treatment, you can never stop, because stopping creates immunity to further treatment. The medication must be taken every twelve hours or you can become resistant to treatment. I hoped Bishop Smith realized these things as well. Bishop Smith assured me he'd find me and let me know the details of our travel, and then, before I could say much more, I was whisked away to talk to more people.

I always tried to remain positive about my status, but as a mother a constant fear hung over my head. I knew that one day I would have to leave my daughters alone and vulnerable. I tried to maintain my courage. My girls are the most wonderful, precious things that have ever happened to me. Like every mother around the world, the fear of them being left alone chilled my bones. Every night since receiving my results I had prayed that God would let me live long enough to see my girls grow, to see that they had a good education and were able to stand on their own, free from the choices that I had had to face. Now here was a man I had never met before telling me he would do all in his power to make this possible. Here I was receiving yet another divine favor. What a mighty God we serve.

This incredible news and the fact that my presentations had been so well received saw me sigh with relief as a feeling of joy and freedom took hold. I spent the rest of my stay walking on a cloud, seeing the sights of magical New York.

One night Moffat and I were taken out onto Broadway for something to eat and I tell you, I had never seen anything like it. There were giant televisions everywhere in the street, and even on top of very tall buildings, all showing gigantic pictures made up of the brightest colors. I screamed, "Televisions in the street! Look! Look! Who put those televisions on the roof?" Our colleague who accompanied us for the night told me that some of the televisions were twenty stories tall!

Some of those televisions showed beauty products designed to help old women look younger. It seemed everyone in America wanted to be young. This is another way New York seems to be the opposite of Zambia. People here spend lots of money on creams to make any lines on their face disappear, while in my country, where the average life expectancy is around forty and declining,[4] beauty is found in gray hair and wrinkles. People crave the wisdom and respect that comes to those fortunate enough to reach old age, knowing that only a few ever get that chance.

Another day, we were taken shopping for Western clothes. Mike Mantel from the Chicago office realized we'd need more clothes if we were to stay in Chicago for the time required to test and plan treatment, so he and Luly from the New York office took me to Casual Corner, a giant store full of brand new clothes. Moffat, meanwhile, shopped with another colleague. I wanted everything inside Casual Corner. The clothes were so beautiful and of such good quality. Mike and Luly helped me choose some items, and then I held a fashion parade, ducking into the changing room to try on the stunning outfits and emerging like a new woman to show my newfound friends. I felt so pretty, it was wonderful.

In the end I chose a red suit. I wanted to be the woman in red, as red symbolizes AIDS. I also got a pink suit and shoes. When Mike Mantel tells this story now, he says he knew I was a talented, persuasive communicator because the shopping expedition cost him hundreds of dollars more than he expected! At the conference celebration dinner that night people were surprised to see me looking like a real American. I guess that's what you call coming to America.

20

Chicago

Next Moffat and I were headed for Chicago. I didn't know much about Chicago besides the fact that it was the home of the Chicago Bulls, a basketball team that everyone knew about back home. When I got home and told people I'd been to Chicago, time and time again people said, "Ah, the mighty Bulls." I began to get some insight into the ability of sports to cross borders and bring people together.

Chicago continued my life-changing, eye-opening journey. It was as though I traveled to another world—not just another continent—on my trip to the States, both in terms of the things I saw for the very first time and the depth of knowledge I gained. The knowledge gave me power. In Chicago we visited people's homes and saw more of regular, daily life than we did in New York. I came to see that people here really did have an incredible standard of living, while in my country many people live on less than $1.25 per day. I continued to get a sense of what was possible.

We stayed at the home of Mike Mantel in the suburbs of Chicago. I later learned that Mike was new to the HIV arena, and he knew very little about this disease—not how it was spread or treated. So it was an extraordinary gesture for this kind man and his family to welcome us with open arms into their home, where, for all they knew, they faced risk of infection.

As promised, Bishop Horace E. Smith arranged for us to have a medical examination with the aim of commencing treatment. For this, we needed to visit Chicago's Northwestern Hospital, which was like nothing I had ever seen. This hospital is housed in a huge building that seems to go on and on forever. Automatic doors lead you inside the modern building where a clean, fresh smell, a reception desk full of computers, and lots of glass and bright, bright lights make it clear you're not in a Zambian hospital.

The hospital has a whole department for people with HIV and AIDS. In it, we came across one lady in a wheelchair who, while clearly in pain from the disease, was at least able to have some independence and live with dignity.

It would have been very easy to feel envious of all I saw. Sometimes, for short bursts of time, I was. After all, Bamaa and Bataa could have survived in this country—of course that is enviable. But in many ways, seeing the contrast gave me the power to explain to those in developed countries how blessed they are and how many advantages they have, and to urge them to take full advantage of every opportunity while being aware there is another side of the world where people don't have any of this.

Bishop Smith was so glad to see us. I knew he had worked hard making arrangements with many different people to get us to this point. He took us to the doctor, who conducted a range of tests on Moffat and me. Interestingly, I found out that my CD4 count had now climbed up to 103. Perhaps it was the good living we had enjoyed since arriving in America.

The doctor asked if I had been feeling sick. I told him I had not. He explained, as Bishop Smith had, that my CD4 count was dangerously low. The CD4 count is one of two measures used to help doctors assess when HIV has progressed to the point where a person requires treatment. The other measure is a person's viral load count, which measures the amount of virus in the blood. There is no hard and fast rule that marks the point when HIV becomes AIDS. One doctor may use a particular CD4 count while another might rely on symptoms to diagnose the progression to AIDS. In any case, with a CD4 count of just 103, it was a miracle I showed no symptoms. I needed to begin medication to control the virus. Moffat's count was even higher than mine, so he didn't need treatment yet. I was excited for him.

Here I also had another question answered. Dr. Tembo had given Moffat and I six months to live though now it had been four years, and we were still OK. I also thought of my parents who, I suspected, were sick with the virus for nine or so years. I learned HIV has several "sub-strains." Sub-strain C, most common in southern Africa, was slow to progress from infection to full-blown AIDS. That meant a person could carry the virus for many years before suspecting anything was wrong, giving it plenty of time to spread. I could not believe all the factors that conspired to give this virus such a head start in my country. I later heard the conditions described as the "perfect storm" for AIDS, and I now know why.

When the World Vision staff in Chicago had heard I was coming, they organized several speaking engagements that gave me an opportunity to touch many parts of the city, including the African American community. As more and more people in Chicago heard my message—in churches, schools and individual homes—they became convinced they needed to make a difference.

I realized the problem in this country wasn't that people didn't want to respond; they had simply never been given the opportunity. The message on poverty, HIV and AIDS was just not getting through. Once people became informed, they wanted to take action. For me, this was the most powerful learning of the trip. As I came to know the American people more, I realized the depth of kindness and empathy in them. It was clear that, once they were empowered with knowledge, their hearts would be broken and they would want to respond.

One of my speaking invitations came from Bishop Smith, asking me to speak at his own church, which is a congregation of several thousand

people, mainly African Americans. It was here in this place of God, surrounded by people who looked like me, that I was most glad I had spoken
to my grandfather about slavery. Ba Khapa's words rang in my ears: *When
you go to America, remember these are your relatives. If they are older like me, treat
them as your grandfather. If they are your mother's age, treat them as your mother.
If they are young, treat them as your children.*

As I spoke to the congregation, one Bible story stood out in my
thoughts: the story of Joseph. To me, at that moment, these brothers and
sisters of mine were the Joseph of today. Once sold into slavery, some had
ended up in a better financial position generations later. Now they had an
opportunity to respond to their brothers in Africa. I later learned this
was not the case for all. Once I finished my address, this gathering of
people who looked like me rose to their feet and cheered and I knew I
belonged. I knew I was among my people. For me it was an emotional
moment; it was a reunion that words cannot describe.

I had the chance to say to these people who shared my roots a message
I want to repeat. If, as an African American, you have any chance to visit
Africa, please come. Please do not die before you come back home. Your
sisters are waiting, your mothers and grandmothers are waiting to welcome you, to reconcile, to embrace you. Please always know Africa is
your home and we welcome you.

Occasionally I came across African Americans who still harbored resentment toward Africa for its involvement in selling their relatives into
slavery, but most of my interactions were with people happy to see a
daughter from Africa. They longed to come and see the beauty of Africa,
the rivers and lakes, the sun that never sets, the animals. Many of the older
men and women craved stories of Africa, asking about the languages we
speak and wanting a depiction of our life there. "In the midst of our poverty and our challenges," I told them, "Africa is a place of the greatest
beauty and joy. It is a continent every human being in the world can call
home." They wanted to hear my story again and again, and they took me
into their homes and hearts. As I spoke to these audiences of my brothers

and sisters, some broke down in tears at the spiritual reconnection with Africa. In the midst of our differences, it was clear that our heart was beating in the same direction. When I had a chance to sing and dance with African Americans, it was clear we were all from the motherland.

Bishop Smith's church, the Apostolic Faith Church, went on to demonstrate great leadership in the fight against poverty, HIV and AIDS. Since that time, thousands of children from Zambia and the Democratic Republic of Congo have been sponsored, and wells and bores have been constructed to provide safe drinking water for village people, all through the bishop's church. As both a bishop and a medical doctor he and his wife, Susan Smith, have taken the issue of AIDS seriously, traveling to Africa twice each year to understand the progress and remaining challenges, which they convey to the church for action. At various times their children join them. When they are in Africa they are with their people.

Bishop Smith's leadership was particularly remarkable in light of a damning report that came out around this time uncovering the widespread attitude of the church toward AIDS. A landmark book called *The aWAKE Project* was launched in 2002, at a Vanderbilt University conference on AIDS and Africa. The book quotes a Barna research poll that revealed that "evangelical Christians are the least likely group to help AIDS victims in Africa—less than 3 percent said they would financially help a Christian organization minister to an AIDS orphan."[1] Surely these are the things that break the heart of God? *My brothers and sisters, are we not the hands and feet Jesus is counting on?*

Like Bishop Smith's church, the groups of students I spoke to in Chicago were not a reflection of the Barna poll but rather wanted to take action, and I experienced great joy interacting with them. My first visit to an elementary school alerted me to the fact that my name would be confusing in America. The teacher told me she caught students peering out their classroom window, looking for my chauffeur-driven limousine and my bodyguard. As I entered the classroom I felt little eyes looking me up and down to check for expensive jewels. The children seemed disappointed when they learned I was a simple village girl who happened to have the blood of the chief's lineage with few material possessions. But still they were inspired to act. Some brought in money from their piggy-banks to buy a goat or a blanket for a child in Africa. Though they perhaps didn't fully comprehend the horror of AIDS, these children were making a difference.

Students inspire me the most, especially since I have always aspired to get to Harvard. I wish I could tell all the stories from every campus, but that is not feasible in this book. I do, however, have to share with you the endeavors of a high school that I have since come to love, Wheaton Academy in West Chicago. "In addition to your formal studies," I began by telling the Wheaton students, "there is an assignment at hand that needs your response." I then recounted for them the story of Zamtan compound's Kakolo Village, where students from one community were regularly killed crossing a busy road to get to school. All too often I hear young people say they can't make a difference, so I ended my presentation by saying, "You are leaders—not just the leaders of tomorrow but the leaders of today. How will you choose to use your time in school? My hope is that you will measure these not by your grades alone or the job you secure on graduating, but that you too will have the courage and conviction to say, 'Not on our watch,' and be inspired to action."

With that, the students of Wheaton Academy were off and racing. So touched were the Wheaton students by this story that they and their faculty leader, Chip Huber, set out to do something greater than the sum of their individual parts: they wanted to build a new school in Zamtan. They opened themselves up to God's work through them and got busy holding homecoming dinners, car washes, fun runs and more to raise money for the school. Some even took trips to Zambia to see the village and meet the children. Here they realized children in Zambia had as much potential as they did themselves; they just lacked the opportunity to nurture it. Thanks to these young people a new school was built in Kokolo Village.

Once their hearts and minds had been opened to the challenges of the village, the Wheaton students could not rest. Next they raised money to build a science laboratory for the students. All this happened just with one group of people who saw themselves as world changers. These were privileged students and they knew it. These students knew they were blessed to have been born in a country that offers them so much, and they were happy to use their privilege to help others.

The person responsible for organizing my speaking engagements was the one other person who really made our visit to Chicago special. Her name was Vanessa Church. The very first time we met, I felt like I had found a long-lost sister. She was an African American woman, close to my bamaa's age, and there was something unique about her. Full of life with a youthful energy about her, she was also wise and thoughtful. Throughout my time in Chicago we got to know each other well as she drove me to my speaking events. We then went on to become close; at times she was my friend, at times she was my sister. Other times she was like a mother to me, and called me the daughter she never had.

Vanessa taught me about life in America while I taught her about her motherland. Learning about my name and my lineage to the chiefs especially excited her. It was funny to me that my name, Princess Kasune Zulu, became such a big deal on this trip. I participated in a number of media interviews where journalists fixated on my name. "Are you a real princess?" they asked time and time again. Their published articles all too often said, "Princess is only her name, not a title." I found this puzzling as we have a great deal of respect for a position in Zambia, no matter how grand or small, and the truth is, my family does have a royal lineage. But this would not have happened in Zambia. Here, though, people were evaluating my heritage and making their own call about its importance. Vanessa was one of the few who never did that; rather, she remained fascinated and impressed. "You really are a princess. You are a princess for the people," she would say. To her it didn't matter that I had little in the way of material possessions. I represented the story of her ancestors coming alive.

Vanessa wasn't just fascinated by stories of life in Africa, however. She was also gravely troubled by the plight of orphans and worked tirelessly to create opportunities for me to share my story. We tried to get as many children sponsored as we could, and each time we were successful we laughed with joy. The success at bishop's church made us especially happy. My heart beat so strongly when I realized how much human beings cared for each other once they knew how to respond.

Vanessa had heard my belief that African Americans were the modern-day Joseph. She realized then just how limited I was in my understanding of American life. I had only seen one side of the story, the side where everyone is doing well, where they have money to give, where there is peace and understanding. To broaden my view, she took me for a drive to a place called Cabrini-Green. I saw right away why she brought me there. This side of Chicago looked very different. There were broken-down cars everywhere and the tall buildings were badly repaired; they looked abandoned. There was no grass, no trees—only concrete, graffiti and broken lights. The glass in the windows was smashed as though someone had been throwing stones. Naively I asked Vanessa why people would want to throw stones through the windows. "Stones?" She sighed. "Those are bullet holes, my dear."

"What about those children playing all around?" I asked. They are the children who live in the projects, the poor of Chicago, I realized. At that moment I had an awakening: not everyone in America lived the life I had dreamed in my head. Yes, many people did well, but many—particularly minority groups—struggled and also needed help.

Vanessa explained that Cabrini-Green was Chicago's notorious public housing estate. Today its population was mainly African Americans.[2] Ironically, the complex had originally been named after Frances Cabrini, the first American canonized by the Catholic Church.[3] It had not been properly maintained, however; that much was easy to see. Home to gangs and violent crime, Cabrini-Green encompassed some of the toughest living conditions in Chicago. The development was torn down in the years after my visit.

Moffat returned to Zambia early. For some reason he had been issued a shorter visa than me. The trip had failed to improve our marriage. In fact, it worsened by the day. We were now living in Lusaka for my work with World Vision, and he went home to be with the girls. I was happy they had their father with them, and truth be told, I was relieved when he left. I had begun to wonder whether our relationship would survive. I had prayed night and day—but Moffat's anger and resentment continued to grow. When I was with him, I was afraid to let my light shine. Still, I promised I'd keep going in the midst of the storm.

On my own last day, Vanessa took me swimming in Lake Michigan. Zambia had many lakes, but I had never been swimming. Now here I was, swimming for the first time so far from home. I loved it, splashing and jumping about in the water, once again I felt free. Looking over the Chicago skyline, I took a moment to reflect. In many ways, meeting Vanessa had heralded a new era for this village girl, who was really beginning to grow.

Still, my heart longed for Zambia. As the plane began its descent over a very different skyline, I was captivated by the natural beauty of Africa: the sunshine and the plains, the slower pace of life. I was home.

21

From the Village to the White House

LIFE CHANGED DRAMATICALLY AFTER THIS POINT. My time in the States opened a lot of doors. I was soon invited to visit Australia, Spain and Canada, and I continued to travel back and forth from the United States while juggling my work in Zambia.

It was also clear something needed to change in my relationship with Moffat. At times I told myself I could endure his barbed tongue. But I changed my mind when I learned Moffat had written to my employer, recommending they fire me. I was shocked he could do such a thing now that I was the primary breadwinner. He put his jealousy and insecurity ahead of our family's livelihood.

I was troubled by the decision before me regarding my marriage. I prayed for a sign, and it seemed this letter was it. Divorce went against every fiber in my being, and my faith. In addition, there was the stigma of divorce. I knew all too well the pain of stinging tongues. But the sting of this relationship was even greater. I knew the choice in front of me. I could make it on my own. We made the difficult decision to separate late in 2002, and the High Court formally granted us a divorce in November 2003.

Fearing the worst, I had saved a little money, which enabled my eight dependents and me to cram ourselves into a tiny, rented, studio apartment. We did not have a bed to sleep on, but at least Rhoda, Saliya, Dale, Deophister, Elvis, Brian, Joy, Faith, Armstrong and I had a safe and harmonious roof over our heads. We had enough food, and the children remained in school. We were happy.

Our little apartment was located in Kabulonga, a wealthy suburb of Lusaka. The president's state house and the residences of various nations' ambassadors are there as well. I chose a small home in an expensive area to be close to the city and to make sure I had a safe place to leave the children when I traveled. Indeed, I am convinced we had the smallest little flat in the whole of Kubulonga. It was located in the Zesco Flats complex, a group of maybe seven small flats set out in a horseshoe shape with a big open space in the middle where children ride bikes and play games.

This is where I found myself, tucked up on the floor, surrounded by sleeping children who snuggled into me, when Ken Casey reappeared in my life. Around midnight one night, while I lay there awake, my cell phone rang.

I remember the children waking and groaning that night at the sound of my phone. I couldn't tell who was calling because the number was withheld. When I answered, though, the voice sounded far away, so I guessed it was an international call.

Because of the faint connection, it took me a minute to figure out that it was Ken Casey. He had been in Zambia just two weeks prior, but I thought he was back in the United States now. My mind raced: *Why was he calling me? Did he come back? Did he need help?* Before I found out what Ken wanted I gave him my neighbor's number, as the connection was too poor to carry on what might be an important conversation. My neighbor had a landline in her home and the reception would be clearer. I woke her whole family as I banged on the door and asked to use the phone.

"Ken, is everything okay?" I asked when we finally reconnected.

Ken told me he was just fine and gave me some surprising news.

"Princess, you are needed at the White House on Tuesday, the twenty-ninth of April, to meet with the president of the United States. Can you make it?"

It was already Friday night. I needed to be in the United States by Monday if I was to meet with the president on Tuesday. "Ken, you know I'll be there."

I didn't know quite what I was getting myself into, but I had a feeling this was a once-in-a-lifetime opportunity, and I knew I had to be there. I was now wide awake with my mind jumping back to my childhood, and Bataa bouncing me on his lap, telling me, "My girl, you will be a Princess among princesses and you will meet with the leaders of the world." I pushed my memories aside as I went back to Ken on the line.

He explained to me that President George W. Bush was considering committing fifteen billion dollars to fight HIV and AIDS in Africa and in some Caribbean countries, including Haiti. He had called a delegation to the Oval Office to explore this possibility and to consider how funds should be spent. Somehow, my name was picked to be one of the delegates. It was such a humbling experience and an honor to be selected.

I would later learn that when the White House called World Vision Chicago looking for me, the staff thought it was a prank and hung up on the caller—not once but twice! I just love the mental picture of my new friends hanging up on the White House.

Timing would be tight, but one thing in my favor was that though America is far ahead of Africa in some ways, we are ahead in time! Thankfully, Washington, D.C., specifically, is six hours behind Lusaka, so this bought me a little extra time. First thing in the morning I rang British Airways, who were able to get me on a flight. A visa wasn't an issue as my by now regular travels to the States meant I had been granted a multientry visa. It looked like I was on my way to the White House!

Once my trip actually started, time went from tight to very tight as I missed the connecting flight that was to take me from London's Heathrow Airport to Washington, D.C.'s, Dulles International. I had to stay overnight in London, and people had to work hard scheduling another plan to get me to the White House on time. I maintained my faith, though; I knew this was my assignment. I would make it on time. (While *I* remained calm, I am sure that, among my colleagues, I sparked an international chain of worry and panicked long-distance phone calls. My colleagues are people of faith, but they have a fear of "Africa time"!)

All told, I arrived in Washington, D.C., as planned, on Monday afternoon, the day before I was due to meet with President Bush. At the airport I learned I was to have a telephone interview with White House spokesperson Caroline Thompson of the White House before I would be able to meet with President Bush. The White House wanted to get to know me prior to officially approving my invitation—which meant there was still no guarantee I'd get to the Oval Office. *Lord, surely you haven't brought me to America to speak on the phone to Caroline Thompson*, I thought as my spirit deflated.

Next, I was handed a letter from my friend Ken Casey, reminding me that President Bush is a man just like any other, put in his position by God's grace. Ken also assured me that when the time came the Lord would give me the words to say. His reminders rejuvenated my spirit. As I read the letter I looked down at my unkept hands and thought of Vanessa Church. She had taken me for my first manicure when I was in Chicago, telling me, "Girl, you are in America now. Those hands need a manicure!" Surprisingly, she was right; the manicure had boosted my confidence as I interacted with people. If ever there was a time for the village girl to look and feel her best, this was it. I decided to take myself to the beauty salon.

With my fingernails and toenails freshly painted in a French manicure, I returned to my hotel room just in time to hear the telephone ringing. I rushed to pick it up and was greeted by Caroline Thompson from the White House. Thanking me for traveling to the United States, Caroline asked me what I would like to tell President Bush.

In the lead-up to my trip, I had thought a lot about what I wanted to say to the then president. At that time in international development and policy circles, the argument centered around whether to fund HIV prevention and education programs or to provide access to treatment for those already infected. The most effective decision was not always taken. Religion, denial, ignorance, stigma and lack of empathy stood in the way of sound responses. The international community was not spending enough money fighting extreme poverty, or HIV and AIDS, and much of what was spent went to education and prevention programs, not treatment.

At the time, the most popular strategy for fighting AIDS was the promotion of ABC, an acronym emphasizing three actions to stop the spread of the virus: *Abstain* as a first priority, or if you are married or in a committed relationship, *Be faithful;* and finally, as a last resort, *wear a Condom.*

Faith-based groups and conservative governments favor this response. I agree, it is important to educate and promote abstinence and safe-sex messages, but the statistics reflect the horrible consequence of relying too heavily on this approach: 33 million infected, 28 million dead. Everywhere the story is the same; when the adults go, the children are left alone. Something had to change.

I passionately believe that alongside these messages needs to come access to treatment. In the United States, over one million are infected, but greater access to treatment means people live a lot longer. In fact, developing countries now see treatment of HIV like treatment of diabetes or other chronic disease. With medicine and a healthy lifestyle, patients can live a long life, but in Zambia, life expectancy was decreasing.

There were many arguments for not providing treatment to Africans: the high cost of patented drugs, lack of sophisticated medical facilities for diagnosis and treatment, and, bizarrely, even the fact that we might not be able to adhere to the strict, 12-hour lifelong medicine regime since we don't wear watches.[1]

The response is complex. Take patented drugs, for example. If patents are ignored and generic drugs allowed, what incentive is there for drug companies to invest the billions required in research and development?

But I also understood profit could not come at the expense of people's lives. AIDS cannot be allowed to be a treatable, manageable condition in one country and a killer in the next. Back then I thought, *we cannot rest until we find a way to overcome these challenges.* Today I thank God that, to a large extent, the issue of generic drugs has been resolved, and many more are now accessing treatment.

I had to convince Caroline Thompson I should come to the White House the next day. There were too many lives at stake for me to fail. I thanked Caroline for this opportunity and then shared my story and my views, reminding her that with millions of children left alone, living on the streets, there is little to stop them from becoming terrorists or troublemakers in the community. We will all be affected and we will all be to blame. If the American government can help provide access to treatment, millions of children can be nurtured and supported by their parents for longer. They can have hope, and become productive members of the global community.

I went on to tell Caroline that you cannot separate education and treatment. They must go hand in hand. Not only must we educate young people about HIV and AIDS; we must educate them, period.

"Princess, you need to tell President Bush this," Caroline said when I was finished. "We look forward to meeting you in person tomorrow."

Hanging up the phone I fell down on my bed in excitement and said, "Thank you, Lord." A representative of the White House called the World Vision office and said they were very interested in what I had to say, so I was officially invited to meet with former president Bush and the then secretary of state, Colin Powell. I had also been chosen to speak to the media at the *stix,* or microphones, after the meeting. Yes! Just as I thought, God had opened doors no human could. I knew he wouldn't bring me this far for nothing.

As the sun rose, a wake-up call and two alarms ensured I would be up and ready in time. I looked down at my freshly painted fingernails and said to myself, "Girl, let's go! This is your day." When I tell this story, people expect me to say the nerves were overwhelming. After all, I was not just going to meet the leader of the free world, but to lobby him to spend $15 billion fighting the disease that has orphaned 15 million children. The stakes were high, and I did feel some nervousness and excitement, but I tell them I had a calmness that came from knowing God had made this possible and equipped me for this day.

By 8 a.m., I was dressed in my favorite African outfit: a deep blue dress with white patterns and white silk edging with a headwrap to match. I did everything to look my best for the White House.

I was picked up by two colleagues from World Vision's Washington, D.C., office who had worked so hard in the background to make this happen, including a senior official named Bruce Wilkinson who would play an important long-term role. On the way to the White House we had to stop at a guardhouse next to some grand, gold-tipped gates. Three guards in firmly creased black pants and crisp white shirts asked us to step out of the car and show our passports. I imagined this was what it was like to visit Buckingham Palace. Since Zambia was a former British colony, this was the main system of government I knew. Once we cleared security, the gates opened and we were directed toward the West Wing. I still didn't feel anything different; I just kept my feet on the ground, lost in the beauty of the surrounding gardens.

Inside, the three of us were invited into a room for some tea. The room was full of dignitaries; I didn't know who they were at the time but they all looked very important. Here I was, an ordinary young woman from Kabwe, Zambia, in the White House with all these impressive people whom I now know to call bigwigs! I took a deep breath as I touched Bamaa's ivory bracelets and imagined Bataa saying to Bamaa, "Joyce. Look. I told you so. Just look at our girl."

For some time we mingled and chatted as a group. Then the moment came. We were called to attention, and the fifteen of us who were to meet with the president were invited to enter the Oval Office. The other guests, including my World Vision friends, were to remain behind.

Looking me in the eye, they told me I would do great.

Of those of us who stepped into the Oval Office, I was the only one who had traveled from Africa and the youngest person by some years. There was a large wooden table inside with place cards at most of the seats. We were invited to find our name and sit down. Opposite me was a place with no name. Wondering who might sit there, I imagined it must have been left vacant deliberately, as there were many important dignitaries around the table and I was just a village girl. Across from me to the left sat the secretary of state, Colin Powell, and next to him, an important-looking German businessman who was friendly and welcoming when we chatted in the previous room. Opposite me to the right sat the secretary of health and human services, Tommy Thompson, and a Catholic cardinal. I don't remember who else sat where, but we were fifteen in total, each at the place matching our nametags, with me opposite an empty seat.

Secretary of State Colin Powell welcomed us, and stated that HIV and AIDS—the weapon of mass destruction of our time, as he described it—is an important cause for the United States of America and the White House. More importantly, he told us HIV and AIDS is an important cause for the president himself, and that the president is saddened by the virus and its impact on humanity. He advised us that the president would be joining us shortly.

We were then asked to go around the table and introduce ourselves. The first speaker encouraged the U.S. government to fund prevention programs instead of paying for condoms, as they felt that condoms promoted promiscuity. Others commended the president for doing what he was doing. As people continued introducing themselves, I learned there was a representative from the Bill & Melinda Gates Foundation and from CARE International present, as well as Uganda's ambassador to the U.S. and me representing World Vision. With HIV being such a challenging, moral issue, the opinions were bound to be as diverse as the groups represented.

When it got to my turn, I simply said, "Hello everyone, I am Princess Kasune Zulu. I'm happy to be here. As a young African living with HIV I thank you so much for inviting me to represent my continent and those who live with HIV and AIDS." I didn't say more as I understood we were just supposed to introduce ourselves.

At about this point, President George W. Bush strode in and greeted us. Here he was, the president of the United States, in the Oval Office where I was seated at his table! I loved the way he entered the room. Peace and calm spread.

Regardless of whether you agree or disagree with a leader's politics—and that is a subject which I simply shall not venture into—it is something quite separate to be impressed with a leader's presence and style. Bill Clinton and President Barack Obama, whom I have seen at events or met in passing, make a similar impact with their presence, and since this day in the White House I have met other world leaders who do as well. President Bush made you calm. He had a welcoming presence that could make you forget you were meeting the president.

As I looked at him walking toward me I wanted to giggle out loud. I don't think I did—or, maybe I did, just in my heart. As we rose together to greet him, President Bush looked welcomingly around the table and encouraged us all to sit down. I was feeling pretty comfortable by now, but this gesture—the president of my second home, the United States, encouraging us to make ourselves comfortable in the White House—took away any remaining nervousness that may have lurked at the back of my mind.

As we took our seats once more, you'll never guess where President George W. Bush sat: right opposite me. That empty seat was for the president of the United States of America. Suddenly, the village girl found herself sitting eyeball to eyeball with the president. At times like this I thank God my skin is black as it doesn't show when I am blushing!

"What's been happening?" he asked. Tommy Thompson relayed everyone's introductions and all that the others had said. Next Tommy

said, "Then Princess Kasune Zulu introduced herself, and here we are."
President Bush turned and spoke to me. He thanked me for my work and
for agreeing to meet with him. Then he encouraged me to share my story.

His recognition of my work was so encouraging and humbling. It is a
hard and lonely journey living with the virus and being a traveling advocate. President Bush made me feel that what I am doing is not in vain. He
made me want to go on. I hold no degrees, and I am not a dignitary. I am
a child of one of the poorest nations on earth, yet President Bush took the
time to say, "Tell me your story." It was a moving moment.

I quickly composed myself and explained that my parents' sickness
forced us to move to the village, that I had to walk several miles every day
to fetch water, that this work made me tired at school, that my parents
lost their fight. I told him that I had to leave school and marry someone
older who could provide for me and my brothers and sisters. I also told
President George W. Bush that AIDS took not only the lives of my parents, my sister and brother but also my life—my innocence, my future.
Yet my reason for meeting with him wasn't to plead my own case, but to
show how my case echoes millions of others out there, to encourage him
to hear the cries of women and children and the anguish of fathers without the strength to protect or provide for their families.

Then I urged President Bush to remember that education and treatment cannot be separated; they must go hand in hand. Only when young
people are educated academically can they get better jobs and learn to
protect themselves. Providing greater access to education is the only way
we can break the cycle of poverty.

I was on a roll, and the president looked interested, so I continued,
pointing out that treatment that allows parents to live longer lets children have a childhood, ensuring they make it through school and grow
up healthy and strong, rather than becoming orphans left to head a
household at a tender age. If my parents had been able to access treatment, I would not be where I am today. I told him my story is repeated
all across Africa—and potentially could have been repeated for my

own daughters. "Before someone sponsored my treatment, there was a time when my blood count was so low that I should have died. Who would have cared for my girls?" I asked him. This is the vicious cycle of AIDS; it hands poverty from generation to generation.

I thanked him, as in truth he was one of the first world leaders to acknowledge this situation. He invited a representative from Africa, someone living with HIV, to sit at his table. People sometimes assume that as a young person coming from Africa, I was naive to the political nuances and blinded by politics—that President Bush said what he knew I wanted to hear, what his advisors told him to say. I tell these cynics I am not naive. My eyes were open. The fact is that President Bush was the first to at least say he cares. In time, his response to HIV would be pulled apart and the flaws uncovered, but we must appreciate that he took a leading role in the fight. That is to be commended, for the biggest challenge in fighting both poverty and the virus is a sense of paralysis and a lack of political will. Future generations will hold us accountable for our inaction. I could have gone on for hours, but it was time for others to have their turn.

There was one other representative from Africa who now lived in the States: Uganda's ambassador, Judith Sekepala. Ambassador Sekepala spoke of how Uganda had reduced its HIV infection rate from 20 percent in the 1990s to just under 7 percent.[2] The success there was due to early and decisive leadership, and a united commitment from the Ugandan government, nongovernment organizations, churches, and traditional and community leaders. They had encouraged abstinence, educated all age groups through frank and open discussion, fought to combat stigma and discrimination, promoted better treatment of all sexually transmitted infections, encouraged a "zero-grazing" push for faithful condom use and improved access to condoms, introduced voluntary same-day-results testing, and improved access to HIV treatment. The results were clear: it is possible to reverse the spread of HIV with education and collaboration.

You could tell President Bush was impressed. Uganda's success appeared to give President Bush hope that the world could fight AIDS. His eyes brightened with excitement at the news that this problem could be solved.

Then he took me completely by surprise and said, "Imagine how Uganda's strategy would have helped Princess!" The conversation once again came back to me, and before I knew it, the president and I were in dialogue. As a woman, I spoke to him about how women have become a source of hope; we don't give up easily. Even in the poorest areas, women have the capacity to give, to fight for life, for the sake of our families and communities. Right now, the burden of HIV and AIDS falls unevenly on women, first because we are biologically more susceptible to the virus, and second because our role as caregiver to the sick means much of our time is spent helping those weakened by the virus: feeding them, keeping their homes, caring for families. This is time that could have been spent productively. It is always the children who suffer.

Soon after I finished the meeting ended. I knew I was lucky to have spoken to the president directly for so long, especially when I realized that some people in the room had not had a chance to speak to the president. He thanked us for our time and asked for our support in encouraging Congress and the Senate to pass the fifteen-billion-dollar bill for HIV and AIDS.

President Bush said his farewells. When he came to me he added, "Say hello to Joy and Faith for me." This was too much; he even remembered my children's names! "Thank you, Mr. President, I shall do that," I replied.

As I had his attention again, it was time for the proud, patriotic Zambian in me to shine. I took the chance to tell President George W. Bush about my country—that even though the former Zambian government hadn't prioritized HIV and AIDS initially, the then current president, Levy Patrick Mwanawasa, and his wife, First Lady Maureen Mwanawasa, are so committed to making Zambia the next success story with much assistance from nongovernmental organizations. "Like Uganda, our infection rates are also now steadily declining," I reported. I wanted to make sure President Bush knew my own country was working hard to reach similar success.

Following our meeting, the president was due to address the larger group before moving on. We were supposed to go to the Rose Garden, but the rains came, forcing us directly into the pressroom—the East Room with its plush blue curtains and the lectern we so often see on television.

There were many seats in the room, as the group was much larger now. I was going to sit in the back since I had had my turn, but the lady from either the Gates Foundation or CARE International asked me to come and sit next to her, three or four rows from the front. Once again the room was full of dignitaries, and most seemed to know each other. They were very comfortable in this setting, which made me want to hide in the background. At this woman's encouragement, however, I joined her.

Standing on the stage, President Bush addressed the group made up of U.S. representatives and senators, the media, dignitaries, the fifteen of us from the Oval Office. He described the reasons he wanted to give fifteen billion dollars to the prevention and treatment of HIV and AIDS across Africa and the Caribbean.

I sensed President Bush looking straight into my eyes as he spoke, engaging me. It made me feel wonderful but also shy and embarrassed. Again I thanked God for my black nonblushing skin. To mask my embarrassment I looked down, like I had lost something on the floor, and then I looked up to the ceiling. But I pulled myself together, took a deep breath and engaged with President Bush.

With the meeting over, the group stood and applauded as the president finished and made his way down the red carpet. People who knew him— or wanted to—made their way toward him so they could speak. As for me, the village girl, I'd more than had my turn, so I made way for others. But it appeared my time wasn't up yet. In another surprise move, President Bush headed straight toward me and kissed me on both cheeks! I was flabbergasted and didn't know where to look. I didn't realize it at the time, but the media cameras caught this kiss on film. Then he was gone.

As the rains had stopped, those of us chosen to speak to the media made our way out to the Rose Garden, and here again I got to speak. I was asked whether today's meeting and the possible fifteen billion dollar contribution would bring hope. "Yes. Absolutely." I told the group of journalists that the crisis in Africa requires immediate attention and the swift passage of this bill, reinforcing that every day of delay will result in the loss of life. While the humanitarian organizations are doing all they can, this problem needs governments, NGOs, churches, individuals—it needs everyone together. "Greater access to treatment means children can live with their parents until they mature, instead of being left alone at a tender age." Those of us chosen to speak continued to answer questions.

Following the White House meeting, the president's bill passed, meaning fifteen billion dollars of U.S. taxpayer funds could be committed to the fight against HIV and other preventable diseases. The legislation endorsing this came to be known as the President's Emergency Plan for AIDS Relief, or PEPFAR.[3] This was generous action taken by a government on behalf of a people, and it has saved many, many thousands of lives. On behalf of the people of Africa I applaud the people of America and other developed countries who have followed suit.

There is more to be done, of course. A full analysis of the PEPFAR funding allocation revealed multiple challenges around complex issues like access to generic drugs and condoms. I was also disappointed to learn that groups receiving funding had to sign a statement condemning sex work and pledging not to work with commercial sex workers, so again this vital, vulnerable part of the equation was left out.[4] This was disappointing since without support there is no way girls will learn the skills to make their way to a better life. Still, by and large, this was a great start. Through initiatives like this, the tide is turning. We see that we can win.

Feeling on top of the world when it was time to leave the White House, I returned to the car with my colleagues who took me for a celebratory seafood lunch. It's funny, the things that stick in your head; I still recall that this was the first day I ate mussels.

That night I felt so fulfilled and accomplished, not just for me but for the impact the passage of the bill and allocation of funds would have on millions of lives. I was full of joy. It felt like the tears of millions were being swept away, their prayers answered. Suddenly part of Jeremiah 1:4-10 came to mind—"Before I formed you in the womb I knew you, before you were born I set you apart; I appointed you as a prophet to the nations"—along with the words of Prophet Zimba: "The American flag has come to a standstill." It was chillingly clear this had been my assignment.

When I woke the following morning at the Hilton just near the White House, I felt free. Jumping up and down on my bed and dancing around my room in my pajamas, I reenacted the things I had said to the president: "Yes, Mr. President." "Sir, future generations will hold us accountable for our inaction." Looking through the hotel window, everything felt and looked beautiful. As a rare treat I decided to order room service so I could celebrate and relax in the comfort of my room.

While I was waiting for my breakfast, I noticed the morning's newspaper had been pushed under the door. Kicking back in bed to read it, my reading came to a sudden halt and a great big "Whaaaaaaat?" came out of my mouth as I saw myself in the *USA Today* being kissed on the cheek by the president of the United States of America! I squealed out loud and laughed. It was not *me* kissing *him* but *him* kissing *me*—and the president kissing an HIV-positive black woman sent a powerful message to the world.

That image sent many feelings through me. President Bush kissing me showed people you can't catch AIDS from a hug or a kiss. I believe that photograph fostered compassion, breaking down the stigma that exists around this cruel, indiscriminate virus and encouraged other world leaders to act. I had to call Vanessa. "Girl, guess what? You go and buy *USA Today* and tell me what you find."

The picture made its way to the U.K, Australia, Kenya, Nigeria, South Africa, Botswana, Singapore and other countries. At last the international community was awakening to the plight of Africa and those in desperate poverty around the world. This was another example of God at work. I felt triumph for every person with HIV, and triumph for my country and for every Zambian and African alike.

Since the publication of that photograph, known among my friends and colleagues as the "Bush Kiss," I have come to know a lot more about the power of meeting an American president. As I continue on my regular travels around the world for work, invariably, no matter where I travel, customs officials ask me, "What is the nature of your visit to our country?" In African countries, as with most developing countries, if I say, "I am with World Vision," my path is cleared. Most people know World Vision, and officials know you are there for a good cause. In fact, a significant part of the Zambian population receive some support from World Vision, whether food or other aid.[6] Not everyone in the U.S. knows World Vision, however, so sometimes it would take me a lot longer to clear customs—until I found a way through. Today, I keep a copy of the "Bush Kiss" photograph in my wallet. One flash of this picture, FBI-style, and customs is cleared very quickly indeed. "On your way, madam."

The Best of Humankind

WHEN I RETURNED FROM THE WHITE HOUSE I had a feeling the trip had been the pinnacle of my work, the culmination of all my activities, the end of my calling. I simply didn't imagine that the journey of life could take me much further. But I was wrong. The White House trip sparked a great deal more interest in my story and a great deal more travel in my life. Inside of me, it confirmed the need to dream big and aim high because all things are indeed possible.

For the next several years, I traveled regularly between the United States, Australia, Canada (which is interesting when you think back to Prophet Zimba's words), Germany, the United Kingdom, and even Spain, Romania, Thailand, New Zealand, Ireland and beyond. On each trip, my mission was to boost awareness of the impact of HIV and AIDS on the world's children and to raise funds for the fight against the disease. I achieved this through presentations to audiences that often included a country's leaders and senior figures.

I have been blessed with opportunities to share with my own late president and First Lady Maureen Mwanawansa, Mrs. Graca Machel

Mandela, UN Secretary General Ban Ki-moon, U.S. Secretary of State Hillary Clinton, UN Special Envoy to Africa Stephen Lewis, British Development Secretary Hilary Benn, other British Parliamentarians and leaders across the world, former first lady Mrs. Laura Bush, and Mrs. Cindy McCain. Meetings scheduled with former British prime minister Tony Blair and Paul Martin, the former Canadian prime minister, were both unavoidably canceled at late notice. I have even met with President Barack Obama, albeit in different circumstances. We happened to share a pew at the Apostolic Faith Church in Chicago when he was running for office—how I wish I had a camera for that occasion! At these meetings and hundreds more in churches, schools, colleges, workplaces, town halls and private homes, I am asked the same question over and over: "Now that we know about the troubles of Africa, what can we do?"

In response to this I have a clear point to make, which I share with you now. I frame my answer by saying I am not a medical doctor, a scientist, an economist or a public-health expert. In these areas I am little more than a layperson. I am simply a woman whose heart is broken by the untold horror of HIV and AIDS and extreme poverty as well as other treatable, preventable diseases like TB and malaria. And I want people to be clear that we cannot tackle these diseases without tackling poverty, for they are locked in a deadly embrace.

Today the rotten reality is that every six seconds of every single day a child dies because they don't have enough to eat.[1] Every fourteen seconds another child loses a parent to AIDS,[2] and every thirty seconds another child dies from malaria.[3] This is the world you and I inhabit together. These are the facts that break the heart of God.

I understand that contemplating these numbers can result in paralysis. They are simply too terrifying and awful to comprehend. We wonder where to begin and just how one person can make a difference. So how is it I can stand before you confident that within our lifetime we will eradicate extreme poverty and preventable disease?

This is the fundamental point I want to make and that I want you to believe at your core—extreme poverty can be solved, not in one hundred years or more but in our very lifetime. This is not my conviction alone—it is a fact understood by the United Nations, by world governments, by economists, by the global ONE Campaign and by the international humanitarian community alike. We who inhabit planet Earth today have it in our grasp to end extreme poverty and preventable disease. We can make the decision that on our watch as the custodians of our planet, we will no longer tolerate the pain and destruction. Surely this is one of the most engaging, uplifting opportunities before humankind today. Can you imagine the joy of being part of the movement that ends the death and suffering brought about by the gross inequalities in our world?

So with this great and very achievable goal in mind, I want to deviate from my story for a moment to respond to the question so often asked of me, "What can we do to end the pain?" First, I say, knowledge is power, so allow me to arm you with the knowledge and the tools you need to become future-makers, leaders of change who will free Africa and other developing countries from the unfair burden of poverty and disease. Are you with me?

We can win because today the grip of extreme poverty affects a smaller percentage of the world's people than at any other time in history. Up until roughly two hundred years ago, most of the world's population, with very few exceptions, lived in dire poverty.[4] But today while the world is home to 1.4 billion who are described as extremely poor and another 1.6 billion who are in moderate poverty, much of the world is richer than it has ever been. So the first important fact that gives me hope is that for the first time in the history of humankind, the number of people needing a hand up is small enough, relatively speaking, to work with. There is more than enough to go round—there are enough people and governments of means to help them out.

The number of people living in dire poverty is not a static figure. With a combination of our support, their hard work, and determination and the right set of external conditions families can lift themselves to a better life. But just as they can climb the perilous journey up the ladder of economic development, they can just as easily fall back down when conditions deteriorate. We must be vigilant and adapt our response as required. The World Bank has advised that due to the global financial crisis, 89 million more people will be living in extreme poverty.[5] A recent study by Plan International predicts that young girls will be particularly hard hit.[6] Likewise, recent food shortages and hikes in food prices, largely attributable to global warming, have seen many more slip back into extreme poverty. Thus, if combating extreme poverty is one of the world's greatest challenges, the other must be combating climate change, for the future of all people, particularly those in the developing world, who will be the hardest hit.

Modern economic theory and recent global experience say that our first goal should be to free people from the clutches of extreme poverty—the poverty that kills, that is so intertwined with HIV and AIDS and other preventable disease—so this is the focus of my attention. I see a brighter future for these 1.4 billion people because a series of road maps exists to lift them to a better life. We know how to make this happen; all that is left now is for us to walk arm in arm across the tallest mountains and through the darkest valleys to reach our destination.

There are several important and helpful policies in place, but the main road map for the alleviation of extreme poverty, the one each and every human being should be aware of, is the Millennium Development Goals campaign. The Millennium Development Goals (MDGs) are eight goals to be achieved by 2015 that respond to the world's main development challenges. The MDGs were agreed to by 189 nations and signed by 147 heads of state and governments during the UN Millennium Summit in September 2000.[7]

The eight MDGs break down into twenty-one quantifiable targets that are measured by sixty indicators.[8] If you are serious about joining the fight to end extreme poverty, I urge you to familiarize yourself with the MDGs as a first step. In summary, the MDGs are to

- eradicate extreme poverty and hunger
- achieve universal primary education
- promote gender equality and empower women
- reduce child mortality
- improve maternal health
- combat HIV/AIDS, malaria and other diseases
- ensure environmental sustainability
- develop a global partnership for development

Included within goal 7, ensure environmental sustainability, is the target of reducing by half the number of people without access to safe drinking water and basic sanitation. Just by bringing clean, safe water to a community we can halve that community's rate of infant mortality.

It must be acknowledged, however, that the reason a country like mine remains in extreme poverty is a tangled web of our landlocked geography, the effects of our colonial history, our own past leaders' corruption and poor leadership, excessive debt burdens, falling copper prices, lack of action from the developed world with respect to foreign aid commitments, and grossly unfair conditions of international trade. It is simply an illusion to suggest a series of eight goals could fix all these woes, but they will certainly go a long way toward improving the lives of my country's extreme poor.

The year 2015 is not so far away, so just how are we faring? A full analysis of how we're progressing toward the MDGs is not permitted here, but let me give you a few highlights. When it comes to one of our most deadly preventable diseases—malaria—as of November 2007, 88 million bed nets had been distributed in high-risk countries.[9] The most recent progress report from ONE, the global campaign organization that has merged with Bono's organization, DATA (Debt, AIDS, Trade in Africa), reveals that "for the first time in decades, the goal of eradicating malaria in Africa is being discussed again and is spurring increased atten-

tion and funding for the disease."[10] *Eradication of malaria?* That hardly
seemed possible just ten years ago. Just look what we can achieve when
we work together. *This is truly incredible.*

Another exciting outcome is the reduction in infant mortality. According to a 2009 UNICEF report, the absolute number of child deaths
in 2008 declined to an estimated 8.8 million from 12.5 million in 1990,
the baseline year for the Millennium Development Goals (MDGs). Compared to 1990, 10,000 fewer children are dying every day.[11] Now clearly
when 8.8 million children die every year, there is still a long way to go,
but through hard work and determination we are taking steps in the right
direction.

How is my landlocked homeland of Zambia faring? I am proud to say
we look set to achieve seven of the eight MDGs: the targets on hunger,
universal primary education, gender equality, maternal health, and HIV
and AIDS are likely to be achieved by 2015. Further, it is possible that
with a concerted effort we have the potential to achieve the targets on
extreme poverty, child mortality, malaria and other major diseases, and
water and sanitation. It looks unlikely that we will succeed with all of
goal 7.[12]

Through the efforts of the government, Zambia is also enjoying other
successes. We are the first country to sign an MDG contract with the
European Union. This contract is a new initiative that will make MDG-
related aid more predictable and long term in nature. My country was
chosen because of its commitment toward the MDG process and because
our government has made such a commitment to improved transparency
and accountability.[13] We have also received generous concessions with
respect to the cancelation of much of our foreign debt, partly as a result
of the hard work of our government and the concessions of the international monetary lenders, and the lobbying of the international community on our behalf. The reduction in our international debt has freed up
money for health care—people who never could have afforded health
care can now be treated. This is all incredible news. Step by step we are

getting there. We have a long way to go but I hope you are starting to get the sense that we can do this.

While it is vital we address poverty and the raft of preventable diseases holistically, we must also keep a specific focus on HIV and AIDS, and the world policymakers have committed to do this. Outside but alongside the MDGs is the world's commitment to providing universal access to treatment for AIDS for all people who require it by 2010. The UN created the Global Fund to Fight AIDS, Tuberculosis and Malaria (GFATM) to meet this goal. An estimated 4.2 million people in low- and middle-income countries are now receiving HIV/AIDS medication, up from only 50,000 people in 2002.[14] While Zambia used to have a woeful three testing centers, it had eighty four by the end of 2005.[15] Millions of deaths have been averted. So many more children can now go to sleep at night knowing their parents are watching over them.

Given the "perfect storm" of economic, historic, geographic and cultural conditions that combined and allowed AIDS to march across Africa, the fact that we are slowly turning the tide is both remarkable and inspirational. This does not mean, however, that we can rest. We are not yet at the 80-percent level that would constitute "universal" treatment—five million people still require treatment.[16] Will we get there by 2010? With the current efforts this looks highly unlikely, as the Global Fund is underfunded by billions of dollars. A specific focus on HIV is vital because HIV infection rates are still far outpacing the number of people put on treatment. UNAIDS reports that amidst this progress in 2008, for every two people who started taking antiretroviral drugs, another five become newly infected. "Unless we take urgent steps to intensify HIV prevention we will fail to sustain the gains of the past few years, and universal access will simply be a noble aspiration," they report.[17]

Of the world's likelihood of realizing the MDGs, UN Secretary General Ban Ki-moon says, "Looking ahead to 2015 and beyond, there is no question that we can achieve the overarching goal: we can put an end to poverty. In almost all instances, experience has demonstrated the validity of earlier agreements on the way forward; in other words, we know what to do. But it requires an unswerving, collective, long-term effort."[18]

That is the question before us: do we have the commitment, the determination, the persistence to make this happen? Do we have the will to make it so? Let's get into some more detail of just how we can move forward.

The cost of the MDGs is obviously a considerable factor. An esteemed economist, UN adviser and author of an extraordinary book, *The End of Poverty: Economic Possibilities of Our Time*, Professor Jeffrey Sachs headed the UN task force that worked out, as best it could given the long-term, global nature of the task, just how much it would cost to realize the MDGs and halve extreme poverty by 2015. The sums required to achieve the MDGs are in the order of 121 billion dollars a year in 2006, rising to 189 billion dollars by 2015 as projects "scale up" in nature.[19] Initially, these sound like enormous sums, particularly given recent global economic challenges. But when we take into account the amount the world's governments are already giving in foreign aid, the shortfall in 2006 was only 48 billion dollars a year for 2006 and 74 billion dollars for 2015, spread between all the developed countries of the world.[20]

So where will the money come from? And what can each of us do to make sure we get there? It is clear governments, both those in the developed and developing worlds, have a role to play, and I am again full of hope that they will deliver us a long way toward our targets. My hope comes from the fact that 189 leaders of UN member countries put their hands on their hearts and pledged to make this happen. Not all of the required money has been committed, but in 2008 a global total of 119.8 billion dollars was committed to official overseas aid—more money than ever before.[21]

Cynics say this is a fraction of what has been promised, though Professor Sachs is optimistic public perceptions reflect support for higher levels of aid. When asked what percentage of the federal budget they think goes to foreign aid, Americans' median estimate is 25 percent of the budget, more than twenty-five times the actual level. When asked how much of the budget should go to foreign aid, the median response is 10 percent.[22] Cynics cite the fact that since the 1970s, developed countries have been promising to commit 0.7 percent of their GDP to overseas aid. In reality, this does not happen. On average, for each of the members of the Organisation for Economic Co-operation and Development (OECD) the actual amount given represents 0.3 percent of gross national income.[23] I have to agree, this is a long way off the committed 0.7 percent promised contribution. In reality, the countries who meet and exceed the 0.7 percent commitment are Denmark, Luxembourg, the Netherlands, Norway and Sweden.[24] They truly deserve our applause. Now, it is not my place to say how much governments should give. All I can ask, in the name of Africa's children, is that our leaders honor the commitments they have made.

The evidence suggests that if we are to meet the MDGs, if we are serious about halving extreme poverty by 2015, we cannot sit back and expect our governments to do the work. Each and every one of us has a much bigger role to play in influencing this outcome. If the first role is to arm yourself with knowledge, perhaps the second role is petitioning your government, making them see this matters to you. If you have the privilege, the freedom and the right to vote in a democratic country, your government is in power by the will of the people *to represent your issues.*

Our leaders act on the issues we say are important—those we shout about again and again and again. On the flip side, when our leaders detect silence and apathy on an issue they assume it is not important to their people. If repeated noise is not made on matters of international development, world leaders assume their people don't care and they lose the incentive to act. When we are silent, our governments believe we only care about issues in our own backyard. They are even inclined to believe acting on international development will cost them votes. Tell them this is not so. Tell them the future of Africa's children depends on them keeping their promises.

As an African woman I was humbled by the heartfelt show of support the people of the developed world made to the developing world through actions like the Jubilee Campaign, ONE and the 2005 Make Poverty History rock concerts. But I beg you, do not fall into the trap of thinking, *Well, that's done, they know we care.* I heard one government official say, "Of course people went to a free rock concert, but do they really care about ending poverty?" We must keep the pressure on our governments. They are our leaders; we need to show them we care and keep them accountable.

I am eager to see how President Barack Obama will respond to the joint challenges of extreme poverty, HIV and AIDS and other forms of preventable disease. Already I'm encouraged. My spirits soared when, on Global Testing Day in 2009, President Obama released a video of himself and his wife, Michelle, testing for AIDS in Kenya as he encouraged all people in America and the developing world alike to know their status.[25]

I am the first to admit there are a raft of reasons developed nations do not meet their commitments, and it is true that some worthwhile commitments happen outside of the MDGs and 0.7 percent GNP commitment. Again, it must be acknowledged that some African governments can, rightly, be viewed with cynicism. After all, according to Transparency International's Corruption Perceptions Index, in 2008 ten of the twenty most corrupt countries in the world are in Africa.[26] Equally, though, we must give credit where it's due, for there are also many strong, fair and visionary leaders in Africa. Countries like Botswana, South Africa and Ghana showcase what is possible in Africa.

While those who live in the developed world must keep the pressure on their governments to honor their pledge to fight poverty through increased aid, debt relief and fairer terms of trade, those from the developed world must remind their governments of their commitment to be transparent and accountable, to make sure resources reach their intended communities and families, to make education and health a priority. We have overcome so much, and we will overcome our current hurdles too. Our people deserve and demand it. We are a continent rich in natural resources and passionate, hard-working people. We must put these to the advantage of all. We are making progress.

The tide is turning and we will win, but if we are to meet the 2015 deadline, our governments need to know we care. Please join with me in telling our leaders the world will judge them not by the promises they make but by the promises they keep. Time is running out. Please don't let the injustice, the inequality, continue on your watch. We are counting on you. I am optimistic today's leaders will choose to leave a great legacy and that their successors will admire and build upon an African legacy they can be proud of.

But we don't get away that easily. Each of us can and must do more than petition our governments. If we look at the money required to meet the MDGs, individual contributions could also get us across the line. One simple sum demonstrates the point: if the 855 million people living in the "rich" world each gave two hundred dollars per year,[27] we would have the amount Jeffrey Sachs calculates we would need to end extreme poverty. It really is that achievable. It is not my intent to instruct people on what they should give; everyone's capacity and circumstance are different, and some direct their giving to other causes. I simply hope that my story, a story that echoes millions of others, will inspire you to join the fight against poverty, HIV and AIDS, and preventable disease. I share with you the following to inspire you to find your own unique, meaningful way to contribute to the fight.

In 2007 I again found myself on Capitol Hill. The funding agreement to continue the PEPFAR funds needed to be reauthorized, and a hearing was held to explore this. Once again I was privileged with an opportunity to advocate for an outcome. The hearing was chaired by the warm and kind, late Senator Edward Kennedy, whose passing saddened me greatly and whose opening remarks have become a source of inspiration to me. Senator Kennedy's words specifically related to HIV and AIDS, but they are also symbolic of the job ahead of us in addressing extreme poverty and other preventable, treatable disease that plagues my continent. I share them with you now.

> At times, this disease has brought out the worst in mankind. Children orphaned by AIDS have been deprived of their rights. Women and girls have been shamefully exploited. And millions of people living with HIV/AIDS have faced stigma, fear, and discrimination. But we've also seen the best in mankind. Nation after nation has pledged to help. Scientists have devoted their lives to finding better ways to prevent and treat AIDS. Doctors, nurses, and other health professionals have worked tirelessly in cities and towns and villages across the world to give hope and help to persons living with AIDS.[28]

I agree with Senator Kennedy, for I have certainly seen the fight against the dual enemies of extreme poverty, HIV and AIDS, and other forms of preventable disease bring out the very best in humankind.

A couple who have become friends, Tedde and Jim Reid of Chicago, toured the Zamtan compound with me. They were so moved by the plight of these periurban dwellers and their lack of access to medical facilities that they and their friends Darryl and Cindy Link, David and Claudia Jackson, and others raised 1.2 million dollars to build a mini hospital in the compound that caters to thousands of people in the community. The medical center is preventing mother-to-child HIV transmission and helping to cure simple infections that all too often take the people of Zamtan's lives early.

The Reids and their friends had the means to contribute significant funds of their own, but not everyone is in this position. Does this mean we should sit idly by? No. If we hear God's calling, if we allow him to use us to be the change we want in the world, whatever our means, the results are profound. For some this will mean volunteering time at home or abroad. For some it will mean purchasing fair trade products that ensure those who grow our coffee, chocolate and flowers receive a fair price for their crops. Others may arrange to commit a service to the poor at their place of worship.

You can even consider a simple gesture like donating money to buy a mosquito net to protect a child against malaria as he or she sleeps. A mosquito net costs ten dollars, including training on how to use and install it properly.[29] This gesture may seem so small, but guess what, you will have just saved a life! Make a pact with your family and friends that when special events come around for the next year, rather than buying gifts no one needs, give a life-sustaining gift. Through many humanitarian organizations you can buy gifts like a sheep for a family in Kenya, a school feeding program for a child in Malawi or something more significant, like the reconstruction of a school. Or why not make a pledge to drink only tap water for a month—no soda or bottled water—and donate the money you save to a charity working to eradicate extreme poverty and disease. You can even donate straight into the Global Fund to Fight AIDS, Tuberculosis and Malaria. Each and every one of us can take the world one inch closer to eradicating extreme poverty and disease or one inch further away with the simple decisions we make every single day. Which will you choose?

Each of us with our own ideology, history, life experience and resources forms a unique and critical piece of the puzzle. The story of nine-year-old Austin Gutwein illustrates this well. In the spring of 2004, Austin watched a video that showed children who had lost their parents to AIDS. He realized these kids were no different from him and yet they were suffering. Undeterred by his tender age, Austin acted. We can all learn from Austin's saying: "As kids, we don't care about the politics of AIDS, how or where they got the disease. We just go out and do something to help."

He spent World AIDS Day on his school's basketball court, where he shot 2,057 free throws to represent the 2,057 kids who would be or-phaned that very day. With other people's sponsorship, he raised three thousand dollars. Since that time, Austin has developed a program called Hoops of Hope that encourages others to seek sponsorship for shooting free throws. At the time of writing, Austin and his fifteen thousand Hoops of Hope participants in seventeen countries have raised over one million dollars to fund the construction of two medical-testing facilities in Sinazongwe, Zambia, as well as funding for a school.[30]

I am filled with relief and joy that the church in the West, specifically, has undergone a great transformation and is stepping up to its role in the fight against AIDS, poverty and injustice in all its forms. While initially the church buried its head in the sand, gradually I have seen the sleeping giant awaken, and I am heartened by the leadership of several churches.

Two examples are Saddleback Church in California and Chicago's Willow Creek Community Church, both of which are making a profound impact. My friends Rick and Kay Warren describe the church as an army of two billion volunteers, an image I just love. As they say, no matter how rural and remote the area in which you find yourself—even in the smallest village, where there is no clinic, clean water, grocery store or school—there is always a church, and a church is there 24/7. Other churches, such as Cornerstone, Menlo Park Presbyterian, Hillside Covenant, Potter's House, Apostolic Faith Church and Westminster, just to mention a few, are responding well. When people's hearts are moved, this is God at work. With over three thousand references to poverty in the Bible, Jesus is asking us to act, and we must hear this call.

My spirit has also been renewed by magnificent groups of students across the developed world who have shown enlightened leadership. At beautiful Pepperdine University in Malibu, California, I was overjoyed to discover students advocating to have AIDS included in the university's curriculum. Given the tools, these young people could not wait to make a difference. They held a "Do You See Orange?" day, an initiative of Acting on AIDS where one in every twenty students wears an orange T-shirt that says "Orphan." This represents the fact that one out of every twenty children in sub-Saharan Africa is orphaned by AIDS,[31] though the rate is one in three in my country.[32] Seeing so many of their friends "orphaned" was a challenging image for students; many of them will go on to become leaders in the fight. What powerful leadership it is for young people to be the ones to speak on an issue that affects their age group so directly. Young people are not the leaders for tomorrow but the leaders for today. We have all been called for such a time as this.

Business must also play a role in the fight, again using whatever talents and treasures are unique to each enterprise. I was brought to tears when I visited McKesson and Pacific Medical, which purchased the goods required for "caregiver kits" and made staff time available to assemble the kits, which were in turn distributed to HIV carers in Africa. These kits contain very basic supplies that enable carers to prolong the lives of those living with HIV and AIDS at home. One of the elements in each kit is Miconazole, the very drug Beatrice and I were sent to fetch for my bamaa, the drug whose frequent unavailability in Africa in 1993 kept me from holding my bamaa's hand as she left this world, the drug that just might have prolonged her life.

Each of these groups has considered the unique resources at its disposal; they have not been discouraged by age budget or bureaucracy. I encourage each and every person to pray, meditate, discuss and imagine the meaningful, unique action you can take. The ways to make a difference are endless.

Once you are inspired, make sure this message is heard by your family, friends, colleagues, prayer partners, fellow students—everyone with an ear to hear. Become a voice for change, an ambassador of hope. We are in this together, and it will take effort from us all. Each of us is part of the solution.

Once you put your mind to it, it's simple to become part of a movement to end extreme poverty. I want you to dream with me. I want you to believe. I know we can go even further than achieving the Millennium Development Goals and providing universal access to treatment for AIDS. So great is my faith in God and my faith in humankind that I just know we will do all it takes to make this happen.

I want you to look into the future with me, to the year 2030, to a world where we all walk together, a world where all lives are valued equally, a world where the MDGs have been realized and exceeded and the results viewed as a triumph of human collaboration. Children of future generations learn about our success at school. Their teachers say, *Just look what they achieved.* So inspired were we by our collective success, we decided to go one step further; we did not stop once we achieved the MDGs. In 2030 Africa has become a prosperous continent, free from international debt and no longer requiring international aid. We are governed by a collection of stable, transparent governments who govern for the good of their people.

I want you to come with me to this place in the future. Join with me, if you will, in imagining the village of my childhood without all the pain. When I dream of this place I see children free to be children, surrounded by parents, laughing and playing, I see safe, secure homes with clean water running close by and abundant crops of food grown sustainably without toxic pesticides that ruin the soil. I see healthy children learning, sitting in desks at school where they have the opportunity to reach their full potential. And when they grow older, the brightest and best of them chooses to remain in the village because here life is rich and there are meaningful, twenty-first-century opportunities for all. Relationships with family, friends and community are held sacred in the land where the sun never sets. People of different faiths respect each other and live peacefully side by side.

This is my dream for Africa. This is my dream for the children. Join with me, please, in making it a reality. Dream and pray with me and fight with me to make this dream real.

23

To All Things a Season

Wⁱᵗᴴ ᴹʏ ᴅʀᴇᴀᴍ ꜰᴏʀ ᴛʜᴇ ᴠɪʟʟᴀɢᴇ of the future shared, it's
time to conclude my own story. It has been overwhelming to see so much
of the world. As someone who genuinely loves people, I thrive on meeting so many people who embrace my message with open hearts and a will
to change the world. I am continually reminded that mine is a truly extraordinary journey for anyone, especially a village girl, and proof that
God works in miraculous ways—that he alone can open doors no human
can, that he uses ordinary people to do extraordinary things.

The virus, and more importantly the way God has encouraged me to
respond to it, has presented me with opportunities beyond my wildest
dreams. As long as people hear my story and respond, I am excited to
keep going. It's like throwing a tiny pebble into a vast lake and watching
the ripples flow all around the world. When someone hears my story,
goes on to change the world and influences others to do the same—that
is what it's all about.

As I followed my call to fight poverty, HIV and AIDS, I discussed my
travel with Joy and Faith, asking if they would prefer me to remain at

home. These are the baby girls I gave birth to, and their well-being has to
be my priority. My heart fills with pride when I think back to their response: "We love you and miss you, Mummy, but the children of the
world need you to keep going, so we're okay." If I ever had to name my
heroes, I could not go past my daughters.

Actually, one reason I continue to work is to fund their education.
With access to medication, my health is holding out well, but it has now
been more than ten years since my HIV diagnosis. God-willing I will see
my ninety-second birthday, but only God knows how much time I have
left. I must make sure that my daughters have a good education—that
their futures are filled with brighter choices and the chance to reach their
potential. A good Western education is expensive, and me continuing to
work and travel seemed to be the only way their education could be
funded. I hope and pray that, as they get older, they will know the sacrifices we made were worthwhile.

So with their blessing I continued to speak wherever I could, sounding
my voice wherever it could be heard. Most of the time Joy and Faith had
our extended family, our "village," caring for them. Eventually they went
to stay in the U.K. with Tunji—a kind-hearted man who started out as a
handsome stranger and became a treasured family friend. The circumstances surrounding our first encounter still make me smile.

Whenever I traveled from Zambia to the U.S. or Australia, my flight
went through London, and on one particular flight, early in 2003, Tunji
and I happened to be seated in the same row, separated by a couple of
empty seats. As soon as our eyes met—before we even spoke—I knew
this man was smitten. To put him off, I strategically placed a copy of my
Australian *Cosmopolitan* article, "I Am One of 28 Million Africans Who
Has HIV yet I Was Forbidden to Talk About It," which featured a large
photograph of me, on the empty seats between us. Then I covered my
head with my *chitenge* and went to sleep. When I woke, I peered through
the cracks in my *chitenge* and still saw nothing but love in this man's eyes.
This was the first time the article failed to work its magic.

Nigerian by birth, Tunji was living as a citizen of Britain and, I learned, was a talented and respected psychiatrist. As time went by, he became part of my life. Quite simply, he was a wonderful man who taught me to love again. As our relationship grew I began to open up to him about Joy and Faith, and how I was struggling to send all my dependents to school. I didn't know what to do. While Moffat remained a loving father, staying with him was not an option for the girls.

Since I traveled so much and could not afford a good boarding school for the girls, Tunji offered to let Joy and Faith stay with him in Kent, in the U.K. Though Tunji and I had become close, I was so independent by then that this gesture of kindness made me feel awkward. I did not want to end up indebted to another man. For more than a year I pushed the offer away, but truthfully speaking, the arrangement made sense in so many ways. Joy and Faith would benefit greatly from a period of British education and from the added benefit of a stable, loving African home environment, and I would have the chance to see them often as I regularly traveled through the U.K. Tunji persisted and finally I gave in. For the next two years the girls lived at his home in Kent and I kept in touch by speaking to them on the phone each day.

This decision to leave my girls with Tunji may appear odd to my readers, but Tunji became part of my extended family, my metaphorical "village." Although this was not an entirely typical situation, it was not altogether uncommon either. Moreover, as we thought one day we would marry, I felt I had to choose what was in the best long-term interest of my girls. It was a painful decision, but if I had to leave this world early, I knew a strong faith in God and a solid education would allow my baby girls to make it in life.

Eventually Tunji and I realized that we were not meant to be together forever. Sometimes God sends people into your life for a specific time and purpose, like he did in this case, and I thank God for sending Tunji to me when he did. I will never be able to thank Tunji enough for all he did during this time. Even after we broke up he insisted the girls remain with him until I was in a stable place where they could attend a good school. What an incredible man. "If I cannot be the tallest tree in the forest, I will strive to be the finest grass in the valley," he would say.

Eventually I was spending more time in the States or in the air than at home, and travel began to take too great a toll on my health, so the decision was made to relocate to my adoptive home, Chicago. The American flag had truly stood still; not only had I visited the White House, I was now coming to stay.

After a period at the Seneca Hotel near the John Hancock building in downtown Chicago, I moved to Oak Park, and while this is a very nice suburb, I stayed on the fifth floor of a cantankerous old building. It would be just my luck that even living in America, hot water rarely ran from the shower; sometimes water didn't come out of the bathroom taps at all. I'd often find myself still bathing the Zambian way, boiling a big pot of water on the stove and then carrying it to the bath.

I lived on my own in Chicago for some time, as I was still traveling too much for Joy and Faith to join me. While I fell in love with the city, in many ways this was a period of intense loneliness for me. By day, my work and the company of people invigorated me, keeping me strong. But at night, for the first time in my life, I was alone. After sharing a home with so many all my life, the contrast really hit me. I often found myself crying at night. I was tired, my legs ached, and the pains in my chest made me continually wonder when I would unite with my girls and my country. I did not let anyone know I was lonely, though. Instead, I prayed for strength and courage every day.

Some nights my loneliness was helped, surprisingly, by the peculiarities of my funny old building and eccentric neighbors who regularly set off the building's fire alarm in the early hours of morning. The wailing siren would jolt us from a deep sleep, and everyone in the building would scamper down the stairs, in various states of dress, where we'd wait until the fire trucks came, only to learn there had been yet another false alarm. This new way of living certainly took some adjusting to, but at least these eventful nights reminded me I wasn't alone.

The truth is, all of us need a shoulder to cry on, someone who can enter into our brokenness at our darkest points. That community or friend can be difficult to find when you're away from home, especially in Western countries, where I have found life to be more individualistic. Every person, though, from the richest to the poorest, longs for this companionship, and when we find it, we are made stronger. We were all created to belong.

For much of the time, my loneliness in Chicago was kept at bay by kind friends like Vanessa Church; Bishop Horace E. Smith and his family, who have become a second family to me; and Mike Mantel, who became my teacher, my dear friend and mentor, and a big brother in the African sense. In fact, I even call him Ba Mike, my Zambian way of saying, "You are a brother indeed." I also cannot forget the kindness of Ernest and Carrie Magazine, a family I met through World Vision who sponsored many children. Ernest reminded me so much of bataa, and Carrie of bamaa.

There is a season for everything, and I am overjoyed my time for loneliness has passed. My daughters are now by my side in the States, their accents evolving to an American, British, Zambian blend. I cannot explain the joy of being together at last. They do miss their bataa, though; he lost his fight in 2007. Joy and Faith have grown into compassionate, kind and generous girls, proud of their heritage and their country. I am so proud of them. Every day I enjoy watching them grow into the beautiful young women God is allowing them to become.

Joy is a great student who enjoys sports, art and drama. Soft and kind with a big heart, she is a peacemaker who always looks out for her baby sister. The two of them are very close—inseparable, in fact, with a special bond. She is also an avid reader of books and aspires to be a doctor to help people in Zambia some day.

Faith is strong and determined and yet has a big heart. When her teacher at her middle school asked what the students would like to do to explore the brokenness in the world, Faith raised her hand and said, "My mom could come and share her story." I could not believe that my own daughter was ready to become a world changer herself. In addition to these qualities, Faith—like many Zambians—loves the Chicago Bulls and is trying to convert her mother.

It is hard to count all the blessings in one's life, but one of my greatest blessings came in the area of my daughters' education. The students of Wheaton Academy wanted to do more than simply raise funds for Africa, so they decided to begin a scholarship program for students from other countries, especially the developing world. Can you guess who they selected as two of their first ten students to receive the scholarship? You're right: Joy and Faith Zulu.

Joy and Faith have had to work hard to catch up to their classmates, since their education started out in a very unconventional way. To that end, they laugh and say to me, "Mum, if you ever happen to have another child, please do her a favor and don't try to homeschool her."

Fountain of Life continues as a charitable organization in Chibombo Village. The school received some funding from the UN and patches of money here and there, but by and large it has been difficult to fund and operate from afar. We now fund an existing school, Shampanole Primary, with nearly four hundred children, mostly orphans. Some of the proceeds from the sale of this book will go not only to the school but also to Liteta Hospital, where my mother died.

As for the rest of my family, my remaining brothers and sisters have all grown and are living between the U.S., Zambia and London. I have officially adopted four other children, including my brother Kelvin's son Armstrong, plus Liaka, Brian, Deophister and Rhoda, who still live in Zambia at my home in Kabulonga. It is not unique to have so many dependents—it is rare to find a family in Zambia these days that does not have orphans staying with them. Kelvin's son Armstrong came to stay with us when he was just two or three years old. I have just received the joyous news that he has been accepted into medical school at the University of Zambia, one of just two universities in the country. His sister

Rhoda finished twelfth grade. I am so happy and proud of all they have been able to achieve.

Life has become rich once more. My health is as good as can be expected. I see a specialist every three months, and my CD4 count has continued to rise to over four hundred. The girls encourage me to exercise, so I have joined a gym.

I found a new spiritual home in an emerging church called River City, located in Humboldt Park area. The church was started by a young pastor named Daniel Hill. With its mission for racial reconciliation, neighborhood development and worship, I knew I had found my church. I love the way that River City welcomes people from all walks of life. It's fair to say that in Chicago's long, cold winter nights my faith has kept me strong. It is what helps me live in hope. It has also broadened my family, as Pastor Daniel and his wife, Liz, have taken us in; their love for Joy and Faith is priceless. Eventually I began preaching at River City, and the congregation, in turn, took the issues of Zambia to heart. Before long, the small but growing church allowed me to lead short trips to Zambia, where it funded a church and prison.

I realized I had truly been accepted into the city of Chicago thanks to the actions of a woman named Clare, who I met through World Vision. Clare had a heart for the plight of the orphans and said she was touched by my story. Unbeknown to me, she took it upon herself to contact the leaders of the city of Chicago, with whom she shared my story. To my absolute surprise and honor, Chicago Mayor Richard. M. Daley named April 24, 2004, Princess Kasune Zulu Day. T-shirts were printed in orange and blue with my name written across them, and the city held events which I was invited to speak at to encourage awareness of HIV and AIDS. I will forever be thankful to the people of Chicago, who have made a village girl feel so at home.

But in December 2005 it seemed Chicago had one more surprise for me. Of course I had come to know it as one of the world's best cities, but little did I know I would find love there as well. It happened, as love so often does, quite unexpectedly. Pastor Daniel had arranged a meeting for me and River City's other pastors at Moody Bible Institute. I needed to print out a document for the meeting, so I headed for the Moody library to find a printer. Seated at a nearby computer was a handsome young man with blonde hair and blue eyes. Suddenly my phone rang. Seeing that it was an international call, I apologized to the young man and tried to take the call quietly. "It's okay. You can talk," he said. I thanked him, embarrassed my phone had rung in such a silent place, and carried on with my business.

Once at the meeting I realized my documents had not printed properly, so back to the library I went. "Oh, you're back," he said in the soft accent of a Chicago native. "My name is David. Who are you?" I told him my name.

"Do you go to church here? I haven't seen you around," David commented.

"I go to River City or the Apostolic Faith Church," I replied, "but I have been invited to Christmas carols at Moody this year."

David gave me his cell number and encouraged me to call if I planned to attend carols.

That very day I had a rare break in my schedule and felt like some company, so I decided to call David. I asked if he'd like to join me for a cup of tea, and he jumped at the chance. We had a fun day, and he asked if he could see me again.

Two days later David took me out again. This time when he picked me up he handed me a single rose. It seemed I still hadn't learned the significance of a rose, as I said thank you and then carelessly tossed it on the dashboard. After our outing, David drove me to Vanessa's house. She was quick to ask, "Who is this white guy you are running around with?"

"He is my friend. He has been driving me around, taking me for tea, and he gave me a rose."

"Where is it?"

"I tossed it on the dashboard."

Vanessa laughed. "Girl, don't you know what it means? I keep forgetting what a village girl you are. A rose means he likes you."

Six days after our first meeting, Dave, realizing a single rose had not made an impact, bought me a beautiful bouquet of a dozen long-stemmed red roses. Finally I acknowledged that this guy was trying to tell me something!

I was slow to respond, however. Things had happened so quickly, and there was clearly a lot about me that David did not know. I knew I could not explain to him what my life was about, so I prepared a pile of magazine and newspaper articles to show him, including the Australian *Cosmopolitan* article that failed to work its magic on Tunji some years earlier. The next time he came to pick me up I invited him upstairs, gave him the pile of articles and left him alone to read.

From where I was waiting in my bedroom, I thought I heard someone crying, so I went to see if he was okay. "What is going on? Please stop crying, David," I said.

As I looked into David's tear-filled eyes, he said, "Can you let me cry? This is heartbreaking." I did as he asked and left him to continue sobbing for nearly an hour. I was sure this was the end of David's affection for me, imagining that he'd finish with a "See you later" and be gone from my life. But his response was different. "Princess, this does not change my feelings for you," he said. "I'm falling in love with you." You could have knocked me over with a gentle breath when David spoke these words.

He continued, "If you had asked me just two weeks ago whether I could develop feelings for someone who is HIV-positive, I would have said no. But now I have to have you in my life."

Here was a man just one year older than me, who had never married before, who was HIV-negative and a devout Christian, who knew I had two daughters, telling me he wants me in his life. I had heard stories like this, but how could it happen to me? I thought I needed to test him a bit.

"I also have many children in addition to my daughters," I began.

"If we could be together, your children would be a blessing."

"Well, David, if you have a heart for me, you need to have a heart for Zambia. I need you to love my country."

"Great! I would love to go with you to Zambia." This guy was in love, and he would not give up.

Within two weeks David had bought a ticket to Zambia, though it would not be until July of the following year that we would travel. Once in Zambia, David felt right at home. He also continued to be encouraged that we should marry from comments like the one my grandfather made.

"This is my new boyfriend, Ba Khapa," I told him as I introduced David.

"Princess, you know in our culture there is no such thing," my grandfather replied. "Here you would be married."

By this time David had met Joy and Faith on a number of occasions, though I had never told them we were dating. They figured it out on their own, however, and in Zambia they came to love him.

As much as I liked David, it was hard to adjust to a loving, affectionate relationship. At times I pushed David so far I wondered whether he would persist, though I always hoped he would. I wanted him to be sure he was making the right decision in choosing to spend his life with me. And I wanted to be certain my feelings for David were not born out of necessity or gratitude. I had proven to myself I could stand alone; this time I wanted to choose love for love's sake, and I wanted to be sure it would last.

I finally stopped my fighting, though, when Dave told me, "If you should ever become sick, it will be my honor to care for you, and your daughters will always be cared for as if they are my own." These words made it clear that he truly loved me, against all odds, and I felt the same for him. So on July 19, 2008, David's wait was over. We were married in a ceremony in front of our family and friends.

AIDS has taken a lot from me, but it has also offered me a big extended family who all wanted to be there to help celebrate our marriage. Three of my four "mothers" who have taken me in were there: Susan

Smith (the bishop's wife), Carrie Magazine and Dr. Phiri's wife, Chilufya Mwaba; unfortunately the doctor could not make it himself, and neither could my California "mum," Pastor Mary Williams Jackson. These special women gathered around and prayed for me, and I felt truly blessed as I prepared to enter the next phase of my life. *What a mighty God we serve.*

My other "dad," Ernest Magazine, walked me down the aisle, and as we set foot in the church he whispered in my ear, "Yes, Daughter, we made it." Looking out among the sea of people during the ceremony, I saw so many faces I love—friends and families from all walks of life: Mike Mantel and his family, my World Vision friends, Jim and Tedde Reid, David and Claudia Jackson, Darryl and Cindy Link, Chip Huber, my brother Muyani and his daughter Diara, Pastor Daniel Hill who did the first benediction, and of course, Vanessa Church. I could not control myself from giggling with delight as I put one foot in front of the other on my way up the aisle.

There was one other important person missing who has not yet been mentioned: my sister Belinda Collins, who has sacrificed so much to write this story for me. Living in Australia and eight months pregnant with my godson, Samuel, she was unable to travel. Tears formed in my eyes as Bishop Smith's daughter read a letter on Belinda's behalf.

Then there was Linda Schoefernacker, eyes full of tears as she watched her first-born son waiting to be married. She is the only remaining parent between David and me, and she was joined by her late husband's only surviving brother, Uncle Dennis. Linda had already assumed the role of loving grandmother to Joy and Faith and has gone on to become a blessing to me to me and the girls.

Finally, standing at the altar, can you guess who was standing beside my husband to-be? Not only were we to make our commitment in the presence of God, but Bishop Horace E. Smith was there to perform the task of marrying Princess Kasune Zulu and David Schoefernacker. I reflected on what a remarkable journey God had taken me on to reach this point—to be standing at the altar waiting to be married to the man I love surrounded by people who love me.

One day, well into the future, when Joy and Faith are educated and
the rate of HIV infection has truly declined, David and I long to head for
Zambia. David loves Africa, and my heart yearns for a simple life surrounded by mango trees underneath Zambia's endless skies, where the
focus is on relationships, family and community. The sound of the drum
beats in my ears; I hear them every day. I long to be back in the arms of
my mother Africa.

Epilogue

W HEN I REFLECT ON MY LIFE, IT'S CLEAR that HIV has been
far from the end of it all. In many ways, living with the world's most infa-
mous incurable disease is a blessing. In fact, it has been the beginning of a
whole new life, for I have chosen to live positively in the midst of suffering,
continually reminding myself that the virus lives in me but I do not live in
the virus. It does not own me or my soul. It is only a visiting stranger in my
body. My willingness to disclose my HIV status and encourage others to
respond has brought about many of my lifelong dreams.

But perhaps HIV's biggest blessing has been the realization that we
need to make every day count. My time is running out. This to me seems
a good lesson to learn, because whether you are a head of state, a church
leader, a scientist, a teacher, a nurse, a parent, a patient, a humanitarian
worker, a friend, every human being on earth has this in common: our
time to make a difference is limited. We may have two years, twenty
years, fifty years, but most of us will never know just how long we have.

When our time on earth ends our life should not only be measured by
how long we lived or what we managed to accumulate, but by what we
achieved in the time we lived, the differences we chose to make, be they
great or small, and how we chose to respond to the least of our brothers

and sisters. We must think hard about the purpose of our life, and be deliberate about the legacy we choose to leave behind.

Whatever passions burn in your heart, whatever promises you have made to yourself and others, do not delay another day in pursuing them in the hope that time is on your side. Time has a habit of getting away from us. Take it from someone who knows all too well that time is running out: when the years have faded and we have all gone and our grandchildren ask, "What did they do?" what do we want the answer to be? Let us stand together and be counted.

My bamaa, Joyce Mwanamusulwe Kasune, during her last year of work before getting seriously sick in early 1992, at Chibombo District Council where she was personal secretary to the governor.

My bataa, Goodson Moffat Kasune, around 1975 in Livingstone. This is the only surviving photo we have of him.

My grandmother (bakaba banakashi) Selina, with her granddaughter Brenda at her village. Behind is the hut my mum stayed in before dying. In 2003 she died of cancer while I was on my visit to the White House.

Me (standing) with my friend Nchimunya N'gandu in 9th grade, Mumbwa Secondary School, 1990.

From the left: Uncle John Banda, Aunty Erika Lukoshi holding her first granddaughter Erika Kaunda Muma, in suit a family friend, my cousin Erika Brenda and her son Danstan Lukoshi, in Chililabombwe, around 1993 or 1994.

Fountain of Life Ministries Community School, at our house that we shared with the orphans. This is the day in 1998 that the Colgate Company donated toothpaste and toothbrushes to the students. Standing are teachers and community parents, and the man by the door is Mr. Banda from Colgate.

My family village. I am fourth from left; Belinda Collins is second from left.

During my broadcasting days at Radio Icengelo, 2001.

Speaking at Apostolic Faith Church in Chicago, one of the early days speaking on the church arising to issues of HIV and AIDS.

Speaking at World Vision's HIV/AIDS Step into Africa Experience at Grand Central Station in New York, 2003.

With George W. Bush, April 2003.

With Senator Hillary Clinton.

Testifying before the U.S. Senate Committee on Health, Education, Labor and Pensions for the reauthorization of the President's Emergency Plan for AIDS Relief (PEPFAR) from $15 billion to $50 billion, December 2007.

At State House in Zambia with the late President of Zambia, Levy Mwanawasa, in 2005. Onlooking is the president of World Vision USA, Mr. Richard Stearns. Photo by Jon Warren.

With UN Secretary General Ban Ki-moon and Ishmael Beah, author of *A Long Way Gone: Memoirs of a Boy Soldier.*

With Stephen Lewis, former special UN envoy for HIV/AIDS in Africa.

With my adopted children in Lusaka: left
standing is Rhoda, Brian, Princess, Dcophister,
Saliya. Front row, seated: Faith, Armstrong, Joy.

From left to right: Faith
(holding dog), Moffat
(father), Joy, Princess, and
Moffat (stepbrother), July
2006, Ndola, Zambia. This
is the last time the girls saw
their father before he died.

With David Schoefernacker, shortly after we met in December 2005. We attended the independence day celebrations for Kenya and Tanzania.

Princess, Faith (left) and Joy under a mango tree in the backyard of our home in Kabulonga Lusaka, Zambia. About ten of us lived here: me, Joy and Faith; my adopted children Laika, Brian, Deophister, Rhoda and Armstrong; and my other two dependents Elivis and Saliya.

Appendix

Join the Movement to End Extreme Poverty and Disease

W E H A V E A D E C I S I O N T O M A K E. Will we be the generation to end the suffering of extreme poverty, HIV and AIDS, and preventable disease? Here are some suggestions on how to join the fight.

1. LEARN, ANALYZE AND QUESTION

Most of the references cited throughout *Warrior Princess* are web-based, so you can access them easily. Below is a list of our favorite sites and books that will help you become a future-maker.

Sachs, Jeffrey. *The End of Poverty: How We Can Make It Happen in Our Lifetime.* New York: Penguin Books, 2005.
> Renowned economist Jeffrey Sachs, instrumental in the creation and costing of the Millennium Development Goals, outlines with hard facts and costing models just how we can end poverty in our lifetime. This book is a must to give you a good grounding on this topic.

Nolen, Stephanie. *28: Stories of AIDS in Africa.* New York: Walker, 2007.
> Powerful stories of Africans infected and affected by AIDS—drivers, teachers, health workers, grandparents and even the great leader Nelson Mandela—to demonstrate the far-reaching, devastating impact of this virus. Each of these twenty-eight individuals represents one million people who have died from AIDS.

Millennium Development Goals <www.undp.org/mdg/>.
> Learn more about the Millennium Development Goals and progress being made. See the United Nations Development Program (UNDP) report "Are We on Track to Meet the Millennium Development Goals by 2015?"

Millennium Villages <www.millenniumvillages.org/>.
> Like a sped-up version of the MDGs piloted in select villages. Watch and see what is possible when we focus our energies. The team, led by Jeffrey Sachs, seeks to prove that we can end poverty from the village up by providing practical, simultaneous interventions in agriculture, health clinics, the provision of schools and water, and more.

2008 Report on the Global AIDS Epidemic <www.unaids.org/en/Knowl-
edgeCentre/HIVData/GlobalReport/2008/2008_Global_report.asp>.
   Every two years, UNAIDS publishes a detailed update on the AIDS
   pandemic that is well worth reading.

The 2009 DATA Report, *Monitoring the G8 Promise to Africa* <http://one.org/
international/datareport2009/>.
   Bono's organization, DATA, and the global activism group ONE have
   combined forces. Each year they release a report to keep us accountable on promises made to Africa.

The Global Fund <www.theglobalfund.org>.
   Learn about progress at the Global Fund to Fight AIDS, Tuberculosis
   and Malaria.

ONE International <www.one.org/international/>.
   ONE is a campaign and advocacy organization committed to the fight
   against extreme poverty and preventable disease, particularly in Africa. Cofounded by Bono and other campaigners, ONE's website provides knowledge as well as actions we can all take.

World Vision <www.worldvision.org>.
   A great resource for learning more about how humanitarian organization World Vision is contributing to the fight.

Global Poverty Project <www.globalpovertyproject.com>.
   "1.4 Billion Reasons" is a compelling 90-minute presentation that
   brings together all the pertinent information on extreme poverty and
   the actions each of us can take to end the suffering. Contact the Global
   Poverty Project today to book a presentation for your college, workplace or church.

Ellyard, Peter. *Designing 2050: Pathways to Sustainable Prosperity on Spaceship
Earth.* Yarraville, Victoria: TPN TXT, 2008.
   Former UN adviser and renowned futurist Dr. Peter Ellyard explores
   how we as a people can live in peace, harmony and abundance with
   our planet in the year 2050. A must for big-picture thinkers.

2. CONTEMPLATE AND PRAY

Pray, meditate, and ask for wisdom, grace and guidance to determine your course of action. This will be a path only you can take, according to your unique means and talents.

3. TELL EVERYONE!

Once you are inspired, make sure you share this message with your family, friends, colleagues, prayer partners, fellow students—everyone with an ear to hear. Become a voice for change, an ambassador of hope. We are all in this together, and it will take effort from us all. We are all part of the solution.

4. PRACTICALLY, WHAT CAN I DO?

Write to your local member of Congress or Parliament. They need to know we care; it really does make a difference. Urge them to keep their commitment to the MDGs, to further reduction of unfair debt and to the creation of more fair global trade practices.

Volunteer with an organization committed to fighting poverty at home or abroad.

Encourage your church, school or workplace to raise money or undertake projects that will help end poverty. Get creative; you are limited only by your imagination. You'll be surprised how quickly you generate a wave of change.

Donate money to an organization fighting poverty, HIV and AIDS. Purchasing this book is a good start, as 10 percent of all sales go to charitable organizations supporting those affected by AIDS.

At the risk of alienating any agencies, we encourage you to research your favorite charitable organization. You'll find helpful lists of reputable charities in <www.givewell.net> or <www.thelifeyoucansave.com>.

For more ideas on how to act check out:

www.one.org/international/   www.oxfam.org
www.worldvision.org   www.savethechildren.org
www.theglobalfund.org   www.plan-international.org
www.virginunite.com   www.doctorswithoutborders.org

Thank you for the difference you will make.

Acknowledgments

Princess Kasune Zulu wishes to thank:

The audiences I have interacted with over the past ten years who have encouraged me to write this book.

My husband, David Schoefernacker, who taught me to love again.

To my daughters, Joy and Faith, and my adopted children, Brian, Rhoda, Armstrong, Deophister and Laika, for their understanding and support and for enriching my life every day.

My mentor and big brother Dr. Mike Mantel, who reminded me not to give up and insisted that this story be told.

Hats off to Belinda Collins, who is so much more than my coauthor, whose gifts and excellence made this book what it is today.

Darren Collins for patiently allowing us to write, and the Richardson and Collins families—thank you for loaning your daughter and sister to me for the past three years.

My friend Mae Cannon, whose efforts made it possible for us to have a publisher.

Mrs. Chilufya Mwaba Phiri and Dr. Mannasseh Phiri, my surrogate mum and dad, for their endless support of this book.

My instructor on understanding AIDS, Dr. Bob Baugher, whose teaching and support has been indispensable.

Al Hsu and the team at IVP for their expertise and patience.

My professor Paul Koptak at North Park University, whose challenge in class to preaching and understanding Scripture was timely and increased my understanding. The more I studied the more I realized how little I know.

Pastor Daniel Hill, my mentor.

My cousin Tubya Kasune, who helped me reflect the current situation in

Zambia and who took time to read the draft word for word.

To my brothers Nathan and Muyani Kasune who made sure that my family was well represented.

My mother-in-law Linda Schoefernacker who read the manuscript before anyone read it and told me how she laughed, cried, had fun and was challenged as she read.

Alex Mukuta and Chola Musukuma from ZNBC for editing local language content. Sherrine Masupelo, whose connections for the local languages were indispensable.

David and Kelsey Starrs for coming to my aid when my laptop broke down in the midst of my final edits and deadline. Such a timely gift. Paul, Susie and the entire prayer group.

To those who gave permission for their names and story to be part of this book—friends and extended family

To all the children, women and communities in Zambia who gave me a chance to enter their lives and hear their stories.

To organizations such as UNAIDS, Eternity Fountain, Oxfam and World Vision, whose expertise deepened my understanding of humanitarian work and the important role of advocacy and being a voice for the voiceless.

Mawi Asgedom, Edward Gilbreath and Victor Weykyoi Kori, whose advice was key in the infancy of this book. Jo Kadlecek, who began this journey with me. Joan Mussa, who encouraged me that God's timing would be right, and Joseph Salesini, for his support.

Above all, I would be remiss if I did not thank God, who had a bigger plan and purpose for my life than I could ever have dreamed of. I am humbled that he saw it worthy to use me for such a time and book as this. This is again proof that God uses ordinary people to do extraordinary things.

Belinda Collins would like to thank:

Princess Kasune Zulu, my sister, for having faith in me to document your story. To do so has been my great privilege and blessing. I hope I have done your incredible tale justice. While the last three years have been tough, a big part of me will be sad when the journey is over. I will miss our eight-hour phone calls, your wisdom and guidance.

My husband, Darren, who graciously gave me the space to make this dream come true, who cooked, cleaned and cheered me on every step of the way. You are one of a kind. Our son, Samuel, for traveling with me to Seattle to write and for bringing such simple, pure joy to our lives.

My family: Ken, Sue and Darren Richardson and Meredith Hennessy, and Nana, Mrs. Ada Richardson, my in-laws Mary and Neale, Mike and Glenn. I doubt a more supportive, loving family exists anywhere.

My extended family, Joy and Faith Zulu and David Schoefernacker, for lending Princess to me. I love you dearly.

Melanie, Danielle, Kate, Rubina, Kate, Vicki, Leanne, Naomi, Adam—all of my family and friends who have been neglected for the past three years.

My wise mentors Professor Louise Rolland, Sue Coffey, Colin Parkes and Dr. Peter Ellyard; Peter in particular for his guidance in creating the "village of the future."

Al Hsu and the team at InterVarsity Press for their expertise, kindness and encouragement.

Dorothy Hansen for her delightful and considered proofreading.

Melinda Tankard Reist and Angela McMahon for editing my introduction, and Melinda, Veronique Filippini, Dianne Clarke and Emily Wood for continued inspiration and encouragement.

Benjamin Scantlebury for patiently creating princesszulu.com.

Simon Moss of the Global Poverty Project and Simon Duffy of World Vision Australia for editorial advice.

David Horgan and Janet Rowe for advice on the world of publishing.

Our lawyer, Lisa Oritz at Perkins Coie, for helping us navigate the world of publishing.

DVA Navion for support with airfares and laptop.

Notes

Chapter 1: Positive
[1]Stephanie Nolen, *28: Stories of AIDS in Africa* (New York: Walker, 2007), p 102.

Chapter 2: "Princess Is Her Name"
[1]Embassy of the Republic of Zambia, "Major Tribes" <www.zambiaembassy .org/zambia.html>.

Chapter 3: My Big Family
[1] S. Kumbula Tendayi, "Zambia," *World Press Encyclopedia* 2003 <www.encyclopedia .com/doc/1G2-3409900243.html>.

Chapter 4: The Short Life of a Baby Named Linda
[1]World Health Organization, "Core Health Indicators—Zambia" <http://apps .who.int/whois/database/core/core_select_process.cfm?country=zmb&indi cators=healthpersonnel>.
[2]World Health Organization, Zambia Statistics <www.who.int/countries/ zmb/en/>.
[3]Elizabeth Davies, "AIDS Reduces African Life Expectancy to 33," *The Independent World* <www.independent.co.uk/news/world/africa/aids-reduces-african -life-expectancy-to-33-553364.html>.

Chapter 6: Be Strong and of Good Courage
[1]Stephanie Nolen, *28: Stories of AIDS in Africa* (New York: Walker, 2007), p. 7.
[2]Ibid.
[3]Ibid.
[4]Ibid., p. 220.
[5]UNAIDS, "2008 Report on the Global AIDS Epidemic," p. 33 <http://www .unaids.org/en/KnowledgeCentre/HIVData/GlobalReport/2008/2008_ Global_report.asp>.

Chapter 8: A Teenage Mother Growing in Faith

[1]World Health Organization, "Core Health Indicators for Zambia," 2008 <http://www.who.int/whosis/database/core/core_select_process.cfm?coun try=zmb&indicators=healthpersonnel>.

[2]OECD Social Institutions and Gender Index, "Gender Equality and Social Institutions in Zambia" <http://genderindex.org/country/zambia>.

Chapter 10: I Have to Know

[1]World Health Organization, "Global Access to HIV Therapy Tripled in Past Two Years, but Significant Challenges Remain" <http://www.who.int/hiv/mediacentre/news57/en>.

Chapter 12: A Fountain of Life

[1]Stephanie Nolen, *28: Stories of AIDS in Africa* (New York: Walker, 2007), p. 255.

[2]Jeffrey Sachs, *The End of Poverty: How We Can Make It Happen in Our Lifetime* (New York: Penguin, 2005), p. 75.

Chapter 13: Hitchhiking with Truck Drivers

[1]OECD, Social Institutions and Gender Index, Gender Equality and Social Institutions in Zambia, "Family Codes" <http://genderindex.org/country/zambia>.

[2]Stephanie Nolen, *28: Stories of AIDS in Africa* (New York: Walker, 2007), p. 46.

[3]Dave Chibesa, "Quelling Chirundu Sex Menace," *Times of Zambia* <http://www.times.co.zm/news/viewnews.cgi?category =8&id=1058570154>.

[4]Nolen, *28,* p. 46.

[5]Ibid.

[6]Ibid., p. 328.

Chapter 14: Meeting Dr. Phiri

[1]John S. James, "Durban Declaration on HIV and AIDS, " July 7, 2000 <http://www.thebody.com/content/art32103.html>.

Chapter 17: "You're Listening to *Positive Living*"

[1]Roll Back Malaria, "Malaria Fact Sheet" for World Malaria Day 2009 <http://www.rollbackmalaria.org/worldmalariaday/docs/fact-sheet-RBM.pdf>.

[2]Ibid.

[3]Ibid.
[4]Ibid.

Chapter 18: My Vision for the World

[1]UNAIDS, "Greater Involvement of People Living with or Affected by HIV/AIDS (GIPA)" <http://www.unaids.org/en/PolicyAndPractice/GIPA/default.asp>.

[2]Peter Singer, *The Life You Can Save: Acting Now to End World Poverty* (Melbourne: Text Publishing, 2009), p. 7.

[3]Ibid.

[4]Jeffrey Sachs, *The End of Poverty: How We Can Make It Happen in Our Lifetime* (New York: Penguin, 2005), p. 20.

[5]Australia's 1987 Grim Reaper HIV-prevention television campaign <http://www.youtube.com/watch?v=U219eUIZ7Qo>.

[6]"New HIV Infections in Australia Up 41 Percent from 2000, Study Finds," October 12, 2006, National AIDS Treatment Advocacy Project (NATAP) <http://www.natap.org/2006/newsUpdates/110906_27.htm>.

[7]Dave Chibesa, "Quelling Chirundu Sex Menace," *Times of Zambia* <http://www.times.co.zm/news/viewnews.cgi?category=8&id=1058570154>.

[8]Lynn Arnold, "Millions Dead and Economic Devastation—This Is the Other War," *Sydney Morning Herald,* November 29, 2002 <http://www.smh.com.au/articles/2002/11/28/1038386256534.html>.

Chapter 19: Coming to America

[1]Elikia M'bokolo, "The Impact of the Slave Trade on Africa," *Le Monde diplomatique,* English edition <http://mondediplo.com/1998/04/02africa>.

[2]Stephanie Nolen, *28: Stories of AIDS in Africa* (New York: Walker, 2007), p. 73.

[3]UNAIDS, *2008 Report on the Global AIDS Epidemic,* p. 215 <www.unaids.org/en/KnowledgeCentre/HIVData/GlobalReport/2008/2008_Global_report.asp>.

[4]Elizabeth Davies, "AIDS Reduces African Life Expectancy to 33," *The Independent World* <www.independent.co.uk/news/world/africa/aids-reduces-african-life-expectancy-to-33-553364.html>.

Chapter 20: Chicago

[1]Jenny Eaton and Kate Etue, "Letter from the Editors," *The aWAKE Project: Uniting Against the African AIDS Crisis,* Vanderbilt University <http://www.vanderbilt.edu/AnS/religious_studies/aidsafrica/theawakeproject.html>.

[2]"Cabrini-Green," *Wikipedia* <http://en.wikipedia.org/wiki/Cabrini_Green>.
[3]"Cabrini-Green," Amanda Seligman, *Encyclopedia of Chicago* <http://www
.encyclopedia.chicagohistory.org/pages/199.html>.

Chapter 21: From the Village to the White House

[1]Stephanie Nolen, *28: Stories of AIDS in Africa* (New York: Walker, 2007),
p. 29.
[2]UNAIDS, *2008 Report on the Global AIDS Epidemic*, p. 215 <www.unaids.org/
en/KnowledgeCentre/HIVData/GlobalReport/2008/2008_Global_re-
port.asp>.
[3]Nolen, *28*, p. 29.
[4]See <www.pepfar.gov>.
[5]Nolen, *28*, p. 49.

Chapter 22: The Best of Humankind

[1]World Food Program, Hunger Stats <www.wfp.org/hunger/stats>.
[2]World Vision, HIV and AIDS Fast Facts, 2001 <www.worldvision.org/
content.nsf/about/press-development-aids>.
[3]World Health Organization, Media Center, Fact sheet 94, "Malaria—Key
Facts," January 2009 <www.who.int/mediacentre/factsheets/fs094/en/>.
[4]Jeffrey Sachs, *The End of Poverty: How We Can Make It Happen in Our Lifetime*
(New York: Penguin, 2005), p. 27.
[5]World Bank, "Low-Income Countries Face Long Recovery—Serious Challenges Require More and Better Support," September 16, 2009 <http://web
.worldbank.org/WBSITE/EXTERNAL/NEWS/0,,contentMDK:22316262
~pagePK:34370~piPK:34424~theSitePK:4607,00.html>.
[6]Plan Australia, Media Release, "Because I Am a Girl, the State of the World's
Girls," September 22, 2009 <www.plan.org.au/mediacentre/mediareleases/
because_I_am_a_girl_-_state_of_the_worlds_girls_2009>.
[7]United Nations Development Program, "About the MDGs: Basics: What Are
the Millennium Development Goals?" <www.undp.org/mdg/basics.shtml>.
[8]Ibid.
[9]One International, "HIV/AIDS and Malaria—the Opportunity".
[10]"The DATA Report 2008," p. 8 <www.one.org/report/en/index.html>.
[11]UNICEF, "Global Child Mortality Continues to Drop," September 10, 2009

<www.unicef.org/childsurvival/media_51087.html>.

[12]United Nations Development Program, "Zambia Millennium Development Goals: Progress Report 2008" <www.undp.org.zm/joomla/attachments/005_ Zambia%20MDGs%20Progress%20Progress%20Report%20Zambia%20 2008.pdf>.

[13]Eurostep, "Commission Signs £225 Million MDG Contract with Zambia" <www.eurostep.org/wcm/content/view/548/158>.

[14]Joint press release by WHO, UNAIDS and UNICEF, "More than four million HIV-positive people now receiving life-saving treatment," September 2009 <www.unaids.org/en/KnowledgeCentre/Resources/FeatureStories/archive /2009/20090930_access_treatment_4million.asp#>.

[15] United Nations Development Program, "Zambia Millennium Development Goals: Progress Report 2008," from the foreword <www.undp.org.zm/ joomla/attachments/005_Zambia%20MDGs%20Progress%20Progress %20Report%20Zambia%202008.pdf>.

[16]Joint press release by WHO, UNAIDS and UNICEF, "More than four million HIV-positive people now receiving life-saving treatment," September 2009 <www.unaids.org/en/KnowledgeCentre/Resources/FeatureStories/archive /2009/20090930_access_treatment_4million.asp#>.

[17]Dr. Peter Piot, foreword to UNAIDS, *2008 Report on the Global AIDS Epidemic,* p. 11 <www.unaids.org/en/KnowledgeCentre/HIVDataGlobalReport/2008 /2008_Global_report.asp>.

[18]United Nations Development Program, "Millennium Development Goals" <www.undp.org/mdg>.

[19]"Costs and Benefits: Expanding the Financial Envelope to Achieve the Goals," Millennium Project <http://www.unmillenniumproject.org/reports/costs_ benefits2.htm>.

[20]"The Cost and Benefits of Achieving the Millennium Development Goals," pp. 253, 256 <www.unmillenniumproject.org/documents/MainReport Chapter17-lowres.pdf>.

[21]OECD, "Development aid at its highest level ever in 2008" <www.oecd.org/ document/35/0,3343,en_2649_34487_42458595_1_1_1_1,00.html>.

[22]Jeffrey Sachs, "Facts on Foreign Aid," Economic Possibilities for Our Time <www.earth.columbia.edu/pages/endofpoverty/oda>.

[23]OECD, "Development aid at its highest level ever in 2008" <www.oecd.org/

document/35/0,3343,en_2649_34487_42458595_1_1_1_1,00.html>.

[24]Ibid.

[25]"President Obama's National HIV Testing Day Message" <www.youtube
.com/watch?v=VWj88CckQW8>.

[26]Transparency International, 2008 Corruption Perceptions Index <www
.transparency.org/policy_research/surveys_indices/cpi/2008>.

[27]Peter Singer, *The Life You Can Save: Acting Now to End World Poverty* (Melbourne:
Text Publishing, 2009), p. 155.

[28]See <kennedy.senate.gov/newsroom/press_release.cfm?id=340A5881-BBF2
-49C5-8519-47F2220A2112>.

[29]ONE International, "Malaria" <www.one.org/c/international/issuebrief
/1030/>.

[30]See <www.hoopsofhope.org>.

[31]Act:s: The World Vision Activism Network, "AIDS" <www.worldvisionacts
.org/?q=aids>.

[32]Stephanie Nolen, *28: Stories of AIDS in Africa* (New York: Walker, 2007), p. 68.